Alexander Robertson

Lectures, Legal, Political and Historical

On the Sciences of Law and Politics

Alexander Robertson

Lectures, Legal, Political and Historical
On the Sciences of Law and Politics

ISBN/EAN: 9783337079291

Printed in Europe, USA, Canada, Australia, Japan

Cover: Foto ©Suzi / pixelio.de

More available books at **www.hansebooks.com**

LECTURES,

LEGAL, POLITICAL, AND HISTORICAL:

ON

THE SCIENCES OF LAW AND POLITICS;

HOME AND FOREIGN AFFAIRS;

AND

JOHN GRAHAM OF CLAVERHOUSE,

VISCOUNT OF DUNDEE,

AND

HIS TIMES:

BY

ALEXANDER ROBERTSON, M.A.

BARRISTER-AT-LAW,

AUTHOR OF LECTURES ON THE GOVERNMENT, CONSTITUTION, AND LAWS OF SCOTLAND, 1875-78;
AND OUR HOME, COLONIAL, AND INDIAN AFFAIRS, 1879-80.

LONDON:
STEVENS & HAYNES,
Law Publishers,
BELL YARD, TEMPLE BAR.
DUNDEE :
WINTER, DUNCAN & Co. 10 CASTLE STREET.
1889.

GENERAL TABLE OF CONTENTS.

MY LORD PROVOST,

I have to thank you for the favour you have conferred upon me by allowing me to dedicate to you the following volume of Lectures.

The first Lecture was intended to prove that there was a legal science which was higher than the rules of any system of national jurisprudence; and that, in connection with the University College of Dundee, there were many strong reasons for the establishment of a School of Scots Law. The second Lecture was intended to show that there was a political science which transcended the principles and practices of political parties; and that, in the government of a great Empire, something more was required than the realization of the wishes of a majority of the electors in any one of the factors which composed it. The scheme of national and imperial governments and legislatures, prefixed to the first and second Lectures, and published in the early part of last year, was intended to indicate in what way Home Rule might possibly be settled on a national and imperial basis. The third and fourth Lectures were intended as an exposition of the principles I had enunciated in the second Lecture, and may be taken as a brief outline of my own political opinions as to our rights and duties at home and abroad. The fifth Lecture was intended to be a true, impartial, and historical statement of the Life and Times of John Graham of Claverhouse, Constable, Provost, and Viscount of Dundee.

Wishing all prosperity to my native place, over which you preside as Chief-Magistrate with such honour to yourself and advantage to the community of Dundee,

I have the honour to be,

MY LORD PROVOST,

Your obedient Servant,

ALEXANDER ROBERTSON.

DANEBURY HOUSE,
KEW GREEN, KEW, SURREY,
27th July 1889.

TWO LECTURES

ON

LAW AND POLITICS.

TWO LECTURES

ON

THE SCIENCE AND STUDY OF LAW

AND

THE SCIENCE AND STUDY OF POLITICS,

DELIVERED AT DUNDEE IN JANUARY 1887,

TOGETHER WITH

A GENERAL OUTLINE OF A SCHEME FOR IMPERIAL AND NATIONAL CONSTITUTIONS
FOR GREAT BRITAIN AND IRELAND,
AND FOR ENGLAND, SCOTLAND, AND IRELAND.

BY

ALEXANDER ROBERTSON, M.A.,

OF LINCOLN'S INN, BARRISTER-AT-LAW

(AUTHOR OF LECTURES ON THE GOVERNMENT, CONSTITUTION, AND LAWS OF SCOTLAND, 1875–78,
AND OF SPEECHES ON HOME, COLONIAL, AND INDIAN AFFAIRS, 1879–80).

DUNDEE :

WINTER, DUNCAN & CO. 10 CASTLE STREET.
1888.

PREFACE.

THE two following Lectures were intended by me to be followed by a series of Political Speeches in the County of Forfar, during the present recess, and as opportunity occurred, or necessity arose between this date and the next General Election, and to be on Home, Colonial, Indian and Foreign Policy, and in further development, historically and otherwise, of my former Speeches on Home, Colonial, and Indian Affairs. As I am told that the Central Conservative Association has made arrangements with various political gentlemen to deliver a series of political speeches at various places in the county, and as I am inclined to think that, for the present, there is a superabundance of political talk in Forfarshire, and in other parts of the country, I do not consider myself called upon unnecessarily to add to the superfluity. I can easily remember the time, not long ago, when a conservative political speaker in any part of Forfarshire was *avis rarissima.* But, inasmuch as sometime ago, and also lately, I announced, in the public press, that I was to deliver two political speeches, at Broughty Ferry and Monifieth, on Home and Foreign Affairs, I shall take the earliest and most convenient opportunities of performing my engagements to my friends at the two last-mentioned places. I think, however, that I should, at once, place in the hands of my friends, and of

the public generally, my two Lectures on Law and Politics;
because (1) the practical aim of the Lecture on Law was to
advocate the establishment of a Law Professorship or Lectureship in Dundee; and (2) the practical aim of my Lecture on
Politics was to prepare the way for a statement by me of the
great political questions of the day.

However, in consequence of the vacancy which will shortly
occur in the parliamentary representation of Dundee, or, at
least, in consequence of the opportunities which, I hope, will
arise at, or before, the next General Parliamentary Election, I do
not feel that there is any imperative necessity for explaining
my political opinions at present.   With pertinacious obstinacy,
I have explained, in Dundee and elsewhere, what these are,
and have made no secret about my preference to represent my
native town of Dundee, in the House of Commons, rather than
any other constituency.   At the General Election of 1885, I
thought my time for contesting Dundee as an independent
Conservative candidate had, at length, arrived.   But, although I
had issued my address to the Electors, I retired from the contest
in order to give the official Conservative candidate the advantage
of having no Conservative opponent, and to save myself the
expense of an unsuccessful contest, and, as future circumstances
might dictate, to reserve myself for a bye-election at Dundee,
or for the next General Parliamentary Election, under favourable conditions.   As regards Dundee, I never believed at any
time, and do not believe now, that any local Candidate, except,
perhaps, Mr W. O. Dalgleish, could be induced, or could reasonably
hope with any advantage, to lead the forlorn hope of the Conservative Party in Dundee at a bye-election, or at the next
General Parliamentary Election.   *Arbores seret diligens agricola,
quarum adspiciet bacam ipse nunquam.*   Nay more, I have

sometimes almost despaired of being able to persuade the great body of my former fellow-townsmen to agree with me that, in the present juncture of public affairs, the interests of the British Empire are best entrusted to an Imperial, Patriotic, and Conservative Government. But I do not despair of being of some use to my friends in Dundee, or elsewhere in Forfarshire, in the future complications which are rapidly approaching, both at home and abroad. I shall, therefore, act in regard to any vacancy in Dundee, or elsewhere in the county of Forfar, as I think best and most advantageous for the promotion of Popular, National, Imperial, and Conservative principles of Government. The present condition of political parties through-out the country is anomalous, and cannot long subsist. The political atmosphere at Dundee, and throughout the county of Forfar, needs to be strengthened and purified by the infusion of strictly national and imperial principles of political action. In such times as exist at present, both at home and abroad, the representatives of a great people ought to be something more than mere parliamentary delegates, or political party hacks. At all events, until such time as I can enter the House of Commons as a free and independent member, able and willing to devote my best services to the local community whose suffrages I asked, and to the community at large, I would prefer not to enter the House of Commons at all.

I have twice offered my services to the Electors of Dundee as a candidate for parliamentary honours, and have twice voluntarily retired from the contest. My friends in Dundee may, however, rest assured that, if, as a candidate, I should enter upon a third parliamentary contest in Dundee, I shall do so with the object of doing my best to uphold the banner of Peace, Prosperity, and Enlightened Progress, and in the full determination that I shall fight the battle to the bitter end; and that, whether defeated or victorious at the poll, I shall conduct the contest on public grounds, and in an honourable fashion towards all my opponents. Either as a Parliamentary Candidate, or as a Representative in the House of Commons, or as a free citizen, I hope, at all events, and before long, to be able to lay before my friends in Dundee, and elsewhere in the county of Forfar, an outline of national and imperial policy, which will be based on something else than the ephemeral and evanescent opinions of any political party. Whether I succeed in my political aspirations or not, and either in Dundee or elsewhere, I am determined to be free, and to do all I can to promote the welfare, happiness, and prosperity of my fellow-countrymen in every part of our great Empire. Although I am an Englishman by reason of my profession and my adopted country, I have never ceased to be a Scotchman; and, in the midst of no small difficulties, I have done all in my power to make myself acquainted with the constitutions, laws, and administrations of England, Scotland and Ireland, and of our Colonies and India, and to teach others what I myself have learned regarding them.

I confess that I have long held, that, all other things being equal, men acquainted with the laws, manners, and customs of a country, and not strangers more or less ignorant of these things, should represent the People in the British House of Commons. Now, since I left Dundee to go to the Edinburgh and St. Andrews Universities, and afterwards to London to practise at the English Bar, I have, for the last 27 years, resided in Dundee, or the immediate neighbourhood, during several months of every year, and have been absent, as a rule, merely when Parliament was sitting. As I shall most probably continue to do the same for some time to come, whether I am returned to Parliament or not, and as I have never failed to keep myself acquainted with the local affairs and interests of Dundee, I am entitled, I think, to look upon myself as a person belonging to the locality. At some future time, and, as I hope, before long, I shall point out how the political knowledge and talents of the Scotch Bar, and of the Scotch people generally, could be more advantageously utilized in the national legislation and national administration of Scotland than they are at present. I shall now merely state that, in my opinion, the time has arrived for a large measure of decentralization as to legislation as well as administration in England, Scotland, and Ireland.

Indeed, in the not distant future, I look upon local county administration, on a popular basis, and also upon national self-government for England, Scotland, and Ireland as inevitable and indispensible. To use the words of Mr Froude, the historian, " we must Americanize our Institutions." I, therefore, hope that the Conservative Party will soon lead the way to a lasting and amicable settlement of the problems connected not only with local county administration, but also with national self-government and Imperial government. Apart from the recent disgraceful obstruction in the House of Commons, parliamentary government has, for many years past, utterly broken down, and has frequently spent its best efforts in vain attempts at national and imperial legislation and supervision, and it cannot be restored to strength, vigour, and efficiency by any mere rules of procedure. Too little time is now given, in the Parliament at Westminister, to National, Colonial, and Indian Affairs ; and the English representatives, and the supporters of the Government of the day, often vote in Scotch and Irish national affairs which they do not understand, and which they are not qualified to decide. Therefore, devolution, by delegation or substitution, of some of the parliamentary functions at Westminster cannot be long delayed, and I have thought, for some time, that the people of Scotland would do a great service to the Empire by formulating a plan of national self-government for themselves, and by showing England and Ireland how national self-government can be made safe and consistent with the interests of the British Empire, and the peace, welfare, and prosperity of the world. As a rough and theoretical sketch of such a plan, capable of being modified and extended to every part of the British Empire, I have to submit to the reader's serious consideration a Scheme for an Imperial Constitution and for National Constitutions. It was drafted in the Easter recess of 1887, and was lately revised; and, with no small hesitation, is now made public for the first time. It was originally, and is now, intended for general application to our world-wide Empire at some future time. Whatever its blemishes, or excellence, practical or theoretical, it will, I hope, show the difficulties to be encountered in any general scheme of national self-government, and may, peradventure, demonstrate the futility of such a scheme, or of a scheme limited to Ireland. It will, I believe, show that proposals for national self-government for the United Kingdom of Great Britain and Ireland are beset with grave difficulties and dangers, which can only be fully dealt with by a general measure applicable to all the Kingdoms of England, Scotland, and Ireland. In my opinion, national self-government is required for England, Scotland, and Ireland; or it is not required for any one of them; and whatever measure of self-government is given to one Kingdom ought to be given to each and all of them. The national executive Government should be co-extensive with the national Legislative powers. The aspirations of the leaders of the Irish Home Rule party, or of the majority of the Irish people, or even of the whole of the Irish people, are not a safe foundation for great, nay, stupendous changes on our present constitution and modes of government. I, therefore, hope that, as in the settlement of the Franchise and Redistribution Bills of 1885, so now, in regard to the great problems of national and imperial government, Her Majesty's Ministers will, in the Parliament at Westminster, make full and distinct proposals in regard to it, and that all the leaders of all the great political parties in the realm will lay aside all partizanship, and try to settle the greatest domestic question of our times on a permanent and patriotic basis. In any such settlement, the Parliament at Westminster must be supreme. According to my view, national self-government is infinitely to be preferred to provincial self-government in any shape or guise. As regards county government, it should, in my opinion, be administrative and not legislative.

Our present unwritten, yet glorious Constitution, is the fruit of the labours of great and patriotic men for many centuries, and should not be abolished or materially modified, until, after ample and mature discussion, a better one can undoubtedly be substituted in its place. Till this great problem of national self-government for England and Scotland, as well as for Ireland, is settled, for the present, in one way or another, Committees of the whole House of Commons, as a rule, should be abolished, and General Grand Committees and National Grand Committees for Public Bills, and also Parliamentary Commissions for Private Bills should be adopted to enable the Parliament at Westminster to do its work in a rational and business-like manner, and in a reasonable period of time.

Moreover, discussions on motions for the adjournment of the House of Commons should be abolished as a general rule.

As, peradventure, a favourable chance may arise for my becoming a Candidate for the Parliamentary Representation of Dundee at the approaching vacancy in February next, my advice to my own personal friends, Liberal and Conservative, in Dundee is not to pledge themselves to any Candidate till the writ is about to be issued for the vacancy. I would even venture to warn all the Parliamentary Electors of Dundee against adventurous strangers and carpet-bag politicians, who are always ready to give any number of pledges, and to break, or disregard, them without compunction. I would also urge upon them to exercise their franchises with an enlightened regard to their own local interests, and to the honour and advantages of their country, and with a deep feeling of grave responsibility at a critical epoch in the history of the Empire. Let all citizens, who love justice, order, and progress, firmly stand up for the Supremacy of the Law in every part of the British Empire as an essential doctrine of good government.

21 LOUISE TERRACE,
BROUGHTY FERRY, FORFARSHIRE, N.B.,
27th December 1887.

Postscript.—2 Plowden Buildings, Temple, London, E.C., 19th January 1888.—From unavoidable causes, the publication of this pamphlet has been delayed longer than its Author expected.

CONTENTS.

1. LECTURE ON THE SCIENCE AND STUDY OF LAW.

I.—LAW IN GENERAL.

II.—THE LAW OF NATURE.

III.—MORALITY.

2. LECTURE ON THE SCIENCE AND STUDY OF POLITICS.

I.—PRIMITIVE OR NATURAL SOCIETY.

II.—CIVILIZED SOCIETY.

III.—CIVIL GOVERNMENT DEFINED.

A 2

IV.—ESSENTIALS OF A GOOD GOVERNMENT.

A GENERAL OUTLINE OF THE PRINCIPLES

OF A

SCHEME FOR AN IMPERIAL CONSTITUTION

FOR THE

UNITED KINGDOM OF GREAT BRITAIN AND IRELAND;

AND FOR

NATIONAL CONSTITUTIONS

FOR THE

KINGDOMS OF ENGLAND, SCOTLAND, AND IRELAND,

AND CAPABLE, WITH MODIFICATIONS, OF BEING GRADUALLY

EXTENDED TO EVERY PART OF THE BRITISH EMPIRE

(Referred to in the Preface).

I. IMPERIAL CONSTITUTION.

1. GOVERNMENT.

1. THE SOVEREIGN of England, Scotland, and Ireland is and shall be Sovereign of British Empire by hereditary title.

2. The Sovereign to be the Representative of the Empire in all international relations, rights, and duties; and as such to declare war, make peace, enter into treaties with foreign powers, and appoint representatives at foreign courts.

3. The Sovereign is and shall be Commander-in-chief of the whole Imperial Army and Navy, and wherever stationed, whether at home or abroad, in peace and war; and, as such, to name and dismiss the officers of the Imperial Army and Navy.

4. The Sovereign shall appoint and dismiss the officers of the Imperial Ministry, namely, the Prime Minister and "the Members of the Cabinet," who shall be responsible to the Sovereign and the Imperial Parliament for the legislation, administration, and supervision of the Empire.

5. The members of the Imperial Ministry, whether members of the Imperial House of Peers, or House of Commons, or not, shall have power to speak in the Imperial House of Peers, or House of Commons, on all matters concerning their own Departments.

6. The Sovereign shall appoint the Judges of the Supreme Courts, civil and criminal, in England, Scotland, and Ireland; and, on the petition of both or either of the Houses of the Imperial Parliament or the National Parliament concerned, may suspend, or dismiss the Judges of such Supreme Courts.

7. The Sovereign shall create, constitute, and maintain an Imperial Court of Appeal, for the final decision of all disputes between the Imperial, National, Colonial, or Indian Governments, or between the separate National, Indian, or Colonial Governments themselves, for the final decision of all appeals, civil or criminal, from each country, dominion, colony, or dependency of the British Empire; and, on the petition of both or either of the Houses of the Imperial, National, Colonial, or Indian Governments, may suspend or dismiss the Judges of such Imperial Court of Appeal.

2. THE IMPERIAL LEGISLATIVE ASSEMBLY.

1. The Imperial Legislative Assembly shall consist of three classes or estates, namely—(1) the Sovereign and the male children of the Sovereign, and the eldest son of the Heir-apparent; (2) representatives of the temporal and hereditary Peers of England, Scotland, and Ireland, and Life Peers nominated by the Sovereign; and (3) Representatives of the Commons of England, Scotland, and Ireland; and shall sit and vote in two Houses, namely, the House of Peers and the House of Commons; and shall assemble, at least, once a year for business at Westminster; and, unless dissolved, shall continue for seven years.

2. The Sovereign and the Imperial Peers shall sit and vote in one and the same house.

3. The Sovereign shall have power to pass, or veto, Bills passed by both Houses of the Imperial Parliament, and to call, adjourn, prorogue, and dissolve the Imperial Parliament.

4 (1). The House of Imperial Peers shall be composed of representative and elected Peers of England, Scotland, and Ireland, and shall be chosen by themselves from the temporal and hereditary Peers of England, Scotland, and Ireland, at assemblies called by the Sovereign for the purpose, in the following numbers, namely, (1) 156 for England; (2) 16 for Scotland; and (3) 28 for Ireland. All the imperial hereditary Peers shall be chosen for life, and vacancies shall be filled up as they occur in each country.

(2). The House of Imperial Peers shall also be composed of men distinguished for high attainments or distinguished services in religion, law, medicine, surgery, art, science, literature, war, diplomacy, commerce, or agriculture, nominated for life by the Sovereign, and never to exceed 50 in number, and to be distributed, as nearly as convenient, between England, Scotland, and Ireland, as follows, namely :— (1) 30 for England; (2) 10 for Scotland; and (3) 10 for Ireland.

5. The Imperial House of Commons shall be composed of Representatives elected by England, Scotland, and Ireland, as follows, namely :—(1) 495 for England and Wales; (2) 72 for Scotland; and (3) 103 for Ireland.

6. No alteration shall be made on the Imperial Constitution, or on the National Constitutions, by the Imperial Parliament, unless the same shall be passed by a majority of two-thirds of the full number, for the time being, of each House of the Imperial Parliament.

7. British Hereditary Peers must choose for themselves, and their successors, whether they shall rank and vote as English, Scotch, or Irish Peers.

8. No Archbishop, or Bishop, of the Church of England shall, as such, have a right to speak or vote in the House of Peers.

8. LEGISLATIVE POWERS OF IMPERIAL PARLIAMENT.

1. All laws as to the British Army and Navy, and as to Postal and Telegraph regulations, coinage and banking, and the imposition of customs and excise

within England, Scotland, and Ireland, and also within the Colonies and Dependencies not endowed with powers to make such laws within their own territories.

2. All laws as to the political rights of citizens within England, Scotland, and Ireland, and the Colonies and Dependencies referred to in § 1.

3. All laws as to commerce and navigation within England, Scotland, and Ireland, and the Colonies and Dependencies referred to in § 1.

4. All laws as to the Imperial Finances, Expenditure, and as to the Dominion, or Colonial contributions to the Imperial Exchequer.

5. All laws as to Colonial and Indian relations, emigration and colonization, and foreign passports.

6. All laws as to Imperial taxes and the appropriation of Imperial taxes to Imperial purposes, or to such purposes as shall be expressly declared to be of Imperial interest.

II. NATIONAL CONSTITUTIONS.

1. GOVERNMENT.

1. The Sovereign shall appoint three separate national Ministries, namely, for England, for Scotland, and for Ireland, to consist of a Prime Minister and "the Members of the Cabinet," who shall be responsible to the Sovereign and the National Parliament for the legislation, administration, and supervision of the nation or country, whether England, Scotland, or Ireland, for which they are appointed.

2. The Sovereign shall appoint the Judges of the Inferior Courts, civil or criminal, in England, Scotland, and Ireland respectively ; and, on the petition of the National Parliament or Legislative Assembly of England, Scotland, or Ireland respectively, may suspend or dismiss the Judges of such Inferior Courts.

3. The members of the three National Ministries may also be members of the Imperial Ministry ; and whether, or not, representatives of the Peers, or of the Commons; and shall have power to speak in the National Assemblies of the nation or country of which they are Ministers on matters concerning their own Departments.

4. The Sovereign shall have power to dismiss the National Ministers, or any of them.

5. The National Parliaments shall, as far as possible, be called, meet, adjourned, prorogued, and dissolved, at times different from those for which the Imperial Parliament is called, &c.

2. THE NATIONAL LEGISLATIVE ASSEMBLIES.

1. National Parliaments or Legislative Assemblies shall be constituted for England, Scotland, and Ireland, and be composed of Sovereign, Peers, and Commons, that is to say, the Sovereign or his or her Representative, and the Representative Hereditary and Life Peers, and Representatives of the Commons, shall sit and vote in one and the same chamber, and shall all vote at one and the same time ; and all the members of the National Parliaments or Legislative Assemblies shall be eligible for election to the Imperial Parliament.

2. The National Parliaments shall assemble, at least, once a year in London, Edinburgh and Dublin; and, unless dissolved, shall continue to exist for seven years.

3. The Sovereign shall have power to pass, or veto, Bills of the National Parliaments; and to call, adjourn, prorogue, and dissolve the National Parliaments.

(1). THE ENGLISH NATIONAL ASSEMBLY.

The English National Legislative Assembly shall consist—(1) of the Sovereign or his or her Representative; and (2) of 156 Representative Temporal and hereditary Peers of England; and (3) of 30 Life Peers nominated by the Sovereign; and (4) of 495 Members chosen by the urban and rural constituencies of England and Wales.

(2). THE SCOTCH NATIONAL ASSEMBLY.

The Scotch National Assembly shall consist—(1) of the Sovereign or his or her Representative; and (2) of 16 Representative Temporal and hereditary Peers of Scotland; (3) of 10 Life Peers nominated by the Sovereign; and (4) of 72 Members chosen by the urban and rural constituencies of Scotland.

(3). THE IRISH NATIONAL ASSEMBLY.

The Irish National Assembly shall consist—(1) of the Sovereign or his or her Representative; and (2) of 28 Representative Temporal and hereditary Peers of Ireland; and (3) of 10 Life Peers nominated by the Sovereign; and (4) of 103 Members chosen by the urban and rural constituencies of Ireland.

2. LEGISLATIVE POWERS OF THE NATIONAL ASSEMBLIES.

1. Unless in so far as limitations may be made by the Imperial Parliament, the Laws to be passed by each National Assembly shall comprehend all state matters connected with police, the administration of justice, and the whole civil and criminal law as regards private rights and duties, the relation of the Church and the State, education, poor law, the cultivation of the soil, and the relations of employers and employees, and also as regards all private bill legislation.

2. All national revenue and expenditure.

3. All laws as to local government, urban or rural, and local taxation.

III. IMPERIAL LAWS TO BE SUPREME.

1. Unless limited in scope, all laws passed by the Imperial Legislature shall be applicable to every part of the British Empire, and shall be supreme.

2. Where disputes between the Empire and separate National, Colonial, or Indian Governments, or between separate National, Colonial, and Indian Governments themselves, the final decision shall be given by the Imperial Supreme Court to be constituted.

3. Appeals from the Supreme Courts of each country, dominion, colony, or dependency of the whole British Empire, may be made to the Imperial Court in all civil and criminal matters tried or decided in the Supreme Courts.

IV. ESSENTIAL AND FUNDAMENTAL PRINCIPLES
OF CONSTITUTION.

1. An Imperial Parliament and an Executive shall be constituted for the Empire. The Imperial executive shall be the Privy Council of the Sovereign.

2. National Parliaments and Executives shall be constituted for separate countries, and, as may hereafter be convenient, for dominions, colonies, and dependencies, and also for three or four or more divisions of India. The National executives shall be the Councils of the Sovereign.

3. The House of Commons of the Imperial Parliament shall have exclusive right and power to grant or refuse supplies for Imperial purposes.

4. Rules of Procedure shall be the same for all Parliaments, Imperial and National; and stages of Bills shall be reduced to—(1) the first reading; (2) discussion in committee; and (3) approval or disapproval on Report of Committee.

5. The House of Peers shall be restricted in numbers on a fixed basis, and no Temporal and Hereditary Peer shall be capable of Election as a representative of the Commons in the Imperial or in any National Parliament.

6. Educational and ecclesiastical matters shall belong to the National Parliaments.

7. No alteration shall be made in the constitution of any Parliament, Imperial or National, without Imperial sanction. Further, all the National Parliaments shall have power to pass Resolutions as to matters of Imperial interest, and transmit them to both Houses of the

Imperial Parliament for consideration, and may make recommendations thereon to the Imperial Parliament. But they shall have no power whatever to pass Laws on any of the matters herein described as Imperial.

8. The state patronage of each country, colony, or dependency shall be under the Sovereign, or his or her Ministers in such country, colony, or dependency.

9. Imperial Ministers shall remain as at present, except President of Local Government Board, Secretary for Ireland, Minister of Education, and Home Secretary.

10. The national Ministers shall be Prime Minister, Lord Chancellor as Minister of Justice, Lord President of the Council, Chancellor of Exchequer, Secretary of State for Home Affairs, President of the Board of Trade Agriculture and Labour, and Minister of Religion and Education; and their salaries shall be paid out of the national taxes of the country for which they are appointed.

11. The office of Lord-Lieutenant for Ireland shall be abolished; and the cost thereof, now paid out of the Imperial Exchequer, shall be capitalized, and appropriated to Ireland; and the capitalized amount shall, with the sanction of the Imperial Parliament, be made available for strictly Irish National objects.

12. The royal constabulary force in Ireland shall be abolished, and its duties in future performed by a purely civilian police force, maintained and supervised as the English and Scotch police forces; and the cost of the royal Irish constabulary force, now paid out of the Imperial Exchequer, shall be capitalized and appropriated to Ireland; and the capitalized amount shall, with the sanction of the Imperial Parliament, be made available for strictly Irish national objects.

13. The Representatives of the Church of England shall, as such, be excluded from the House of Peers; and the two Houses of Convocation of Canterbury and York shall be erected into a General Assembly or Convocation of the Church of England, and with same or similar powers as the Church of Scotland has in Kirk-Sessions, or Vestries, Provincial Synods, and General Assemblies; and Private Church Patronage in the Church of England shall, on payment of compensation, be abolished and conferred on Churches, except high church dignities, which should be conferred or sanctioned by the Sovereign.

14. To the Imperial Exchequer shall belong—(1) Customs; (2) Excise, except Licences; (3) Stamps; (4) Property and Income Tax; (5) Post Office; and (6) Telegraph service. And by the Imperial Exchequer shall be paid—(1) Permanent charge of Imperial Debt; (2) Imperial Civil List; (3) Imperial Annuities and Pensions; (4) Imperial Salaries and Allowances; (5) Imperial Courts of Justice; (6) Imperial Army and Navy; (7) Salaries of Imperial Ministers; (8) Postal and Telegraph Service; and (9) Maintenance of Palaces and Public Buildings.

15. To Local National Governments shall belong —(1) Land Tax and House Duties; (2) Crown Lands; (3) Interest on Advances for Local Works; and (4) Duties on all Licences to Trade. And by the Local National Governments shall be paid—(1) National Civil Lists; (2) National Salaries and Allowances; (3) Cost of National and Local Courts of Justice, civil and criminal; (4) National Contributions to Science and Art; (5) National Contributions to

Police; and (6) Cost and Maintenance of National Public Works and Buildings.

16. For an eternal Union for the protection of the realm and for the welfare of the British Empire.

LECTURE

ON THE

SCIENCE AND STUDY OF LAW

(DELIVERED IN THE ALBERT INSTITUTE, DUNDEE, ON 11th JANUARY 1887).

I.—LAW IN GENERAL.

INTRODUCTION.—The subjects of my present Lecture are (1) the Science of Law, or of the rules prescribed to mankind as members of the human family and as members of a state ; and (2) the Study of Law. I, therefore, propose to demonstrate that Law is a Science, and that it is worthy of study, and to point out to you what are the relations of the Laws of Nature, of Morality, and of Jurisprudence to each other.

Justice as defined by Justinian.—In the Institutes of Justinian, " Justice is defined as a constant and perpetual wish to render every one his due." This definition, which is adopted from the works of the great Roman lawyer Ulpian, was taken by him from the Stoics. But it is a definition which is inapplicable to

B

the whole mass of rights and duties protected and
enforced by legal remedies.   In the system of Roman
law, morality and law are blended.   But the distinction
as to what ought to be done, or not done, and what
is commanded or forbidden by positive human law, is
useful and necessary, and is universally recognised in
all systems of modern law.   Human tribunals cannot
judge of the rights and duties of men by the affections
of the mind.   Still, those affections are often essential
factors in the decisions which must be given in many
of the affairs of life, and more especially in all matters
which involve the consideration of the motives, and of
the praiseworthiness or culpability of men.

Hooker and others on law.—Of law as a principle
universally diffused and permeating the world, Hooker,
in his great work on Ecclesiastical Polity, thus writes
in the highest and sublimest strains of eloquence : " Of
law, no less can be said than that her seat is the bosom
of God; her voice, the harmony of the world; all things
in heaven and earth do her homage; the least as feeling
her care, the greatest as not exempt from her power;
both angels and men and creatures of what condition
soever, though each in different sort and manner, yet
all with uniform consent, admiring her as the mother
of their peace and joy."   Thus speaks the great
Edmund Burke : " That the law is the highest ideal
yet approached by us towards reason and justice in
their practical applications in the affairs of life."
Similarly, Cicero, in his speech for Cleanthes, said,
" that the laws are the foundation of liberty, and the
fountain of equity."   Not less firmly have the greatest
lawyers and statesmen of our own and former ages,

and of all civilized countries, held that law was founded
on moral rectitude and the principles of eternal truth.
In fact, religion, justice, and law, all stand or fall
together; and, like all the sciences, show forth the
glory of God, who reigns in heaven over all the earth,
and whose highest and grandest attributes are truth,
justice, and mercy.

Erskine's definition of law.—According to Erskine,
law is frequently used, in a large acceptation, to express
the method of God's providence, by which the material
world is preserved in such a manner that nothing in it
may deviate from that uniform course which He has
appointed to it. In this sense, I may here observe
that it is applicable to the brute and inanimate creation
as well as to human beings endowed with reason.
He proceeds to say, that the word, in its strict sense,
is peculiar to intelligent beings, endowed with conscious-
ness and liberty of will, and who consequently have
an inward power of acting and forbearing, and who, by
disregarding the prescription of law, contract guilt,
and render themselves obnoxious to punishment. It
is in this strict sense that I have to show that law is
a science.

Law as a science.—Now, law is sometimes used for
what is, or is not just, and sometimes for what is
prescribed. In either of these significations, law is a
science; for science is neither more nor less than a
body of general rules or principles systematically
arranged; and law is the body or system of rules
prescribed to man as a human being, or as a member
of a state. Natural law deals with man as a human
being; positive law deals with man as a member of a

state; and international law deals with the relations of states as states amongst one another, and also with the relations of members of different states. As a science, law, in its strict sense, deals with the permanent and invariable facts of human nature, as displayed in the physical, logical, and ethical nature of man. Looking at law as a body of truth systematically arranged, and in its most abstract meaning, and as comprehending what is or what is not just, we are brought face to face with the great moral law, which is deducible from the nature of man as a rational creature in regard to his actions towards God, his neighbours, and himself. In other words, we come into contact with the duties which we owe to God, namely, *e.g.* reverence and obedience; with the duties which we owe to our neighbours, namely, *e.g.* justice and truth; and with the duties which we owe to ourselves, namely, *e.g.* self-preservation and temperance. Unless man were capable of acting in conformity with some general rules of conduct, he would not be capable of reasoning on his actions, but would be the pitiable victim of every momentary feeling or passion, and would, therefore, be rationally unaccountable to God or man. That he is susceptible of reasoning, and that he is not the pitiable victim of such temporary feeling or passion, but is a being capable of taking the widest survey of his actions, and is capable of acting or forbearing, is universally apparent to all men who are not fools or idiots. This proposition is a necessary axiom in all our systems of science, religion, and education. We know that we can decide between what is or is not just, and we know that we have the power to do or not to do what is just. I, therefore, come to the conclusion that we are moral beings, endowed by God with the powers of making, or of obeying general rules as to our conduct, and therefore that there is a science of human law in regard to man as a moral being.

Law as a command.—But, as I have said, law is sometimes used for what is prescribed. In this sense, law is the command of a sovereign, containing a common rule of life for his subjects, and obliging them to obedience. In this definition, the chief element with which we are concerned is the statement that there is a common rule applicable to the different matters which are of common and public interest to the subjects of the same sovereign. Infinitely diversified as are the various relations of one person to another in their different relations in life, and of all to the state, the vital factor of every well-governed state is, that the law is the same to all in regard to every important relation of the citizens.

Law as an inviolable decree.—Another definition of law I ought to notice. It is this: an inviolable decree ordering what is right, and forbidding the contrary. This, I think, is as good a definition of law as any with which I am acquainted. Observe, that a decree is the command given in reference to some particular subject; also, that it is liable to be violated or disobeyed; and further, that the thing ordered is right; or in other words just; and that what is contrary to that which is ordered is forbidden.

Laws must be possible, intelligible, and commanded.—Whatever be the sovereign power in a state, all laws ought to be possible, intelligible, and commanded. If a law is not capable of being performed, it cannot be a rule of conduct; for a law which is not capable of being performed is absurd on the face of it. If it is not intelligible, it is liable to the same objection. And if it is not commanded, it is from its very nature no rule of conduct.

Laws must have a sanction.—Added to all laws there must be what is called the sanction or punishment, that is to say, the penalty for disobedience. This sanction is always laid down in every good law of a civilized country, and as little as possible is left to the discretion of the judge; for such discretion is apt to degenerate into partiality, and even the abrogation of the law itself. But, of course, the exact degree of punishment is not easily fixed in many cases; for it must be laid down according to many varying circumstances in particular cases, which cannot be known beforehand. Laws are often harsh, cruel, and tyrannous. But the laws should always be just. The supreme power should always have the happiness of the subjects in view; for thereby will the honour and glory of the sovereign, and the prosperity, welfare, and security of the subject, be secured.

Law as defined by Blackstone.—I have yet another definition of law to submit to your consideration, and its fulness will enable me to dispense with any comment upon it. I refer to the definition of law given by Blackstone in his Essay on Bailments. It is in these words : " Law is the science which distinguishes between the criterion of right and wrong ; which teaches to establish the one, and to prevent, punish,

and redress the other; which employs in its theory the
noblest faculties of the soul, and exerts in its practice
the cardinal virtues of the heart." These brief observations must here suffice for what I have to say as to
law as a Science.

*Law divided into natural, international, and
national.*—Of this science of law, a threefold division
has been made, namely, natural, international, and
national. The law of nature is derived from man's
nature, and therefore directly from God himself. The
law of nations is derived from reason, and has been modified, in many important respects, by international
conventions, and comprises all the duties which one
independent state or body politic owes to another. The
national, sometimes called the municipal, law is derived
from reason and convenience, and comprises all the rights
and duties which can be legally enforced in any independent state or country. Beyond saying that the law
of nations comprehends the international rights of
peace and war, the security of ambassadors, the
obligations arising from international treaties, and,
generally speaking, the enforcement of the contracts
made by the citizens of different states, I cannot enlarge
upon the law of nations. I shall, therefore, at once,
proceed to the consideration of the law of nature, and
of the national or municipal law; that is to say, of
law as a system of rights and obligations—divine
and national—in reference to man as a human being,
and as to man in a state of civilized society.

II.—THE LAW OF NATURE.

Law of nature as defined by Grotius.—The definition of the law of nature, as given by Grotius, is in
these words: "It is the dictate of reason; and an
action is good or bad by its agreement or disagreement
with the rational and social nature of man." Whatever is ordered or prescribed by reason must be right.
No doubt, the reason or the intellect of an individual
may be deranged by natural weakness or disease; but
the reason of man, in a perfect state of health, must be
right and true. If not, there is no basis for any
scheme of human nature, *i.e.* nothing upon which we
can depend, unless the transitory and unreliable
opinions of mankind. But man is endowed with intellectual faculties, which, if necessarily finite and
insignificant compared to the mind of God, whose
characteristics must necessarily be infinitude and
perfection, are capable of reaching to a high, a very
high, degree of perfection. Therefore, since God has
justice and goodness as His chief attributes, we may
reasonably infer, that we, His creatures, are also
possessed of those attributes, in some, even although
far from a perfect degree. As a matter of fact, demonstrated by experience, we know that we are capable
of forming such ideas of justice and goodness, and even
of regulating our conduct according to them. That
there are some persons who do not, or who cannot
do so, is no reason for saying, as a general rule, that
such powers do not exist.

St. Paul and others quoted.—St. Paul says, that the law of nature is written by God upon the heart of every one of us. Cicero, in the fragment preserved by Lactantius, lib. 6, cap. 8, says: "It is not therefore one law at Rome, and another at Athens; one to-day, and another to-morrow; but it is ever the same, exerting its obligatory force over all nations, and throughout all ages." It is, therefore, immutable, and is implanted in our nature by the Deity Himself. "The law of God," Carlyle says, "is as much now in the world, and is as clearly revealed as at Sinai, *e.g.* in the intellect, in the starry heavens, and in the sense of right and wrong in man." Here we stand at the fountain of all law. "For," says Edmund Burke, "if there is no God, good, just, and true, above us, there is no contract or obligation incumbent on us, unless by our own will, which will be determined by our own power." But, if duty is determined by power merely, there are no moral duties at all; for moral duties are essentially from God, and conscience, and will; that is to say, from the Author of Nature, and from the principle of man's heart applicable to what is right and wrong, and from that other human principle—the will—which carries the conclusions of the intellect into effect. The conclusion of the whole matter is, that the law of nature is the origin and foundation of all law. In adopting this opinion, the great Lord Bacon, in his work on the Dignity and Advancement of Learning, uses these words: "For there are in nature certain fountains of justice, whence all civil laws are derived but as streams; and like as waters do tincture and taste from the soils through which they run, so do civil laws vary according to the regions and governments where they are planted, though they proceed from the same fountains."

The law of nature suitable to man.—Now, this law of nature as regards man is such that it is suitable to his natural constitution. Its fitness and wisdom, in fact, are founded on the general nature of human beings. Moreover, it has been prescribed by the will of the Deity, and has been enforced by the sanctions of shame, remorse, infamy, and misery, and the expectations of the world to come.

The objects of the law of nature.—The objects of this law are God, our parents, and our fellow creatures. Towards God, we owe reverence and obedience; towards our parents, honour and obedience; and towards our fellow creatures, the performance of all our obligations and engagements. Under the last-mentioned class of duties, we may include all friendly offices in society, *e.g.* to do to others as we would that they should do to us; to take care of our preservation; to restrain our natural passions and appetites within due bounds; and to cultivate our faculties to the utmost of our power. These duties are clearly traceable to our nature as intellectual and moral beings, and as creatures deriving our nature from God, and as being under an obligation to use these powers for other and higher purposes than mere enlightenment.

All laws of nature not enforced by national law.— Some of the laws of nature are not enforced by the laws of any country, *e.g.* charity, benevolence, and temperance. Others of them are so enforced wholly, or in some degree, by being subjected to fixed rules, *e.g.* where the duty of providing for children is determined by specific portions being appropriated to them; and where, while the liberty of making wills is conceded to all, the law divides a man's property in certain proportions amongst his relatives and next of kin in the event of no specific instructions being given.

National laws based on natural laws.—Now, these rules, built on the foundation of the law of nature, are not only convenient, but necessary; for where freedom is permitted to man, it is morally desirable that it should be exercised in order to fix what is right and wrong, and settle the rights of the parties interested. Indeed, men, and also nations, should live by rules; that is to say, by just principles towards an end. If this were not so, man's noblest faculties would be of no use to him, and his duties would be a mass of single instances without principle or coherence. This end or purpose, in the region of moral law, is happiness, the desire for which is implanted in us by God Himself. "Happiness," says Vattel, "is indeed the centre of the duties which men and nations owe to themselves, and this is the great end of the law of nature. This desire is not only powerful, but it is the end which all men have in view." If men were just and enlightened, the law of nature would be sufficient for the individual and the state. But they are not so; for ignorance, self-love, and passion often render the sacred laws of human nature, and indeed of all laws, human and divine, ineffectual.

Positive laws necessary.—The necessity for establishing positive laws, and also the duty of enforcing them, and even of punishing transgressors, are thus apparent.

Yet it is no less true that "the fear of God is the beginning of wisdom," and that he who fears God has nothing to fear.   Where there is no law, there cannot, properly speaking, be any transgression.   When we do not know that we are breaking the law, we can be guilty of no moral wrong.   But, in the protection of the rights of other individuals, and for the maintenance of good order in the state, we may reasonably enough punish transgression of laws, of which the transgressors may be studiously or unhappily ignorant.   In making laws to decide the rights of individuals, or to maintain order in the state, we cannot always allow ourselves to be met with the answer, that the law was unknown until the offender was brought before the judge.   God alone can properly and fully judge of the motives and actions of men.   At His judgment seat, and, I fear, nowhere else, men will get absolute justice, and be punished or rewarded according to their deserts, and according to the eternal laws of truth and justice.

III. MORALITY.

Morality and jurisprudence co-related.—From what I have already said, it is perfectly clear that there is a close and marked co-relation between morality, or the science of ethics, and jurisprudence, or the science of law, *i.e.* the science of the just and the unjust. The essential characteristic of law is generality; and of morality, individuality.   But, in the progress of society, "moral claims become legal rights, and moral ties become legal duties;" or, once more, they become "the expression of the highest moral sympathies and habits of a people." Right is the central term of the science of law, and also of morality. Thus, for example, the tendency of civilization is to place men and women on terms of equality, for the purposes of moral and social advantage. In barbarous ages, the tendency is to make them unequal, and to subordinate the women to a state of degrading slavery to the men. Primitive law is harsh and cruel in all its aspects; civilized law is mild and generous. "Law and morality both imply," writes Sheldon Amos, "a law of right sentiment, and a command to obey the law, and a corresponding degree of moral and legal responsibility for not obeying them." Law is, in fact, the hand maid of morality. To express morality in adequate language is often impossible; but to express law in adequate language is always possible, and is absolutely essential.

Morality and positive law defined.—Morality may be defined as the free actions of men as susceptible of rule; and positive law, as what is due to others, and may be enforced by law. Morality and law both deal with human actions as right or wrong; but their spheres are not co-extensive. Morality has its origin in the conscience of mankind: positive law has its origin in the commands of a sovereign and human lawgiver. As the eye is formed to enable us to see external objects, so the mind is given to us by God to distinguish not only what is true and false, but what is right and wrong. But conscience is peculiarly that faculty of the mind which instructs us as to what law we should follow. Conscience is our moral oracle.

Like all the human faculties, it is capable of improvement and increased discernment. To enlighten the conscience as to moral rights and obligations is no less a duty than to improve the mind in the due appreciation of all things true and false. Unless our moral perfection be reached, and unless, when reached, be acted upon, man's noblest faculties are useless to him. On the other hand, jurisprudence, being the science of making and expounding laws, and applying them to human actions, is, as I have said, very closely allied to the science of ethics, which is called morality; for, as we have seen, morality deals with human actions, and is distinguishable from law, justice, or the science of jurisprudence, by the origin rather than by the nature of the acts. Both jurisprudence and morality deal with human actions as right or wrong by different standards. Their rules may be, and often are different, and even contradictory; but, in a perfect system of both, there should be no such difference, or, at least, no such contradiction.

Principles of jurisprudence.—The first principles of jurisprudence are simple rules of reason, experimental, essential to society, and pervade all law. "The science of jurisprudence," says Edmund Burke, "is the pride of the human intellect, which, with all its defects, redundancies, and errors, is the collected wisdom of ages, combining the original principles of justice to the infinite variety of human affairs." He also says that "justice is itself the great standing policy of human society, and any grave departure from it seriously lies under the suspicion of being no policy at all." Morality, that is to say the science of ethics, is derived from "*mores*," meaning customs, or the free actions of men considered as susceptible of rule and direction. Were men not susceptible of rule and direction, they would not be morally responsible for their actions, because their actions would not be free and spontaneous determinations of their minds. Every voluntary action is imputable; and the essential character of moral action is imputation.

Duty of obedience to the moral law.—Hence, in this aspect of our subject, we come into contact with the duty of obedience to the moral law, and its fruits; and of disobedience, and its consequences. Harmony between God's commands and men's actions is the highest virtue, and brings the truest happiness. On the other hand, antagonism between God's will and human action is the worst form of vice, and brings the highest degree of misery. Virtue brings us health of body and mind, the enjoyment of property, and confidence, esteem, and friendship. On it depends the public security, the tranquillity of families, and the prosperity of the state. It comprehends the grand principles of religion, temperance, modesty, beneficence, justice, and sincerity. On the other hand, the evils of vice are enfeeblement of body and mind, distempers, poverty, misery, violent and dangerous parties, fear, dishonour, punishment, contempt, and hatred. Neither rank nor wealth determines true happiness; but poverty, ignorance, and pain are real evils. Vattel holds that virtue is the true path to happiness, and that a virtuous nation is most happy, flourishing, and formidable. He wisely and truly adds that piety and religion are the purest sources of felicity.

IV. RELATIONS OF LEGISLATION AND POSITIVE LAW.

Legislation is in the supreme power.—The legislative power in a state resides in the supreme power as the head and chief over all things within its territory, regulating the interests and duties of the citizens towards each other, and towards itself, and towards its various delegates in the government. As supreme, this chief and superintending power cannot divest itself of its supremacy without endangering its existence. This supreme power can fetter neither itself, nor its successors; for it is a rule of universal jurisprudence that *posteriora derogant prioribus, i.e.* that posterior abrogate prior laws. To secure the greatest liberty to all, with the least restriction to any, is the great problem of legislation; but, alas! unfortunately, the legislation of most ages often merely reflects their ignorance and prejudice. To defend bad laws as either necessary or just, in consequence of their being passed by a representative assembly of the people, is absurd. Laws are good or bad as they approximate most nearly to the condition of society for which they are enacted; and popular representative assemblies frequently fall into legislative blunders as great as monarchs or aristocracies. Still, the right of legislation is vested in the sovereign power alone, *i.e.* in the supreme power of the state; for none other than such power has the right to exact obedience. This sovereign or supreme power must be the supreme power in an independent state; for, if it is less than independent, it is no longer supreme, and, in the exercise of legislation, would be subject to a higher or supreme power.

Subject states.—A subject state is a state which has only a limited power of legislation. Such were the Roman *Municipia* and tributary kingdoms of the Roman Empire.

Sphere of positive law.—I have already said that God has defined all our moral duties, or duties under the law of nature, by a fixed, determinate, and immutable law, and has yet left us ample scope for the infinite and complicated variety of human life, according as our positions are changed in time, or place, or stage of civilization. What things are thus allowed to us, we are not obliged to use; but we may give them up by entering into society, in whole or in part, as the common interest shall require. Such things lie within the sphere of a possible positive law, or general regulation by the head of the state. To define the rights and obligations enforced by the state, and to support these rights and obligations, are the proper subject matters of positive law. Of these rights and obligations, the main branches are ownership and contract, and civil injuries and public crimes. The laws of nature do not require to be formally promulgated to give them binding force; but positive laws do require to be formally promulgated before they are binding. Positive laws cannot be known till they are made and published by a human lawgiver. After the promulgation of a law by the legislative power, the law is binding on all the subjects of a state, and ignorance of its existence is no excuse for a breach of its command. Natural laws, springing from the human conscience, are inherent in man's nature, and require no extraneous human power to enact or to publish them.   For example, in regard to inheritance, it is true that every person, so long as his right is not limited by some indispensible obligation, *e.g.* to provide subsistence to his children, may, by the law of nature, chose the person to whom he would leave his property after his death.   But in England a father can bequeath or devise his whole property to strangers to the exclusion of his own children ; and in Scotland, he can only exercise this natural right to a certain limited extent.   Children, I think, all of us here will admit, have a natural right to inherit their father's property in equal proportions, and whatever may be the nature of that property, whether real or personal.   But this principle of natural law is of itself no absolute reason against the regulation of inheritance by last will and testament, or by descent, or even by deeds of entail, *e.g.* by deeds of entail to support noble families, and invest sons as principal heirs for the purpose of maintaining a condition of society, which necessitated such a departure from the law of nature.

Erskine on positive law.—Erskine describes positive law thus : " Hence things which natural law had left mankind at liberty either to do or forbear, and these only, are matter of positive law, which is therefore defined by Aristotle, ' that which treats of things which were indifferent before the enactment, but became necessary afterwards.' "   " This," continues Erskine, " points out the true reason why positive law is not, like the law of nature, immutable, but may, and, in many cases, ought to be altered or abrogated according to the changes wrought by time on the riches, the commerce, or the manners of the people." Clearly, then, the object of positive law ought to be to promote the common good of the state.

Positive law divided into public and private.— Positive law is divided into public and private. Public law is where the public weal and the preservation and good of society are more immediately in view. Under public law may be comprehended : 1. the constitution of the state ; 2. the administration of the government ; 3. the police of the country; 4. the public revenues; 5. trade and commerce; and 6. punishments, crimes, &c. Under private law are included the civil rights of individuals. All these branches of public and private law are well deserving of careful study by all who would have themselves considered as educated citizens.

Humanity of the modern criminal code.—Now, I may here take leave to observe how great has been the progress of the humanity of the criminal code in our own country and in all modern European states. Many noble and generous-minded men have devoted their lives to the abrogation and mitigation of the severity of the criminal laws of ancient times, and have left imperishable results as the effects of their philanthropic aims. Now, however, there is a danger that, in pity of human frailty, and in the dislike and horror of inflicting physical pain, and in the hope of softening and civilizing the great outcast masses of society, we are endangering our own happiness, peace, and prosperity, and doing little permanent good in raising the criminal classes to a higher standard of human life and happiness.

V.—SOURCES OF MODERN JURISPRUDENCE.

Roman law, feudalism and chivalry.—The chief
sources of the modern jurisprudence of all European
nations, and also of the colonies of these nations in
various parts of the world, are the civil and the
feudal laws, and, in no small degree, the laws of chivalry.   Strange to say, the laws of chivalry did much
to abolish the separation of moral duties in peace and war
(*vide* Ward's Inquiry.)   Indeed, from the 10th and
11th centuries of the Christian era, brutality was less
and less exercised, and the amount of ransom claimed
from a prisoner was restrained, and good faith was
more and more observed amongst enemies.   Again, the
relations of supreme law over vassals prevented, and
always mitigated, the horrors of war.   Subsequently,
about the sixteenth century, the supremacy of the
Pope of Rome was frequently used in the best interests
of great lords and sovereigns, as well as of priests
and bishops.   Beyond all question, the laws and
government of Imperial Rome, and also of Papal Rome,
speak from Rome to the nations of Modern Europe in,
and largely influence, the laws and principles of the
legal tribunals and the forms and principles of government of all of them, whether Protestant or Roman
Catholic.   This observation is true in a high degree as to
Scotland ; for the Roman law was long the legal rule
as to all the relations of life in this country; and, modified as to heritable property by the feudal system,
which very slightly affected legal rights as to personal
property, is still the chief element in the laws of

Scotland. Hence, in Scotland, the words, "the common law," by themselves, mean the civil or canon law, or both; while, on the other hand, the common law of the realm means the ancient usages of this country as distinguished from the Roman law or feudal customs. In England, I may here notice in passing that the common law means the law of England anterior to the existence of the statute law of England.

History of the civil and canon law.—The Roman civil law grew up by the accumulation of private commentaries on the Twelve Tables, and by the harmonizing influence of a succession of great magistrates and learned and experienced practitioners. It was digested by the Emperor Justinian in the year 533, and an abridgment was soon afterwards published. In 534, a collection or code of constitutions of the Roman Emperors from Adrian downwards was published. These latter were called "Novels," and, together with the digest of Justinian, formed the *corpus juris civilis*, or body of the civil law of Rome. The canon law derives its name from the Roman word signifying a rule. Under the directions of the Popes of Rome, it was composed of the ordinances of the churchmen assembled in councils or synods, and is largely formed on the civil law.

Excellence of both.—There is no wonder that these two grand monuments of antiquity have been highly valued in ancient and modern times; for the civil law was the offspring of philosophy and science, and its authors were not merely lawyers, but statesmen and philosophers, and its rules of private, international, and natural law are excellent. The Roman civil law is methodical in its arrangement, and even ornamental in its style.   Its great principles of justice, fixing the boundaries of right and wrong, are a series of excellent rules admirably adapted to the affairs of human life. Moreover, it is an excellent repertory of those rules which ought to guide the national conduct of states towards each other, and contains in its bosom the law of nations as well as the law of nature.   Nay more, in private affairs, the civil law was the common law of continental nations, and throughout all their wonderful vicissitudes and transformations, has had, and still has, an important influence on their laws, old and new, or digested and codified, in every country in Europe. The more the civil laws of Rome are studied and adopted, the better will it be for modern nations. Feudalism engrafted on the civil law many principles which are inconsistent with modern European society; and we are now gradually retracing our footsteps towards the Roman ideal of law.   Thus, the civil law of Rome knew nothing of the distinction of real and personal property as regards inheritance, and has no special favour for the first-born son as heir at law, and did not bestow the landed state of an ancestor on an eldest born son or nearest male heir.   Another name for the Roman civil law was the Pretorian law, which, although strictly applicable only to the decisions of the Roman Prætors and supreme civil judges before the Roman empire was established, took this name in consequence of the Prætors having had the chief work of building up the civil law, as I have said, on the foundations of the Twelve Tables.   This Pretorian law was founded on the universal principles of equity,

and is one of the grandest monuments ever erected in
the world by human skill, art, and intelligence. As
the civil law was the law of Pagan Rome, so the canon
law was the law of Christian Rome; and, in many respects, naturally followed the civil law, and differed very
little from it. Again, as the Roman Emperors claimed
the allegiance of the civilized world till the Roman Empire
was overthrown by the barbarous races by whom it
was overrun in the fifth century, so the Roman Pontiff
claimed the allegiance of the Christian world till the
great Protestant Reformation of the Church in the
sixteenth century. The Pope did so on the grounds that
he was the representative of the Emperors of the city of
Rome, and vicegerent on earth of God Himself. The
Pope has not altogether abandoned his pretensions as
the supreme monarch of all monarchs. Although he
has been deprived of his temporal power at Rome, he
is, perhaps, after all, the most powerful personage in
Europe, or in the whole world. As his temporal
authority has diminished, his spiritual power has increased.

Feudal Law.—The time and manner of the introduction of the feudal law has been subjected to much
dispute in this country and elsewhere. The truth of
the matter seems to be, that feudalism as a system of
law was introduced into England and Scotland by the
Normans. After the Norman conquest of England,
large numbers of Normans settled down with their
followers in England, and spread themselves as far
north as Scotland; and by the generosity or weakness
of the Scotch Kings, and the generosity or weakness
of the fair owners of large landed estates in Scotland,

obtained large landed properties by marriage.   From
and after the Norman Conquest, and probably long before, intimate relations existed between the nobles of
England and Scotland, and also, when at peace, between
the kings of the different parts of the whole island.
As a matter of fact, the Roman civil government,
which for four or five centuries nearly covered the
whole of England and Scotland, contributed a great
deal to the intercourse of the various races inhabiting
the island ; and the Christian religion, with its bishops
and abbots and priests, helped to hand down the
sacred torch of religion and civilization in the
whole of Europe to the Middle Ages.   On the
other hand, feudalism breathed of war, and its
supporters did not modify its peculiar character.
Essentially it was a system based on self-defence, in
which the old tribal relations of chieftain and clansman
gave place to a wiser and stronger bond of union arising
from the relations of lord and vassal, and in which the
blood relationship and obligations of a decaying civilization gave place to wider and more enduring relationships of owner and tenant, landlord and vassal.

Revival of civil law.—When the warlike and
barbarous rivalries of lords and kings began to give
way in this island, the shackles of the feudal law began
to be loosened and fall off, and then recourse was had
to the civil law of Rome for wisdom as to what our
laws ought to be.   As the English and Scotch began
to be more commercial in their habits, and less devoted
to war, the civil law was more and more consulted in
England and Scotland for the determination of disputes
amongst the citizens of both countries.   Strange to

say, English lawyers have generally been reluctant to admit their obligations to the civil law of Rome ; but the greatest lawyers of England have no doubt or hesitation on this matter. Thus, Chief Justice Holt says: " Inasmuch as the laws of all nations are doubtless raised on the ruin of the civil law, as all governments spring out of the ruins of the Roman Empire, it must be admitted that the principles of our law are borrowed from the civil law, and therefore grounded upon the same reason in many things; and is a subject worthy of scientific curiosity and of the study of those who are to profess and practise the English law."

Feudal and commercial age.—We have now escaped from the feudal age, and are gradually escaping from the feudal laws ; and we have entered upon the commercial age, and are gradually returning to the enlightened principles of the Roman civil law. Between the feudal and the commercial periods there are essential differences. Thus, for example, the fundamental bases of the feudal period are force and combination against force, and of the commercial period are contract and order. On things purely rational the feudal laws are silent. In the civil law, the rights and duties of the citizens to each other have been reduced to the law of contract. This analysis is somewhat violent, but it is not without its value. Still, let us never forget that to understand a system of law as a system of government, we must know the occupation, and the morals, and the politics of a nation. Moreover, we must also remember that evil and corrupt manners and customs, and internal weakness and disorder, will overthrow the best laws in the world.

Mighty Rome herself became corrupt ; and her excellent laws did not save her from the barbarian.
History shows that the Romans, as well as ourselves,
have advanced from barbarism to civilization ; and that,
under various impulses and necessities, they and we
have arrived at a high degree of civil and political
liberty, of physical and intellectual development. Let
us, therefore, be on our guard against the corruption
and weakness by which they were overthrown.

*Decisions, institutional writers, and history as
sources of law.*—Before closing this branch of my subject, I must not omit, and can merely here add, that
as part of the customary law of the land, we must
include judicial decisions, and the works of the great
institutional writers on the law. These, so far as consistent with the great principles of law and justice,
and not contrary to the statutory law of the realm,
are parts and portions of the law of Scotland. The
great sources of the law of Scotland are fully and
admirably expounded in the great legal institutional
writers of Scotland. Of these writers I must mention
Stair, Erskine, and Bell, with whom all students of
the law of Scotland must make themselves thoroughly
and deeply acquainted. Nor must such students forget the history of their country, illustrating and explaining the laws which have been made, whether by
the King, or the Parliament, or the Judges of the
Supreme Court. Of course, where statutory enact-
ments exist on any branch of law, they are the very
soul and essence of the law, and override all other
means of ascertaining what the law is.

Action and reaction of the national condition on national law.—I could have wished that time would have allowed me to give a few illustrations of the way in which manners and customs act and react on a nation in regard to the administration, and even the body, of the laws ; but I must press onwards to other matters, and shall here make only one or two observations on the kindred point to which I have just referred. Thus, in the height of the supremacy of the Church of Rome, the clergy were the great and almost universal judges on all disputed subjects, both human and divine. Afterwards, in the feudal ages, the great lords and their deputies were the ordinary judges, and the clergy were gradually deprived of their jurisdiction in civil matters, and restricted as much as possible to matters spiritual. Lastly, in the commercial ages, the progress of thought and political action in Europe is clearly advancing towards the universal supremacy of the civil judges of the state in all matters civil and criminal.

VI.—NECESSITY FOR CODIFICATION.

Our laws should be based on civilized society.—Our laws should be founded on the constitution of man as a member of civilized society; on the highest and noblest opinions entertained about his relations to a civilized or an enlightened state of society; because these should be suitable to a civilized state of society. Yet, we still hold by our old fancies about our feudal relations, as if they ought to be based on a state of society long

ago extinguished ; and we live, so far as an enlightened
system of law is concerned, as if we were just emerging
out of a state of barbarism.   Surely, this is absurd and
ridiculous ; and productive, as we know it is, of the
most unfortunate consequences.   Of course, ignorant
people say that the lawyers in Parliament are to blame
for this state of things.   But I am very far from being
of this opinion.   If the work of codifying our law is
to be done, it must be undertaken by the lawyers, who are, and have always been, the greatest and
most effective reformers of the law.   How a codification
of the law should be executed, and by what kind of
persons, I cannot now discuss here.   At present, I am
merely concerned with the duty of the nation to undertake the codification of the law as a great, useful,
and necessary work.

Our laws largely unintelligible.—All laws should
have a simple distinct meaning ; and yet, how different
from this is the fact !   With our popular, democratic
assemblies and Parliaments, which have largely degene-
rated into mere speaking machines, and with the hap-
hazard mode in which we make laws, based on numerous
debates, amendments, and compromises, we really cannot expect anything else to happen.   What a burlesque
of law must exist, when the most learned in the profession are often ignorant of the rights of individuals
in the most common and trumpery case, and when
learned councillors of the law are obliged to finish their
opinions with the advice that, as the case submitted to
them for their opinion is so difficult, an appeal should
be made to the courts for the purpose of having the
point in dispute settled !   There is no necessity for

coming to the conclusion that, in such an advice, the learned councillors are dishonest. All that can justly be inferred is, that when such an opinion can be generally and honestly given, the law is in a scandalous condition.

Statute law of England and Scotland.—The condition of the statute law of England was thought disgraceful by Chief-Justice Coke, who lived about 250 years ago. Had he lived in our day, how scornful and severe must now have been his censure! How he would have mocked "at the provisoes and additions, and many things on a sudden penned or corrected, by men of none or little judgment in law!" Yet our Scottish statutes, which for the last two or three centuries have become both numerous and verbose, were formerly models of what statute law ought to be. Even the great Lord Bacon praised the old Scottish statutes as almost unsurpassable for their perfection and directness. But, then, we must remember that the statutes which he praised were actually written out in their legal and legislative form by lawyers who knew the law, and were specially trained and experienced in putting the resolutions of the Scottish Parliament into legislative form. This they did at the end of the session, and thereafter obtained the sanction of the king to the statutes framed on the resolutions of the Parliament. Unfortunately the lawyers so employed were suspected, and rightly suspected, of always giving a doubtful point in favour of the king, and the result was that the resolutions were abandoned, and fully drawn-up bills took their place.

Coke on English statutes as badly drawn.—Chief-
Justice Coke, referring to an ancient custom of drawing
up statutes in England, says : " If acts of parliament
were, after the old fashion, penned by such only as
perfectly knew what the common law was before the
making of any act of parliament concerning that
matter, as also how far forth statutes had provided a
remedy for former mischiefs, and defects discovered
by experience, then should very few questions arise,
and the learned should not often and so much perplex
their heads to make atonements and peace by construction of law between insensible and disagreeing
words, sentences, and provisions, as they now do."

His censures applicable to our present statutes.—
How true these words are to the present state of
our statute law! Therefore, how necessary it is to
have all our laws, and especially all our statute law,
arranged and codified in a simple, clear, and proper
form ! If we cannot have a code for the Empire, let
us, I say, have at least a scientific code of the statute
law of Scotland. I believe that neither time nor
money should be spared to carry out the minor, and
even the major scheme to a successful termination.

Legal materials voluminous and chaotic.—Notwithstanding what I have said about an actually existing
science of law, I am justified, I think, in saying, as I
long ago said, that the time has arrived for the codification of our laws,—a codification which, in the
narrowest sense, would comprehend a scientific arrangement of our laws for reference, instruction, and
judgment. Long and justly there has been heard a
loud cry amongst us for the simplification and pub-

lication of our national laws; for they have now grown
to enormous proportions by legislative statutes and
judicial decisions, and the results are chaotic in the
extreme, and involve a gigantic amount of useless
labour to all who are obliged to learn the principles,
or who engage in the practice or administration of our
laws.   But still, if the materials are voluminous and
chaotic, they are valuable and rich for the building up
of a code of law suitable to the wants and aspirations
of our modern society.

Essential characteristics of a code.—As far as possible,
such a code should be digested and composed by the
most learned and experienced men in the country, and
on a scientific basis.   It should be certain in its commands; symmetrical in its form; consistent in its
language; and logical in its divisions: of course it
should also be published and made exclusively binding
on all the subjects of the state to which it extended.

Codification required at once.—Taking the sources
of our law as springing chiefly, not only from the civil,
but also from the feudal laws, I have almost said
enough to show that the laws of this country should
be reduced to an intelligible and scientific form.   But,
when we are obliged to add the numerous statutes
which have been passed by the Scotch Parliament
before the Union, and by the British Parliament since
the Union, the case is very much stronger.   Nay more,
when we are obliged to add the infinite number of
decisions which have been given by way of interpretation of the law, and not unfrequently making vital
changes thereon by what is known as judge-made law,
I think, I have stated an irresistible case for the re-

duction of our laws to scientific order.   Take any
science you think fit—chemistry, astronomy, or natural
philosophy—and think what would have been the condition of any one of them, unless, according to the
progress which had been made, it had been reduced to
scientific order ! How impossible to master even one
of the natural sciences!   How much beyond the power
of the human mind to grasp the great principles which
have been discovered and demonstrated !   Nay, when
we recall to mind the changes which have been made
in the constitution of society, and the alterations
which, even in recent times, have been made as to
real and personal rights, we immediately perceive the
absolute necessity for setting about the work of codification at once.

I have now said enough as to law in general, and
its sources, and its codification, and I must now come
to the practical aim of my discourse.   I have, therefore, to submit to you that it is desirable to establish,
as soon as possible, a course of lectures in Dundee on
commercial law ; and to hope that, before many years
have passed over our heads, a full course of legal
education in Scotch law may be obtained in the town
by all who wish it.

VII. DESIRABLE TO ESTABLISH A COURSE OF LECTURES

IN DUNDEE ON COMMERCIAL LAW.

*Lectures suitable for imparting an elementary know-
ledge of science.*—Every age must be taught in its own
language; and oral instruction, in the general and
elementary principles of the sciences, has always been
found agreeable and effective. Sir James Mackintosh
says, that " public lectures, in all ages, had been used
for giving elementary instruction in all sciences, and
is the most convenient mode to awaken the attention,
abridge the labours, guide the inquiries, relieve the
tediousness of private study, and impress the principles of science." Now, in Dundee, we have a large
number of young men engaged in legal and commercial
pursuits, and to whom, at an early stage of their
careers, a knowledge of the general principles of law,
and especially of commercial law, would be of the
utmost importance. No doubt, all the citizens of a
free country, in one way or another, and most generally
after a bitter experience of its unsatisfactory results,
or of its expensive enjoyment, gradually become
acquainted with a large body of the laws of their
country. But what I would urge upon you as a
desirable, and even necessary, thing would be a general
course of lectures on the general principles of the law
of Scotland, and on its commercial laws in particular, and
on the means and remedies provided for enforcing such
laws.

General principles alone should be taught.—The laws of Scotland are of considerable magnitude, and great study is required to master them.   But the great fundamental principles are ever the same, and must be taught by the wise of every age, *e.g.* those as to property and marriage.   For property is the foundation of civil society, and the rights of acquisition, alienation, and transmission are subservient to the subsistence and well-being of mankind.   Again, marriage is almost universally admitted to be the most effective means of carrying out the intentions of the Creator, and highly productive of the happiness and of the welfare of the human race.

Great power in general principles.—The knowledge of the general principles is enough for most people. When this knowledge has been thoroughly acquired, great progress has actually been made in legal science, and great power acquired over the whole body of the law ; for the propositions in law are, or ought to be, as capable of demonstration as the propositions of geometry.   But, for those who are to spend their lives in the practice of the laws, deep acquaintance is essential, and for their needs ample provision has been made at our old Scotch universities.

Study the force of the words of the law.—Do not, however, forget that to know the law is not to know the words of the law, but the force and virtue of its words.   Words are the servants or the symbols of thought, and were invented for the plain and perfect description of things.   The student of the law must, therefore, search out the reason of the law, and that by diligent and earnest search ; for the reason of the law is its life and soul. He should bring the law to the test of reason and truth. He should examine contrary reasons, and follow out those which are reasonable. He should also write out his ideas ; for, when he reduces his ideas to writing, he most effectively discovers whether or not he has really made any advance in his studies. Words being the symbols of thought will have very different meanings to different persons ; for the thoughts and the symbols of men regarding the same things are very different.

Legal interpretation.—To get at the right meaning of a statute or a legal decision, we should try to discover what are its common reason and intention. Having ascertained these, we have got at the kernel of the whole thing, and can start afresh with a new or well-demonstrated proposition as confidently as the rich merchant can go into the market, and buy goods by means of his stored-up capital. We can even go farther; for we have now the means of making discoveries for ourselves by purely logical processes. For example, we can obtain considerable results by the simple process of analysis, and by applying the rule that where things are allowed, everything following thence is allowed; and again, *vice versâ*, where things are forbidden, everything following thence is forbidden. A perfect lawyer is a rare person ; for he requires the highest and most varied powers—intellect, reasoning, and soul ; taste, imagination, and eloquence. Great lawyers are, in the estimation of all those whose opinion is worth having, and always have been, ornaments of their profession and country.

Duties of lawyers.—For those who would study and
practise the law aright, I would say, widen and deepen
your highest and most generous sentiments; be diligent, simple, and dignified; await with calmness the
noblest rewards which can be conferred upon, or crown
human life.   Remember that you must have regard to
future results as well as present advantages; and that
it is your duty to prefer the noblest to the less noble
in all things.   Never forget that the courts of justice,
in which you will be called upon to practise, are tem-
ples of justice; that you are, or will be, or hope to be,
servants of the law; and that, in your practice, you
have to deal with the highest practical ideas which
have ever been reached by your countrymen in their
progress and aspirations towards justice, which is one
of the head corner-stones of Almighty God, who rules
and governs all things in justice and equity.   True,
study is, at first, difficult and irksome; but it afterwards becomes easy and agreeable.   Besides, high
rewards and honours are always in store for the successful practitioners of the law.

Aim of the course of lectures should be useful.—The
aim of the course of lectures which I now advocate
ought to be to give useful instruction, and should be
confined to the requirements of youthful students of
law, and of young men engaged in commercial pursuits.
It should be strictly elementary, practical, and methodical.   It should be elementary, and not too much
devoted to details; because it is desirable to confine
the attention of the students to general principles
alone, and their necessary elucidation.   It should be
practical; because it ought to have a direct bearing

on the daily lives and future studies of the students.
It should be methodical ; because by such a mode of
study alone can any real and abiding progress be made
in any science.

Method of great importance.—Method is the life of
everything, and especially of study.   Lord Bolingbroke
says of method, that " we may acquire by it less learning, but more knowledge; and as this is collected with
design, and cultivated with art, it will be, at all times,
of immediate and ready use to us."   Indiscriminate
and unmethodical readers or students have been well
compared to such as have no fixed habitation, who
dwell everywhere, reside in no place, and cannot belong
to any country.

Such a course of lectures highly useful.—Even as I
have circumscribed my suggestion for a legal course of
lectures in Dundee, I venture to think that the subject
is of considerable extent ; and, in its minute details,
is not free from complication.   Still, I think, experience shows that the uses of public lectures to direct
the studies of the young, and to expound principles,
and to cite authorities, are very great.   Lectures are
attractive and enticing to the young, and a great help
in the progress of their studies.   No doubt, the art of
teaching is a great gift, and requires sympathy, and
patience, and knowledge.   But, even under grave
disadvantages, it is still the most perfect form of
gaining an elementary acquaintance with any department of knowledge.   We must not forget that,
if we are to prosecute our studies to a higher plane,
and become deeply versed in any branch of science,
we must betake ourselves to the closet, far apart

from men and things, and there commune with nature, law, and truth, and their greatest teachers.

Style of such lectures.—Such lectures, as I have suggested, should be in the form of pure didactic teaching; and should consist of neat and accurate statements of great principles, and their chief consequences and deductions; and should not aim at being brilliant with the varied lights of poetry, or dressed in the varied garb or colours of philosophy.

Course should not be too ambitious.—Above all things, the course should not be too ambitious. Let us, I say, direct our attention and confine our objects to meet the practical requirements of the time and place, of the present and immediate future. Some, I believe, do not feel inclined to take so modest a view of the requirements of a legal lectureship in Dundee such as I have just indicated, and would prefer to see a fully-equipped chair of Scotch law, and even a school of Scotch law in all its branches, established in Dundee. The time may come for this larger scheme. Certainly the time has not yet come; and the necessity for doing something to commence the work is strong and urgent. Still, I can perfectly well understand that the recent Act of Sederunt, by which those who intend to practise as solicitors are not obliged to attend law lectures at the old universities (*vide* Journal of Jurisprudence, 1886), should give a strong impetus to the early establishment of a regular and fully-equipped school of law in Dundee. In the meantime, let us consider what we require, what funds are or can be at our disposal, and what are our materials and tools, and we will then see what sort of a building can be erected.

Funds required for scheme for five or three years.—
Now, to carry out this modest scheme which I have
sketched, three things are required, namely, (1) funds
for a lectureship ; (2) funds for studentships ; and (3)
funds for scholarships. Roughly, I estimate that £500
a year would be required for the scheme : that is to
say, £300, at least, a year of a fixed salary to the
lecturer; £100 a year for four studentships of £25 a
year each; and £100 a year for two scholarships of £50
a year each. In the event of such lectureship being
established, I believe about fifty or sixty students could
be induced or forced to attend, and if the lecturer were
fairly successful as a teacher, he would have a larger
class of students than any professor at the Dundee
University College. The lecturer on law should be
expected to deliver about fifty or sixty lectures in the
course of the year; and ought to hold regular examinations of his students on the subjects of the lectures,
and also on the legal subjects prescribed. To give the
experiment a fair chance of success, provision ought to
be made for five years, or at least three years maintenance of the lectureship, studentships, and scholarships,
or for a total of £2,500, and not less than £1,500; or,
omitting the studentships and scholarships, for a total
of £1,500 or £900. I have calculated that the
permanent and efficient endowment of a law lectureship,
and of four studentships and two scholarships, would
require £10,000 or £12,000.

It would not be difficult to get the necessary funds.—
We are no doubt passing through a painful ordeal;
and till lately have had no great prospect of any
immediate improvement in our local industry. But, I

venture to believe, that if a strenuous appeal were
made to the wealthy and enlightened merchants
and lawyers of this town, no great exertion and no
great labour would be required to raise the necessary
funds. Much has been done of late years in our midst
by the generous and enlightened benefactress who
founded the Dundee University College. But much
yet requires to be done to bring the University College
to a state of perfection in regard to the requirements
of the age, and the necessities of this town and its
vicinity. Moreover, I have been informed, and have
good reason to believe, that, if something were done to
set this scheme afloat, the Trustees of the late Dr. John
Boyd Baxter might be inclined to afford pecuniary aid
in forwarding a project which could not have failed to
appeal deeply to the late Dr. Baxter's own soul, as
a plan not unworthy of high commendation and considerable pecuniary support. Of course, if the late
Dr. Baxter's Trustees, or others, should, by their
enlightened generosity, establish a fully-equipped
school of law in Dundee, and suitable for Dundee and
neighbourhood, no one shall be better pleased than I
would be.

[*By a strange irony of fate, while these pages are
passing through the press, appeals, after considerable
litigation in the Court of Session, are now before the
House of Lords for judgment as to* (1) *whether Dr.
Baxter accounted to his late wife for her separate
estate; and* (2) *whether he knew how to make his last
will and testament effectual to carry out his intentions
in regard to the disposal of the residue of his estate.*

Forensic studies a branch of university education.— I need hardly say that forensic studies are properly a branch of university education, and might naturally expect to be received not unfavourably within the halls of the Dundee University College, where ample accommodation, I believe, already exists for the execution of the scheme I have suggested for your consideration.

Conclusion.—Notwithstanding the long continuance of bad trade, Dundee is a rich community, and has many far-seeing and enlightened citizens, who are deeply impressed with the great advantage of solid and useful knowledge. To my old native town, and to my old former, even I might say present fellow-townsmen, I think, I shall not appeal in vain, to help forward a scheme not unworthy of their best assistance. I, therefore, beg leave to urge upon all interested in furthering education in Dundee, the great duty and privilege of providing the pecuniary means for a thorough course of instruction in Dundee in the elementary and general principles of the law, and especially of the commercial law, of Scotland.

LECTURE

ON THE

SCIENCE AND STUDY OF POLITICS,

OR ON

THEORY AND PRACTICE OF GOVERNMENT

(DELIVERED IN THE ALBERT INSTITUTE, DUNDEE, ON 12TH JANUARY 1887).

———

INTRODUCTION.—In the present Lecture, I propose to treat of the subjects which fall under the Science of Politics; or, in other words, which form the general principles of human society. Whether Politics is a Science or an Art, or a Science and an Art, or a branch of a Science or Art, will be most conveniently discussed in detail on some future occasion. As I have explained in my last Lecture what I understand by Science, I need not repeat what I then said.

I. PRIMITIVE OR NATURAL SOCIETY.

Originally the world common.—At first, the world was the common property of the human race. Gradually, all the land has become the property of individuals, races, and states. But the open sea is, and ought always to be, the highway of nations, and the common property of mankind.

Golden age of romance.—Poets and romancers
paint a golden age as existing in the infancy of the
world. But neither history, nor reason demonstrate, or
render probable, such an age at such a time. True,
there did not then exist the same amount of competition between individuals and nations for wealth
and honour and power as exists in the present age.
On the other hand, the primitive inhabitants of this
earth could not have been anywhere so well and so
amply provided with all the necessaries and luxuries
of life as we are now. The life of primitive mankind must have been coarse and uncertain, and
devoted to the acquisition of the bare necessaries
of life. Men begin to accumulate stores of wealth
and power when they have a reasonable prospect
of enjoying them. In fact, men first began to
emerge out of barbarism as soon as the right of
individual acquisition began to be asserted, and its
advantages began to be appreciated. Dominion and
property put an end to the primitive mode of living,
that is to say, to the primitive stages of hunting and
fishing, and the most rudimentary forms of husbandry.

Family life.—The family life, and then the village
life, were the primitive and barbaric elements of
civilized society. The family life determined the
relations of domestic society, in which the head of the
family was lawgiver, judge, and priest, as well as parent
and food provider. From it, indeed, a number of human
relations, actual and possible, moral and legal, have
their origin. For example, the maintenance of wife
and children, the rights of divorce and of inheritance,
and, briefly, all the rights and duties involved in the

Patria Potestas. Sheldon Amos writes that, ."In ancient Rome, and to a certain extent in the continental countries which have based their laws on the Roman and canon law, the family appears as a small society, every member of which has his place assigned by law, and has his rights and duties in respect of every other member carefully determined." It was the same in Scotland, England, and Ireland in primitive times.

Village life.—The village life is created out of the combination of several families. However originated, whether by the natural combination of the different branches of the same family, or by the settlement of different families in one place, the village community soon becomes organized under some family or chief, pre-eminent amongst the rest for wealth, or wisdom, or military glory. This primitive condition of society has succeeded well amongst all Aryan communities, and has not been altogether destroyed in India even to this day. It has its peculiar laws and customs quite independent of the general regulations which, in the course of time, and usually by conquest, are imposed upon the village communities of India and elsewhere by their conquerors.

Observations as to village life.—The primitive state of village society has its dangers as well as advantages. For, while it largely contributes to the material happiness and prosperity of individuals and of the village groups, it always carries with it a weakness against external and internal foes, a low degree of patriotism, and a deficiency of permanent vitality. This is as true of the great

majority of the Irish people at the present
moment as it was true of the Scotch Highlanders two
or three centuries ago; for these two sections of the
Celtic race when, in similar degrees of civilization, have
shewn small regard for the greater nationalities of
which they form parts. Various devices have been
adopted to remove the defects of this primitive state
of society. As yet, the proper measures of centri-
fugal and centripetal forces, of local and central government, are very far from being well ascertained or defined,
either in India or here at home in Scotland, England, or
Ireland. The true relations which must be established
between the different parts of the United Kingdom
of Great Britain and Ireland, and between them and
the different parts of the British Empire, must soon
be determined. They are, however, too deep and
complicated to be discussed on the present occasion.
From the state of things in the most ancient period
of the history of the world, we may catch a glimpse
of a great question of modern times in all great
empires. Verily, "There is nothing new under the
sun."

II. CIVILIZED SOCIETY.

*Civilization is an advance on the primitive state of
mankind.*—We must not suppose that the primitive
stage of society was essentially different from the
modern or civilized stage of society. Man has not
changed his nature by entering into civilized society.
He has merely advanced in the scale of his being, and

utilized powers given to him by God for higher purposes. So far as civilized society has modified the original, primitive nature of man, it has enlightened and strengthened his nature. Nay more, to all the beauty and variety of the relations and offices in government, civilized society has given rise. Man's body and faculties shew that he was fitted for society; and so does the diversity of his talents. Civilized society is based on the nature and constitution of man, or, in other words, on humanity or human nature. In this nature and constitution, there are three great principles, namely, (1) natural law, which includes religion, (2) self-love, and (3) sociability. Of humanity, there are three springs whence all human rights and duties originate, namely, God, property, and society. When those three classes of duties are understood and obeyed, man reaches the highest ideal perfection of his existence. Our systems of humanity, or of human life, its origin and its present and future conditions, are based on the essential identity of the nature of man in his primitive and civilized conditions. In both conditions, he is a being subject to reason, and endowed with the attributes and responsibilities of conscience, or the power of deciding between right and wrong, and of choosing the one and rejecting the other. As subject to reason, man is capable of rising to an appreciation of the very highest ideas of the Divine nature, and, in a limited degree, of putting those ideas into practice in his daily life. We were not created to be the victims of passing whims and fancies, or of wild irregular passions; but we are bound to rule and guide our conduct by reason, and by human laws, and in conformity to God's commands.

Primitive and civilized life compared.—Man, says Aristotle, is a social animal; and, in his opinion, all mankind are agreed. But, while primitive society is greatly in need of all things, civilized society makes ample, varied, and admirable provision for men in all the things which contribute to the happiness and enjoyment of life. Civilized society is also distinguished for the highest, the best, and the purest thoughts and sentiments which can aid, benefit, and adorn mankind. Whatever poets may imagine, or romancers dream, the primitive state of man was, and, as far as it still exists, is the very reverse of all that we see and enjoy in modern or civilized society.

Law of nature is not abrogated.—The law of nature, or the law of primitive man, *i.e.* the law to which man is subjected in virtue of his nature as a human being, endowed with reason and conscience, is not abrogated by his entering into society. It continues to exist, although modified, in civilized society. It is merely sublimated, and purified, and ennobled. This law of nature is the substantial and only reliable basis, except force for a season, of any long enduring condition of civilized society.

Society is an enduring or permanent contract.— Edmund Burke says: "Society is a contract; but is not to be taken up and dissolved according to the fancies of parties. It is not a contract for the sale of calicoes. It is not temporary; but it is permanent. It is a contract in all science, in all art, in all virtue, and in every performance." It is, in fact, a union of the past, present, and future generations of a certain limited and determinate portion of the globe, with all its rights and privileges, and along with all its disadvantages and responsibilities. Men are not, now at least, in the first place, voluntarily members of civil society, but must be taken as consenting to membership. Men, as physical beings, are doomed to weakness, decay, and death. But, notwithstanding the perpetual changes taking place by death, the State exists; and, for anything we know to the contrary, a State may exist for ever.

A state is a moral essence.—From popular use and political discussion, the word "state" has become indecisive, and ambiguous in meaning. Sometimes it is used as meaning—(1) supreme political authority; (2) executive authority; (3) nation as an aggregate body of persons connected by blood, language, history, or habitation; and (4) a population contrasted with government. Without examining these different significations, I have to say that a state is, in truth, a moral essence; that its moral existence is its essential and its highest characteristic. Consequently the state is properly enough regarded as possessed of will, conscience, and moral responsibility. The laws of a nation are the expressions of this national conscience. But the laws of its decay and death are not yet sufficiently known to enable us to build up a reliable theory in regard to them. Still, all the essential institutions of a state can be resolved into those of government, family, property, and contract. These four elements are not created by, but are independent of, the state, and are principles upon which a state

E

rests. Sheldon Amos writes, that the complex life of a state depends on liberty to pursue industrial occupations, undertake commercial enterprises, cherish family ties, and gradually and surely mature social bonds, and gradually cultivate the various sentiments and emotions of humanity. He further writes that liberty is freedom from restraint to commence, prosecute, and conclude all the objects of human life. In other words, the common aim of the state is ideal, and for the well-being of every atom of the community. Again, Burke says, that "moral essence makes a nation. The majesty of the throne, the dignity of the nobility, the honour of the gentry, the sanctity of the clergy, the reverence of the magistracy, the consideration to law and the property of individuals, and the respect paid to the personal property represented by corporations: all these united are truly the body politic in all countries. They are so many receptacles of justice." To preserve the integrity of the national life is the final end and supreme object of the national corporate existence.

Vattel's definition of a nation or state.—Vattel says: "A nation or a state is a body politic, or society of men, united together for the purpose of promoting their mutual safety and advantage by their combined strength." He further says, "that, by the act of civil or political association, every citizen subjects himself to the authority of the entire body in everything which relates to the common welfare."

Territorial ownership.—Vattel also says, that a nation comes to have a peculiar exclusive right of property and dominion by settlement, appropriation, and cultivation. Now, this right of property comprehends—(1) the dominion by which the nation, or political society, alone may use the country for the supply of its necessities, and may dispose of it as it thinks proper, and derive any advantage it is capable of yielding; and (2) the empire, or right of sovereign command, by which the nation directs and regulates, at its pleasure, everything that takes place in the country. This right of acquisition has important bearings as to the colonial possessions of our own and other countries. For example, when a nation takes possession of a distant country, and settles a colony there, that distant country, though separate from the principal establishment or mother country, necessarily becomes part of the state, equally with its ancient possessions, and is entitled to all the advantages, and subject to all the dangers, as the mother country in peace or war.

Property is public, common, and private.—This right of property is divided into public, common, and private. Public property belongs to the nation, and is reserved for the necessities of the crown or the republic. Common property belongs to all the citizens who take advantage of it according to the necessities, or the laws which regulate its use. Private property is possessed by individuals.

Eminent dominion annexed to sovereignty.—The eminent dominion of a state or nation is annexed to the sovereignty, and consists in the right of the sovereign power to dispose, in case of necessity, and for the public safety, of all the wealth contained in the state. This is a prerogative of majesty. When the property of a corporation, or of an individual, is taken away or alienated in a case of public necessity, justice demands that the corporation or individual should be indemnified at the public charge; for the burdens of the state ought to be supported equally, or in a just proportion, by all.

Rights of private property.—As regards private property, I have to say that, as a general rule, every proprietor has a right to make what use he pleases of his own property, and to dispose of it as he pleases, when the rights of third persons are not invaded. Proprietorship is the right to dispose of a thing in substance, and is a right which is being vigorously attacked by the strange and crude ideas of fantastic dreamers at home and abroad. No doubt property has its duties as well as its rights. But the times will be full of danger when, under the subjection of the pre-eminent prerogative of the sovereign power, whether monarchic, aristocratic, or democratic, or a sovereign power combined of all the three different simple forms of government, a man is not entitled to acquire, use, and transfer, what he has acquired from parental affection, the love of friends, or his own industry and forethought. Of course no sane person would deny that the sovereign power has the right to subject private property to regulations of policy, *e.g.* to prevent deer forests from being established or continued when, and where, corn fields are necessary. For the public welfare and the safety of the state are principles of higher importance and of wider scope in the scale of government than the maintenance of any other national principle whatsoever. What would be the use, or advantage, of maintaining the rights of private property as inviolate, when the safety of the state itself was in danger of being destroyed? When men enter into, or form members of a civilized society, they are bound to do all they can, and, in case of need, even to sacrifice themselves and their property, for the good of their country.

Aims of different states diverse.—The aims of different states and different forms of government are diverse and multifarious. Thus, the aims and objects of a Christian and of a Pagan state are essentially different; and so are the aims of Protestant and Roman Catholic states. In our own country, we have tried to give the widest scope to human activity, and to the attainment of all rational desires. How far we have succeeded in our object it is difficult to say. But, on the whole, and in the whirlpool of diverse aims—educational, religious, scientific, artistic, and industrial—our country has, at all events, reached the goal of human perfection as nearly as any other nation which has ever existed; and has also been able to do great things in the world by advancing the interests of science, and religion, and material progress in our own country, and throughout the world.

III.—CIVIL GOVERNMENT DEFINED.

Good government and party government contrasted. —In speaking to you of civil government, I am, on the present occasion, and in this hall, to treat of wise government, and not party government, and have to say that the chief ends of good government are happiness, justice, and national defence; and of party government, selfishness, personal aggrandisement, and neglect of national interests. Government, in the sense of good government, implies the superintendence of the fortunes of the community, present and future, and power over the physical strength of all the community for all and every citizen, within or without its territorial boundaries. Nowadays, when we have such a host of party politicians, who are all aiming at making the world perfect and happy in their own little span of life, we are kept in a state of turmoil, and are not allowed that rest which is needful to mind and body for the due performance of our daily tasks. We ought, however, to remember that politics are only the means to an end, and that that end is good government. To reach this end, restraint is as necessary as liberty. Without restraint, the forces at work will be apt to do an immense deal of mischief. To hear some people talking about government, one would suppose that its end ought to be to allow every man to do what he thought fit; and yet the truth is, that its end is to allow men to do what they think fit only in so far as they do not injure the like freedom of others. Good order is the foundation of all things in government, and also in most other things. Some people in our own country speak as if the nation had the power of declaring what was true and false, right and wrong; and as if Parliament was omnipotent over all the principles of justice and injustice. True, the people are the ultimate sources of power, and Parliament is the final court of appeal, in this country; but neither the one nor the other can, by laws or resolutions, determine what is absolutely right or wrong. No doubt, civil governments have not to deal with absolute, but merely with relative duties. But still, general principles are the only reliable grounds for safe reasoning; and the difference between the professor and the statesman is, that the former is a man with a theoretical, and the latter is a man with a practical knowledge of government. We need both in the world. The place of the one is in the college hall; and of the other, in the senate. Most unfortunate is that country which is governed by theorists and doctrinaires; for they always bring their country to ruin. On these points, I may here quote the words of Burke, who said that "the majority cannot alter the moral any more than the physical nature of things." In another place, he says, " one cannot dispense with the obligation of public faith, nor can any number." Wisely, in another place, he says that "the duty of statesmen ought to be to give, not to receive, information from the people, who are not capable of it by nature, or called to it by the constitution." Most unwisely, some public men in our own times think, or at least say, the very reverse.

All must be subject to the body politic.—Limiting then, my future observations to good government, the first remark I have to make is that, in a civilized government, every one must be subject to the body politic. In possession of the best constitution and laws in the world, and striving at all times to improve them, we must never forget that obedience to the supreme power is an essential condition of civilized society. If obedience is not thus acknowledged in the body politic, everything is, or is rapidly tending, towards anarchy, confusion, and disorder.   Of late, in the sister country of Ireland, we have had ample and sorrowful evidence of what a country must be when obedience to the laws is not a cardinal doctrine, acknowledged and acted upon by all the people. Here in Scotland, and across the border in England, we have peace, tranquillity, and liberty; and across the Irish Channel, we have practically civil war, disorder, and despotisn.   Long ago Burke said : "A first and primary necessity alone justifies anarchy; and then reason, order, peace, and virtue are subverted by lawlessness, disorder, war, and vice."   When a state of civil war exists, very little regard is paid to the interests of the country, to patriotism, or to the honour or safety of the country.

Political power ought to be exercised beneficially.— Burke lays down that " political power ought to be exercised for the benefit of those over whom it is exercised or claimed.   It is an artificial authority, in derogation of the natural rights of man, and not for the private advantage of the holders.   It is a trust of which the essence is .   .   .   .   . cessation when not duly exercised—when it ceases to be used for the only lawful purpose for which it exists, and substantially varies from such purpose."   To fix the limits of duty and right in a state is true statesmanship ; but to do this with reasonable accuracy is no easy task, and requires long and assiduous training All politicians are not statesmen, nor are all members of Parliament politicians.   A statesman ought to aim at the advancement of freedom and justice as his highest objects.

Not to discuss forms of government.—To discuss the various forms of government, and to show the various advantages and disadvantages of each, would here, at this point, have been interesting and instructive. But I have not time to do more than to indicate and explain the essential parts of a good constitution.

Tendency of modern governments is towards democracy.—Permit me, however, here to make a digression, and to observe that, in my opinion, the tendency of all modern European governments is towards democracy. Beyond all doubt or question, this, if true, is an important fact which cannot wisely be ignored. Thus, *e.g.*, the more democratic the government, the more persons require to be consulted as to the laws to be made, amended, or abrogated. This, I may say, is the political consequence of a democracy. The legal effects are no less striking and important. Thus, for example, as Sheldon Amos points out—(1) unless a permanent legislative commission be established to adapt the proposals of the representative legislative body, law becomes a mass of unintelligible compromises, and without unity or distinct meaning, and is often contradictory, ineffective, and absurd ; and (2) much legislative work has to be delegated to subordinate bodies, such as the Privy Council, and different local governmental boards and judicial councils ; otherwise the national legislative body is not able to get through the work of the year. Lately, in this country, session after session, we have had painful experience of this growing legislative incompetence of our supreme representative legislative Assembly ; and delegation of legislative powers has become an imperative necessity.

Tendency of representative legislators is to divest themselves of responsibility.—Another aspect of this matter is the increasing tendency of our representative legislators to throw upon the people, who are the electors, the responsibility of deciding great affairs of national moment.   This is a grave dereliction of duty as well as of almost unpardonable cowardice.   On the other hand, there is also an increasing tendency in a democratic state not to be satisfied with the mere choice of representatives by the people, but of giving such representatives specific directions in all national public matters of great importance.   Sometimes these directions eminate from the general body of the electors ; sometimesfrom the general body of the supporters of the representative ;   sometimes from a secret committee of his followers ;   and   sometimes from a powerful local magnate, territorial or commercial.   The results are partly good and partly evil, and the predominance of good or evil depends on the political knowledge and self-control of the people, and the political knowledge and self-reliance of the representatives.   Unfortunately, no   nation   in   Europe   has   the   necessary   amount of political knowledge and self-control required, and public affairs are apt to be decided by the loudest tongues and keenest pens, and not by the wisest heads and the most patriotic hearts.   " But," as Sheldon Amos and others have said, " a wisely trained and patriotic statesman will look to the past as well as the present, to the whole as well as the part, and should oppose all unjust or inexpedient outcries however vehement."   Such a statesman should and will be faithful to the people, and neither the master nor the

slave of the people.   Let us now consider the essentials
of good government.

IV. ESSENTIALS OF A GOOD GOVERNMENT.

(1). PUBLIC AUTHORITY REQUIRED.

Simple forms of government.—Clearly, then, a public
authority is essential to regulate the common affairs
of every political society.   Now, the fundamental
regulation which determines the manner in which the
public authority is regulated, is what forms the constitution of the state ; how and by whom governed ;
and the rights and the duties of the governors determine
the character and general tendencies of a government.
When a sovereign is at the head of a state, and is responsible to none for his conduct in the management
of public affairs, the government is monarchical.   When
a few of the highest, or most powerful, citizens hold the
reins of power, and are responsible to none for their
actions in the conduct of public affairs, the government
is aristocratical or oligarchical.   When the government
rests on the basis of popular rights, and the people are
ultimately the rulers, the government is democratical.
A pure democracy would be a government in which
the people actually and directly governed themselves,
and actually passed all laws.   But the democracies with
which the world is best acquainted are those governments in which the people choose representatives to act
for them in the senate, and in which those representatives
are, as a matter of fact, entrusted with the supreme
legislative and executive functions of the state.   These
three simple forms of government may be modified
almost to any extent by a mixture of two or three
of the simple forms of government.

Laws are political, constitutional, ·and civil.—In their legislative capacity, the sovereign powers enact laws which are regulations of the public authority, and are of three kinds, namely: (1) political, regulating the public welfare; (2) constitutional, regulating the constitution of the state; and (3) civil, regulating the rights and the duties of the citizens amongst themselves. The political and constitutional laws are fundamental, and should be suitable to the genius and circumstances of the people.

Attacks on the constitution are capital crimes.—To attack the constitution of a state by violating the constitutional laws, is a capital crime against society. The constitution of a state is never openly attacked, and is always secretly attacked, at first. We should, therefore, be alert and vigilant to watch the attacks made against the constitution. Upon the constitution of a state, changes are to be undertaken with the greatest caution, and with a due regard to prudence and well-established forms. When changes are proposed to be made on the constitution, we ought to consider how far such changes are capable of increasing the better government of the nation. If they are improvements, they should be adopted; and if they are not, they ought to be rejected. The sovereign power in a state exists for the safety and advantage of the people; and whether there are two or more sovereigns or sovereign powers, or there is only one sovereign or sovereign power, can make no difference as to the duty of exercising sovereign power for the benefit of the nation. The theory and the practice of the British Constitution are that all things are to be done for the common welfare and happiness of the people. In state affairs, the sovereign power ought to listen only to the dictates of justice and sound policy, of wisdom, prudence, and moderation ; for the sovereign power is the representative of the nation in its rights and obligations, and must exercise the former, and discharge the latter, with a due regard to the honour of the nation, and the interests which it may have at stake. The sovereign should, in fact, act as a wise and tender parent and faithful administrator. He is the guardian of the laws ; and his person is sacred and inviolable. But a tyrant is neither the one nor the other. At Rome, Nero was declared a public enemy by the senate. He was, in truth, a human monster, and acted like a madman.

(2). DEFENCE AGAINST EXTERNAL ENEMIES.

National defence is necessary.—One of the ends of political society is to defend the nation against all external insult and violence. If a state is unable so to do, its organization is imperfect ; and it should, at once, set about to provide a remedy. If it do not, history shows that it will not long subsist. The duty of national self-defence is necessary for the perfection, and even the preservation of a nation.

Valour is also necessary.—The duty of repulsing all aggressors to secure its rights, and to render itself respectable, is a primary necessity, and an elementary duty of every state. Valour is one of the chief means by which this is secured. In the olden times, the whole of our male population, capable of bearing arms, were bound to discharge this duty ; but, in Europe, for the last two centuries, this duty has been performed, for the most part, by standing armies.   It is well that every nation should preserve its valour, and also its skill in the use of arms ; for experience amply shows that a cowardly and undisciplined force is unable to repulse a warlike enemy, trained to the use of arms. Success in war is less dependent on numbers than valour ; and a brave nation has often defended its territories from aggression against a countless host of unskilful or timid soldiers.   The small band of heroes at Thermopolæ defended Greece against the gigantic Persian forces.   The battle of Bannockburn may remind us what can be done by bravery and patriotism.   The history of Britain proves what can be accomplished by brave men, led by skilful commanders, in every part of the world.   The Romans became the conquerors of the world by their military discipline, frugality, bodily strength, and dexterity, inured to labour and fatigue.   The same qualities have now made the German people the greatest military power in the world.   They have also made us great and powerful by land and sea. Some people talk slightingly of national prestige, but such persons talk about what they do not understand. Character alone often protects and defends a nation. A nation's strength consists in the military virtues, and the material riches of the citizens ; and all wise statesmen will do their utmost to increase these national advantages to the utmost of their ability.

Advantages of national honour and power.—We cannot lightly despise the glory of a nation any more than the honour of an individual.   A nation should hold fast by its glory, and do all it can honourably to increase it. So should an individual his power and honour. The glory of a nation is the clearest evidence of its power. It is the outward symbol of its greatness. When a national reputation for honour and valour has been established, the nation is illustrious, courted, and feared. When it is not, there is a danger of its being insignificant, avoided, and despised. True national glory brings with it a favourable opinion of wisdom and discernment, and is acquired and maintained by the great and noble actions of its great men; that is, by their justice, moderation, and greatness of soul. Not only should princes and ministers act worthily, but all the people should endeavour to act from pure, noble, great, and honourable motives. The nation that so acts will be an honour to itself, and a blessing to all mankind. The philosophers, statesmen, and orators, the inventors, and literary and scientific men, improve and promote the happiness and welfare of the human race. Those men who do not act worthily of their ancestors, and their country, disgrace themselves, and cast a stain on their country. The rulers of the state, by acting or speaking unworthily, are not deserving of the high honour of speaking or acting in the name of a just, honourable, and high-spirited nation.

(3). PROTECTION OF THE CIVIL RIGHTS OF PERSON AND PROPERTY.

Free use of property and personal abilities essential. —Civil society ought to be capable of enabling its members to gain a subsistence by their own labour and

industry; and to make a free and the best use of their
worldly means and personal abilities. Unless this is
allowed, a nation has no right to expect its citizens to
dedicate themselves to its service.   As a rule, in all
modern European nations, all are allowed to work, or
to leave the country.   This rule did not always exist;
and many vexatious laws were passed in this and other
countries to prevent the people from moving about
from one part of a country to another; and especially
to prevent them from carrying their acquired skill to
foreign countries.

Restrictions on labour abandoned.—Formerly, it was
generally supposed that it was the duty of the state
to take care that there should be a sufficient number
of able workmen in every useful and necessary trade
or profession, and to prevent the emigration of such
persons. This policy has been abandoned. Still, even
now, there are certain stringent regulations of, and
interferences with, the members of the learned
professions; because they are considered as a sort
of officers of state.   Vattel says that "a state
ought to encourage labour, animate industry, excite
abilities, propose honours, rewards, privileges, and so
order matters that every one may live by his own industry."   This country formerly acted in this way;
and, no doubt, helped herself forward to be the greatest
and most powerful nation in the world.   We are now
so rich and strong, and believe so much in the virtue
of commercial freedom, that we have abandoned our
old commercial policy, and are foolish enough to suppose
that other nations will adopt our commercial principles
and policy in consequence of their beauty and perfection

in our eyes.   I shall now speak of the two forms of productive labour, namely, industry applied to the soil, and industry directed to commercial pursuits.

Cultivation of the soil is necessary and honourable.— The cultivation of the soil is useful, necessary, and honourable ; for it is the chief and primary source whence the sustenance of men and beasts is obtained. In an agricultural country, it greatly adds to the wealth of the community ; and, in this and in most countries of the world, involves a great capital and employment of labour.

Soil should be cultivated.—To compel the cultivation of the soil is no necessary violation of private property; but may be simply the enforcement of a national duty. This duty of cultivating the soil was once enforced by legal pains and penalties both in England and Scotland; but it is now effectually left to the discretion and the interest of the landowners and occupiers of the soil. But our old agricultural laws, applicable to a condition of society no longer in existence, by which valuable improvements made by the occupiers were, without compensation, handed over to the landowners, have been wisely and justly abrogated, and compensation for the agricultural improvements made by occupiers has been raised to the dignity of a legal right.   Before this change was made in the law, gross injustice was often done to many of the tenant-farmers of Scotland, England, and Ireland.

Agriculture should be promoted.—As the progress of society is from the life of the hunter or fisher to that of the husbandman, so the next step is towards industrial trades and commerce.   Although we live in an in-

E

dustrial age, the quiet virtue of the life of the agriculturalists is not to be despised, and everything should be done to enable the husbandmen to reap and enjoy the reasonable fruits of their labours; for they are the backbone of the country, and have many of the virtues which increase the importance of every civilized nation.

Home and foreign commerce is useful.—In the early stages of society, men barter what commodities they possess for what they require, or wish to obtain. As society advances, barter gives place to exchange, and generally by means of third persons. This exchange is what is strictly designated as commerce, or buying and selling. It enables individuals and whole nations to procure those commodities which they need, but cannot procure at home. Commerce is either home or foreign. Home commerce is useful by furnishing all the citizens with the means of procuring what they want in the way of necessary, useful, or agreeable things. "It causes," says Vattel, "the circulation of money, excites industry, animates labour, gives subsistence to a great number of people, and adds to the population and power of the state."

Foreign commerce increases the national wealth.— Foreign commerce does those things for us, and also provides what our own national resources could not produce. By trading with foreigners, a nation often procures such things as neither nature nor art can fnrnish in our own country. If properly directed, foreign commerce increases the riches of a nation, and may become the source of wealth and plenty to all who engage in it. The greatest traders with foreign countries have been the Carthaginians, the Dutch, and the English, the United States of America, and the various English colonies and dependencies which are part and portion of the great British Empire.

Every nation is at liberty to engage in commerce or not.—Whatever we may think to the contrary, every nation is at liberty to engage, or not to engage, in commerce, and on such terms as it thinks fit. Permission to trade is a right granted by one state to another, or to the world in general. We, at one time, had very close and stringent rules as to commerce between ourselves and our colonies and dependencies and other nations. But we have now adopted the principle of a free and unrestricted exchange of commodities with all nations, and have merely limited this right by fiscal considerations. We now give no bounties to our own traders, and have long ago abolished all monopolies in trade. How far we have been wise in opening our ports to the world, and neglecting advantageous stipulations towards ourselves, is too wide a subject to enter upon here. Unless I am greatly mistaken, we are shifting our position, and tending towards some form or system of reciprocity, which, strange to say, has never been wholly abandoned by the most ardent free traders in negotiating commercial treaties between this and other countries. In a perfect system of free trade, there should be no commercial treaties at all. When the democracy has been fully enthroned in this country, we will, most probably, follow other democracies in their commercial policy with foreign countries, and insist on real commercial free trade treaties; or, in other words, endeavour to approximate to the old and

partially abandoned system of granting favours when
we receive favours.   No doubt, we shall also do our best
to include the whole of the British Empire, and all its
vast colonies and dependencies, with all their wonderful
and gigantic capacity for trade and commerce with the
mother country, in one and the same imperial fiscal
and commercial union for every part and portion of
the British Empire.   Our trade with our colonies and
dependencies has lately been enormously increased,
and is increasing at a rapid rate.

Gold and silver are useful in exchange.—In the first
ages of the world, after the introduction of private
property, people exchanged their commodities for those
things which they wanted.   Afterwards, gold and silver
became the standard value of things.   When stamped,
they are of great use in commerce, and greatly facilitate
commercial transactions.

(4). TRUE HAPPINESS OF A NATION.

Felicity is the aim of all men.—Felicity is the aim
of all mankind ; and the desire for its gratification
having been implanted in us by God Himself, the
Author of our being must be held to have intended
that we should be happy.   In the pursuit of happiness,
grievous mistakes may be made by us just as in every
human pursuit.   But our mistakes may well be our
instructors ; and, taught by the lessons of bitter experience, we may rise higher and higher, after fearful
blunders, in the realization of happiness.   Our passions
often carry us headlong into low, contemptible, and

grovelling forms of vice. But reason, with her powers of comparison, and of deciding between true and false, good and bad, and between things to be followed and those to be avoided, has always the power to remain the mistress, or ultimately to assert her power on our future conduct.

Its pursuit is a duty.—Endowed by God with the capacity for happiness, the pursuit of happiness is a duty which we owe to ourselves and others. To find out happiness, we must devote ourselves to the acquisition of useful knowledge; the adoption of a wise discipline in art, science, and literature; and to the practice of justice, piety, and religion. Instruction is not sufficient to make us happy. Still, enlightenment is the best security for the happiness of the individual, and the best pledge for the obedience of the citizen. To search out the truth, and to act on it when found, are the most worthy functions of a rational being. Man becomes perfect, so far as he can become so in this world, by the possession of natural and acquired faculties to obtain, and activity to put him in possession of, felicity. The ideal man of the ancient Greeks and Romans was, "the honest, wise, and pious man," and he indicates what, in their estimation were, and what, I think should in our estimation be, the highest attributes of mankind. These attributes are justice, wisdom, and religion, and to these I propose to direct your attention under the next and last branch of my present Lecture.

(5). THE CHIEF ENDS OF CIVIL SOCIETY.

(a) *Safety of the state is one of the chief ends of society.* —The government can increase the wisdom of its subjects by directing the energies, the knowledge, and the virtues of the governors and the people to the safety of the state, one of the chief ends of civil society. The love of country is an excellent and necessary virtue. Indeed, patriotism should always be raised to the highest point in every civilized community. To be prepared to sacrifice all things for our country is true magnanimity and the highest wisdom. Plato truly says that "we are not born for ourselves, but for our country and our friends." Where ardent love of country or patriotism exists, the nation is raised to the highest pitch of glory. The love of country is natural to all men ; but it is often weakened by tyrannous, unjust, and cruel rulers. Free nations are, morever, lovers of freedom, and passionately interested in the glory and happiness of other peoples and countries, and wish them also to be possessors of the highest degree of liberty and freedom.

(b) *Justice.*—Justice is one of the principal duties of a nation. But justice does not merely consist in the enactment of good laws. It comprehends the duty of enforcing the law, and taking measures to have it dispensed to every one in the most certain, speedy, and least burdensome manner. Men have given up their natural liberty to enjoy peaceably what belongs to them, and obtain justice according to law. If it be not so obtained, confusion, disorder, and despondency arise, and the civil virtues are extinguished, and the bonds of society are weakened.

Good laws required.—The laws should be just and wise. If men were enlightened and just, the laws of nature would be sufficient for civil society. But ignorance, self-love, and passion often make the laws of nature, and sometimes even the best civil laws, ineffectual. Hence, there is a necessity for establishing positive national, or municipal, laws. In this way, the law of nature is changed into the civil law, which should always be simple, fixed, and certain. Altered and amended under various natural and unnatural impulses, at different times, and in different stages of civilized society, it becomes, in a new garb, the law of the land. The civil law ought not to be unchangeable, like the laws of the Medes and Persians, but ought to be amended to suit the necessities and the condition of a nation. As a child outgrows the laws of his infancy, so a nation outgrows the laws of its infancy; and new and amended laws and discipline should be adopted in both cases.

Laws must be enforced.—We must never forget, however, that the best laws in the world must be enforced, or they will be useless. What is the use of laws unless they are enforced? Laws are intended to rule and guide the conduct of the citizens. Unless they are obeyed, or enforced, what benefit can they be to any one? On the execution of the laws of the land depends the national tranquillity, happiness, and glory. Under weak and incompetent hands, the most just and

enlightened laws bring national disaster and disgrace.
One of the wisest maxims of every good government is,
that whoever breaks the law of the land must be punished.
The only exception in this country to this rule is, that the
sovereign can do no wrong, and is therefore exempted
from punishment. This rule does not apply to the
ministers of the British crown. To pardon offences
against the state, to reconcile civil justice with mercy
mild, is a prerogative of sovereignty; and, in all
civilized countries, is entrusted to the sovereign power.

Punishment should be certain.—Punishments ought
neither to be uncertain, nor too severe. In all the
most important cases, and when left to the discretion
of the judges, they should be fixed by law absolutely,
or within certain limits. They should never be
extended beyond the just objects of all punishments, namely, the safety of the state, and the
protection of private persons and their property, and
the reclamation of the offender. They should be
established with justice and wisdom. They should be
kept within limits by established forms of law.

Limits of punishment.—The state has no right
of punishment, unless some fault has been committed
against it, or its subjects, or against the human race under
the laws of nature. In the latter class, are poisoners,
assassins, and incendiaries by profession. These attack
and injure all nations by trampling the laws of all mankind under their feet. They also violate all public
security, and are the enemies of the human race. But
even these must be tried, and condemned, and punished,
by due course of law; and, as often as possible, they
should be punished by the states of which they
are citizens.

(c) *Wisdom.*—Wisdom was the second characteristic most highly esteemed amongst the ancient Greeks and Romans, and is also very highly valued by all the civilized nations of modern times. The great end of government being the happiness and the glory of the people, the governors and the people ought to direct their energies, their knowledge, and their virtue to the national happiness.

Useful knowledge increases happiness.—In what way, and how far, can government increase the happiness of its subjects by means of wisdom? It can do so by imparting knowledge to the young in such matters, things, and subjects, as may be useful to them in their daily lives, and in their various trades and professions. It can also do so by encouragements given by the state for improvements in the arts and sciences which are useful and ornamental in a state of civilized society. Tyrants fear knowledge; wise sovereigns promote it. Wise men are not slaves, but faithful subjects. Literature and arms soften, refine, and inspire the love of virtue. Most assuredly, it is desirable and necessary to inspire the people with the love of virtue, and the hatred of vice; for virtue is the true path to happiness, and a virtuous people are the most contented, happy, flourishing, and formidable in the world.

(d) *Governments should advance the national interests and glory.*—The government can also increase the wisdom of its subjects, and augment their true felicity, by advancing the interests and the glory of the country. To do this has been the great aim of all true patriots and the best of mankind. They who injure their country are infamous, and deserve the severest condemnation; and, in serious and grievous wrongs, deserve the most condign punishment. On the other hand, the rewards of the true patriot are the highest and best which can be conferred on a human being. They are greater than riches; greater than learning; and greater than eloquence. When Nelson said that "England expects every man to do his duty;" when Bruce addressed his followers in the heart-stirring words which begin with "Scots wha hae wi' Wallace bled;" they stirred up the most patriotic feelings in the bosoms of their followers, and excited them to glorious deeds, which have been the wonder and the admiration of the whole world, and will be so as long as the world admires true heroism and devotion to the interests of one's country.

(e) *Religion.*—Religion is the third of the principal duties of a nation. Man is a religious animal, and religion is at the basis of all civilized society. The foundation of true religion consists in obedience to the will of God, reliance on His declarations, and imitation of His perfections. As I believe that politics and religion are indissolubly allied, I have no hesitation in saying that piety and religion are essential to a nation's happiness. Piety is that disposition of the soul that leads us to direct all our actions towards the Deity, and endeavour to please Him in whatever we do; is of universal obligation; and is the purest source of felicity. Enlightened piety in a people is a permanent support of lawful authority; and in a sovereign, is the best pledge of a people's happiness. But I must not here, or at this time, enter the field of controversial religious politics.   I merely observe that religion is either internal or external, and that internal religion, or liberty of conscience, is a natural and inviolable right of every human being; and that external religion, whether established by the state or not, is a proper subject of state regulation.   Blind piety is superstition, and produces bigots, fanatics and persecutors, who may certainly be subjected to the laws of the state. Internal religion aims at getting just ideas of God, His laws, His creatures, and the ends of the creation; for, without such ideas, we cannot reasonably hope to please Him.   It is purely a matter between God and every individual human being.   Internal religion is based on the natural and indefeasible right of the liberty of conscience.   As a rule, all men may be, and in every well-regulated state, are free to think as they please, without regard to the good of society; but they are not free to act as they please, without regard to the laws and regulations which have been made for the good of the state.   A state religion, when established, or endowed, by the state, has been so established for the safety and advantage of the state.   When it is not efficacious for these objects, it ought to be brought into harmony with the main purposes of its existence.   If it cannot be so brought, it may not unreasonably be abolished altogether as a state-established, or state-endowed, religion.

Is the soul immortal?—Here we approach a grave and tremendous subject, full of doubts and fears, and yet not without consolations of the highest and most enduring nature.   It is this: Is death the end of all? or is the soul immortal?   The properties of body and

soul are different. For example, the body has extension, and the soul has thought, pure and impalpable,
as their essential characteristics. We must, therefore,
conclude that body and spirit are essentially different.
Again, God is a Spirit, whose power pervades all
space, and whose power is infinite and beyond finding
out. We are, therefore, led to believe that the soul
of man, as a spiritual essence, participates in the nature
of the Supreme Being. We are also led to believe that
the excellency of the soul is opposed to the theory
of its annihilation, when what we call death comes
upon us. Moreover, the natural aspirations and
desires of the soul are opposed to the theory of its
annihilation at the time of death. God, by His very
nature, cannot be a deceiver of any man, and the
aspiration after immortality has been the most universal and all-pervading belief to be found anywhere
in the world. These considerations are not absolute
proofs that the spirit of man is immortal, but they are
sufficient to fix, settle, and determine our duty. The
world is like a beautiful palace, perfect in all things, for
use and ornament. Is it possible that it is in the domain
of the spiritual world that the beauty and perfection
of the workmanship are not to be found? No; never.
It cannot be so. I cannot believe it.

Harmony of the universe.—The key to the riddle
of all our doubts, questions, and knowledge, as to
the relations which connect man with this fair, beautiful,
and wonderful world, and with the strange, unknown, untrodden world beyond it, is to be found in
the universal harmony of the universe, material and
spiritual. This universal harmony is to be found in

the universal reign of law and order throughout the length and breadth of the universe at all times, in all places, and under all the various aspects and natures of things material and spiritual; and in nothing being created in vain by an all-wise God; and in the impossibility of thinking that He will not bring all things in heaven and earth to a wise and successful end. Can we suppose that the Supreme Being has provided no remedy against evil deeds, which are unpunished and unexpiated here? No. Can we imagine that He has no reward to give to those of His creatures who have obeyed His laws to the best of their ability, and yet have been reviled, misrepresented, and tortured for His sake? No. If we could so believe, what becomes of the Divine wisdom, goodness, and justice? Men can, and do, lie and deceive one another. God can neither lie nor deceive. I, therefore, hold that there is a life beyond the grave; that the soul of man is immortal; and that, in the world to come, there will be a great day of judgment to all men; that they will be dealt with and judged, rewarded and punished, according to the deeds done by them in this life; and that they will be mercifully, yet righteously, judged by the great Creator and Father of us all. Therefore, let us always act justly and righteously; and, to the best of our ability, let us do all we can to understand and to imitate the Divine perfections of truth and justice and mercy.

Conclusion: We should study the science of politics.
—I have left myself very little time to enlarge on the duty of studying the science of politics, and greatly fear that I have almost exhausted your patience and

forbearance.   A few words, however, are all that are
required as to this duty on the present occasion; for the
study of the science of politics is clearly both
interesting and instructive, and deeply concerns our
highest interests as individuals and as citizens.   We
have great responsibilities to discharge as citizens of
Great Britain; and for good or evil, we have great national
powers entrusted to our care.   Therefore, let us see that
these responsibilities are rightly and fully discharged.
This is neither the time nor the place to enter into a consideration of the existing complicated and inflammable
state of public affairs both at home and abroad.   Here,
and for the present, I have confined myself to the
general principles at the basis of society, and have
studiously avoided all matters involving party badges,
or party names, or party predilections.   I have briefly
tried to determine our relations, our rights, and our
duties, to the state, and to our fellow-men, and to God.
How far I have succeeded in my aim is not for me to say.
But I confidently submit to you that the subjects
which I have been discussing to-night are honourable
and useful in the highest degree; and, therefore,
worthy of your best consideration and deepest study.

WINTER, DUNCAN AND CO., PRINTERS, DUNDEE.

POLITICAL ADDRESSES

ON

HOME, IRISH, AND COLONIAL AFFAIRS

(DELIVERED AT BROUGHTY FERRY ON 29TH MAY 1888),

AND ALSO ON

INDIAN, EGYPTIAN, AND FOREIGN AFFAIRS

(DELIVERED AT DUNDEE ON 30TH MAY 1888).

ENLARGED AND REVISED.

BY

ALEXANDER ROBERTSON, M.A.,

BARRISTER-AT-LAW,

AUTHOR OF THE GOVERNMENT, CONSTITUTION, AND LAWS OF SCOTLAND, 1875–78 ;
OUR HOME, COLONIAL, AND INDIAN AFFAIRS, 1879-80 ; AND
THE SCIENCES OF LAW AND POLITICS, 1888.

DUNDEE :

WINTER, DUNCAN & CO. 10 CASTLE STREET.

1889.

PREFACE.

THE two following Lectures were written out in the month of May 1888, for delivery at Lochee and Monifieth, and were, in all their substantial features, actually delivered at Broughty Ferry and Dundee on the 29th and 30th May of that year. With a few minor and unimportant exceptions, the Lectures, as they are now published, express my present opinions on the great political questions of our Home and Foreign Policy under discussion. As a matter of fact, I had revised these two Lectures at the end of last year, and had brought them down to that period, and had intended to deliver them at Monifieth and Lochee during the Christmas recess; but the grave and serious illness of my mother prevented me from carrying out this latter project, and I accordingly restored them to the original form in which they were written. For example, in my first intended Lecture for Christmas, I had properly omitted all reference to the social, the agrarian, and the political agitation of the Irish Parliamentary Party. But in the first Lecture now published, I have allowed what I said in last May about that Party to remain. I myself regret that the Leader of the Irish Party did not get a Commission to inquire into the authenticity of the calumnious letters, and that he was not left to take all necessary and legal steps against his calumniators in the ordinary courts of law.

If the Government had wished a Public Inquiry into the civil strife of Ireland during the last ten years, they ought to have asked for it deliberately, as had been done in all Parliamentary Inquiries hitherto. *The Times* must now protect itself against its own illegality as best it may. The Government should stand fast by their impregnable position that the present Parnellite Inquiry is a Private, and not a Public Governmental or National Inquiry.

The reader will kindly observe that the headings of the first Lecture were, by mistake, continued on pages 187 to 241, and that the headings of those pages should have been —Indian, Egyptian, and Foreign Affairs, and not Home, Irish, and Colonial Affairs.

One deep and abiding regret attaches itself in my mind to the present publication. The two Lectures now published were to have been dedicated to my mother as a slight proof of my filial piety and reverence. But, alas! before they had passed through the press, death had taken her away from this world to her eternal rest, peace, and happiness.

With these few explanations and personal observations, I now submit the two following Lectures to the careful and candid consideration of the general public.

21 Louise Terrace,
Broughty Ferry, 29*th April* 1889.

CONTENTS.

CONTENTS.

2.—ADDRESS ON INDIAN, EGYPTIAN, AND FOREIGN AFFAIRS.

I.—PRELIMINARY.

II.—INDIAN AFFAIRS.

1.—INTERNAL.

(1)—GENERAL.

(2)—BURMAH.

2.—EXTERNAL.

(1)—GENERAL.

(2)—AFGHAN POLICY.

(3)—RUSSIAN POLICY IN CENTRAL ASIA.

III.—EGYPTIAN AFFAIRS.

IV.—FOREIGN AFFAIRS.

1.—THE EUROPEAN SITUATION.

2.—THE BALKANS.

3.—AUSTRIAN AND RUSSIAN POLICY.

4.—FRENCH AND GERMAN POLICY.

5.—RUSSIAN POLICY IN EUROPE AND ASIA.

ADDRESS

ON

HOME, IRISH, AND COLONIAL AFFAIRS

(DELIVERED AT BROUGHTY FERRY ON 29TH MAY 1888).

I.—PRELIMINARY.

GENTLEMEN,—Some considerable time ago, I publicly announced that I was to deliver a political address at Broughty Ferry. With your permission, I now proceed to fulfil my promise.

We live in a democratic age.—In this country, the sovereign reigns, but does not rule. The House of Lords no longer holds its ancient place of predominance in the government of the state. In the last resort, the House of Commons decides on the policy of the British empire at home and abroad. Hence, the people of this country, by their representatives in the House of Commons, have now the grave and serious responsibility of finally deciding on the national policy of the British empire. They should, therefore, make every effort to be equal to the duties involved in maintaining the glorious inheritance which has been handed down to them as the fruits of eight centuries of increasing glory and renown. We must never forget that the

F

wealth of the empire, the political freedom enjoyed
by every part of our wide-spread dominions, and our
efforts to advance freedom and justice, civilization and
Christianity, throughout the empire, and even throughout the world, are unsurpassed in the annals of any
other people, ancient or modern, in the world.

Great and interesting questions await and demand
solution by our imperial legislature.   In our home
policy, the greatest questions which have to be solved
are these : How can the great mass of the people be
regenerated from the misery, degradation, poverty,
and vice in which too many of them are engulfed ?
How can the great mass of the people honestly and
justly obtain higher wages and better food, houses,
clothing, and education than hitherto, for themselves,
their wives, and their children ?   How are these
aims to be satisfied ?   Can they be realised by themselves, or by the government ?   Must they be obtained
by their own thrift and industry ; or by a re-organization
of social and economical forces, acting through the
intervention of the state ; or by new arrangements
with their employers by co-operation or co-partnership?
Whatever may be the ultimate, or immediate, solution
of these problems, great and strenuous efforts must be
made to improve the moral, material, and social
wellbeing of the nation.   All class legislation must be
abolished in every department of the state.   Hurtful
privileges and exemptions of every kind must be
abandoned.   Legislation and administration must be
based on what is advantageous and suitable to the
whole body of the people.   The problems can no longer
be settled by the wishes or votes of the landed or of
the commercial aristocracy.   Nay more, the hereditary

principle of the House of Lords will and must be greatly modified before long. In my opinion, it might well be modified by a large reduction of our hereditary legislators on the principles of representation applied to the Scotch and Irish peers, and by a large infusion of life peers into the House of Lords as representatives of the great and permanent interests of the country at home, and of our gigantic empire beyond the seas.

The laws of the state should approximate to natural laws.—Natural laws should be carried out in preference to all merely state or municipal laws, in so far as the laws of the state interfere with natural laws. But, in all cases, obedience to the laws of the state is an imperative duty in every well-regulated state. Modern Socialism contemplates gigantic alterations on the existing laws and constitution of every country. It aims at an impossible ideal. I hold, as a fundamental principle of good government, that we should have complete freedom to live and act within the scope of the laws of our country, and on the basis of individual property and freedom, and that the state laws should approximate as nearly as possible to the great and eternal principles of liberty and justice. No country can be great or prosperous without fixed laws, largely founded on liberty and justice. We must, therefore, direct our attention, as a great and civilized nation, to the social and material wellbeing of the great masses of the people. We must encourage thrift and temperance, courage and justice, and do all we can to help the poor and the down-trodden and the starving to rise to a higher sphere of wealth and living here at home, and also abroad in our immense colonial possessions, which are parts of our imperial inheritance, and in which there are millions of acres of good, free, and virgin soil waiting to be cultivated, and to return a great reward to the tillers of the soil. Let each and all of us, then, do our best to perform the duties of our different stations in life. Without dogmatizing on our beliefs or theories, and without bowing down to any man, or body of men, in a sort of fetish worship, let us try, in all cases, to discover how far the instincts of the people are true and legitimate, and how far we can truthfully say, and wisely believe, that the voice of the people is the voice of God. For my own part, I do not believe that ignorance is wisdom in politics, or in any branch of human knowledge, or that a majority of men, as such, have a right to rule over themselves or over other people.

Political leaders required.—I protest against the conduct of some political teachers, who, by their works, profess the most profound respect for the opinions and views of the great mass of the people who are parliamentary electors in this country, and yet show their most profound contempt, in practice, for the principles they profess to have adopted. Popular leaders should be men who lead and instruct the people in all that is best and noblest in our national life and political philosophy. But many popular leaders of the present day are men of the most determined self-will, and merely pander to popular ignorance and prejudice, or they are men who wait for evidences or proofs of popular opinion before they act. I protest against men of education and experience becoming the tools of the ignorant mob. Leaders should be men who lead; and not men who are led. Such men are needed in every age to make a country great, morally and materially. We need men who will stand up for righteousness and justice to all sections of the people. We need men of capacity and foresight in national affairs. We need men who have the interests of the country at heart, and prefer these national interests to all personal or foreign interests. We need men whose greatest aim in the world is to raise their country to the highest pitch of honour and glory, of happiness and prosperity. We do not need men greedy of public office for their own glory and aggrandisement. We need bold and determined leaders of the people in our national affairs. We need men who know their own minds, and are straightforward, honest, and courageous. But not a few of our politicians are without sound political principles, and are carried hither and thither by every whiff of doctrine. Such persons are credulous and dangerous, and have no sense of political duty, unless to follow the lead of the political party to which they belong. Alas! many of our so-called leaders have deserted the ever-enduring and well-established doctrines of every civilised government in regard to the necessity for absolute submission to the laws of the government under which they live. They forget, however, that the people of this country admire pluck, justice, and wisdom, and that the people will follow the men who advocate what is based on right principles, and not on passion or base expediency. Public men naturally wish to be popular; but they should never seek popularity at the expense of enlightened patriotism. They ought to remember that they can gain a high and permanent niche in the history of their country in no other way than by attending to the permanent facts and lessons of history and politics. Men who would be statesmen should purify the sentiments, and improve the characters of the nation in truth, honesty, and justice. If that is their duty, how, I ask, do many politicians in this country perform it? Is not our political life becoming a low, degraded trade without any high or fixed principles?

The great problem of legislation.—Radical politicians say, that the government of the country should be carried on in conformity to the wishes of the multitude. I do not agree with them in their aims or methods of government. I hold that we should aim at national liberty and intelligent government, which are based on a full appreciation of the moral, religious, political, and industrial relations of men as individuals and members of the state. These relations give us the sum total of our present degree of civilization. Briefly, the great and essential differences between liberalism and conservatism are these: liberalism is popular; conservatism is national: liberalism is sentimental; conservatism is rational: liberalism is based on feeling; conservatism on reason.

Politics is a great and difficult study.—When we calmly look at political matters we will soon discover that they require as much ability and study as the most difficult subjects of human speculation; and that, if we follow the uneducated bent of our own minds, or of the minds of other people, we will become the dupes of political and economical fallacies, which have been exploded long ago, and will neglect the true means of happiness and wealth, and will end our lives in disappointment and ruin. Democracy, pure and simple, is dogmatic and impulsive, not practical and rational. It is a thorough-going destroyer. Indeed, it would destroy everything in our existing political institutions and laws. Let us, therefore, be on our guard against it in good time, and before it is too late.

I must now ask your calm and impartial consideration of some of the great political questions of the day as to our Home, Irish, and Colonial Policy. First of all, then, I wish to direct your attention to our Parliamentary Procedure.

II.—HOME AFFAIRS IN GENERAL.

1.—REFORM OF PARLIAMENTARY PROCEDURE.

Parliamentary devolution indispensible.—Many years ago, Sir Robert Peel said that eight or nine hours a day were spent in the House of Commons in aimless and fruitless talk. Within the last few years, especially since the last Parliamentary Reform Bills, the useless talk in the House of Commons has become a perfect nuisance and a grave public scandal, and desultory and inconclusive debates have been largely increased.

The right to ask the Queen's ministers for explanations of their policy and their conduct of public affairs is a high and valuable privilege, and ought not to be surrendered. But that so much of the time of the House of Commons should, on every day of its sittings, be wasted by a host of useless questions, is a grave public scandal. If all useless questions were disallowed in the House of Commons, there would be two or three hours every day of the most valuable time of the sittings of the House saved for really useful public business. In July 1882, Mr Gladstone was compelled to acknowledge that the important question of Parliament was not liberty, but the delegation of authority to do the work of the nation.   In August of the same year, he said that the House of Commons was reduced to impotence; that there was the greatest need of drastic rules of procedure; and that utter ruin had been inflicted on the governmental measures of the session then about to end.   Accordingly, an autumn session was begun in October 1882, and was continued for six weeks, and the whole of this period was devoted by the House of Commons to this great and important subject.   Although a form of clôture, which was intended to stop the endless flow of vapid and useless talk in the House of Commons, was then passed, and Grand Committees for law and justice, trade, shipping, and manufactures, were created; still not much good has been effected, and the House of Commons has since been compelled to pass more stringent rules than had ever existed before in any period of its history.   In 1882, Mr Parnell asked, and others have since proposed, that the Grand Parliamentary Committees should be made national.   But Mr Gladstone objected to Mr Parnell's proposals on this point, and said that, if such Committees were granted to Ireland, they must also be granted to England and Scotland.   For nearly five years, the clôture was scarcely ever enforced, and the public time in the House of Commons was wasted as much as before; and the Grand Committees, being too large, did little or no good.   In July 1887, Mr Gladstone said that Scotch and English affairs were neglected at Westminster; and that, in the future, there would be still less time for such matters.   Every year demonstrates the truth of Mr Gladstone's observations on this point. Parliamentary obstruction in the House of Commons has been scotched in the year 1888, but it must be completely extinguished. To discuss the Trafalgar Square riots for two nights was an outrageous abuse of the time of the Imperial Parliament. I hold that loquacity is the great obstructive in the House of Commons; and that we can never get rid of this arch impostor until we conduct our public business on a more rational basis than at present. In the House of Commons, every year, we have a mass of irrelevant and useless amendments on bills, and a consequent waste of public time. Every session we have much useless discussion on crude and immature legislative proposals. Parliament exists for the passing of useful laws, for the remedying of grievances, and for the granting of necessary supplies, and does not, and ought not to, exist for useless discussion. The conclusion to be drawn from this condition of affairs is, that we must have decentralization, and some form of Home Rule for England, Scotland, and Ireland. This conclusion is, I think, slowly but surely penetrating the minds of all thoughtful politicians. Possibly, I do not say necessarily, the solution will be found in having one Legislative Assembly for each country, and one Imperial Parliament for the Empire.

Waste of time on the Queen's Speech and granting supplies.—Two great sources of wasting the public time in the House of Commons spring (1) from discussing the Queen's Speech at inordinate length, and (2) from an old, and now useless, practice of moving for the removal of grievances before grants of money are made to the Crown for the ordinary and necessary expenses of government. Flagrant instances of the waste of the public time in the House of Commons might easily be found in recent debates on the Queen's Speech. In February 1887, the debate in the House of Commons on the Queen's Speech was continued for more than two weeks, and was productive of no good result; and in the House of Lords, it was finished at a single sitting. The useless and frivolous chatter in the House of Commons on that occasion had, at last, to be stopped by the Speaker of the House interfering in the discussion, and taking the evident sense of the House for the closure of the debate, and thereby putting an end to the wordy war. About the same length of time was again spent in the House of Commons on the Queen's Speech in 1888, and to the utter weariness and disgust of the nation.

The House of Commons has no effectual control over the public expenditure.—As a matter of fact, even although it was by the power over the public purse that the House of Commons attained its present great, indeed supreme, power in the state, yet, strange as it may seem, it is true that the representatives of the people, as such, have, in general, no effective control over the national expenditure. The ministers of the day and the permanent officials of the government in office have practically the absolute disposal of the national finances. Long days and weary nights are spent in the House of Commons over the public expenditure, and all in vain in the way of effecting any substantial reduction on the constantly increasing and heavy burdens of national and local taxation.

Naval and military expenditure.—In all our public departments, we have great waste and muddling. The highest market-price is often paid for inferior and foreign articles. Ships, barracks, and public buildings are built at enormous cost; and when blunders are made, or frauds detected, nobody is responsible, and nobody is punished. Every year, we pay £7,750,000 out of the national exchequer for pensions; and since 1883 the pension list has risen £1,000,000. On the abolition or reorganisation of public offices, the general principle which has been adopted is, to grant pensions on the basis of estates for life to the holders of the offices abolished; and, by this means, men, in the prime of life, retire from the public service with large pensions. What says Lord Wolseley about the army? He says that we have 140 generals in our army, and that 100 of them are not employed, and are useless and expensive besides. What says Sir Edward Reed about the navy? He says that we pay £3,000,000 for services in the navy, and about £2,000,000 for no naval services whatever; that we pay £17,600 for 17 admirals who are employed, and £166,990 for 281 admirals who are unemployed. The control over the naval and military services needs to be made direct and concentrated; responsibility for every department should be clearly and distinctly laid down and enforced; and neglect of duty in these services, and in fact in all the services, should be made swift and sure. All the military and naval services should be under one head, able, from his knowledge of military and naval requirements, to combine and harmonize the management and conduct of all naval and military affairs, and with properly qualified persons in all naval and military departments, as in every well-organized business house in this country. I hold that the military service should be presided over by a military officer; and the naval service, by a naval officer; and that a civil or parliamentary head should be responsible to Parliament and the country for both services.   At present, and for a long time, we have been living in a fool's paradise, and we are in danger of being rudely awakened from our torpor and indifference by some great national disaster.   Our trade, our credit, our possessions at home and abroad, and our honour are insufficiently protected on land and sea ; and yet the people are ready to pay a fair and just price for safety and protection.   Surely, we must squander a lot of money on our army, when we cannot place a single corps d'armée of 50,000 men on the continent of Europe in the event of war breaking out at the present moment. Yet our army costs almost £21,000,000 a year. Again, surely, we must uselessly squander a lot of money on our navy, when we have several warships without guns or their full armament.   Yet we spend £13,000,000 a year on the navy.   In the last twenty years, we have spent £300,000,000 on our army and navy.   Have we got value for this immense sum of money ?   I venture to say that we have not.   What is the use of warships without guns and armaments and ammunition and men ?   None whatever.   They are worse than London lighters, or Broughty Ferry fishing-boats; for such warships deceive us into a feeling of security, which is perilous and groundless, and might be extremely dangerous.   We need our great rivers and great commercial ports to be defended ; and yet they are in a disgracefully defenceless condition.   We should not allow this state of matters to continue for a single day longer.

The empire must be defended.—We have a great

empire to defend, and yet we do not take adequate steps to defend it. Surely such negligence is disgraceful to the people of this country, and most of all to our rulers. Who are really to blame? Certainly not the people; for they would support any government which would take the steps necessary for our safety and defence. Who, then, are to blame? Why, of course, the governments in and out of office for a long time past. However, the nation and the present government are becoming aroused to the vast importance of this great and important matter, and are determined to allow it to be neglected no longer. Too long, our politicians have been political Hamlets, " sicklied o'er with the pale cast of thought," and yet deficient in action ; or they have been crazy fanatics, filled with fantastic dreams of universal brotherhood and peace, and thinking that sufficient for the day was the evil thereof. Life, says Goethe, is like a game at whist. In whist, fate may deal the cards; but much depends on the skill of the players. Providence has entrusted to us great duties to perform in the progress of humanity and in the civilization of the human race. Let us take care not to neglect to perform those duties. By all means, let us take due precautions to protect and defend our shores on land; but, above all things, let us take ample means to protect and defend ourselves, by our navy, which is our first, best, and most reliable bulwark, from all external attacks at home or abroad, or on the ocean, on which we are at present supreme. The supremacy of our navy must be the basis and backbone of our power and sovereignty.

Remedies proposed as to parliamentary procedure. —As to parliamentary procedure, the remedies I

would venture to propose (1) as to the Queen's speech
would be, that it should be read as a mere simple
programme of measures for the ensuing session, and
not liable to be discussed, unless on a direct motion
of no-confidence in the Government of the day;
and (2) as to questions, that they should be largely
diminished by a committee of the House; and (3) as to
discussions on the estimates and votes of supply,
that, in future, there should be three grand practical
Committees of moderate dimensions, say of 30 or 40
members, engaged at one and the sametime on the
Army, Navy, and Civil Service expenditure. By
these remedies, as I think, a great improvement and
saving of time would be effected for really useful
public work. When the government in office is to be
attacked, it ought to be so on a clear and distinct
motion. The universal rule ought to be, that no
extraneous discussions were admissible under any circumstances, and that any member offending against
this rule should be severely punished. The estimates
and the supplies would be far more effectively discussed
before committees of 30 or 40 for each of the great
departments of the state, than they are by the present
arrangements.

Bills read too often.—Another point deserves our
serious attention. I mean the way in which all bills,
public and private, are treated after they are laid
before Parliament. Public bills, according to the
ordinary and orthodox way of discussing them, are
read three times in each House of Parliament.
Between the intervals of the second and third readings, they pass through committees of each House.
The first reading is, as a rule, purely formal, and is

taken on the motion for leave to introduce a Bill;
but it takes up much of the time of Parliament, and
instructs no one. Drastic alterations as to the stages
through which public bills pass the two Houses of
Parliament ought to be made; and the parliamentary
procedure as to private bills ought to be completely
changed and remodelled. Two readings in each
House, together with full and rigorous examinations
in committee of every bill, are amply sufficient for
the discussion of any bill, public or private.

*Committees of the whole House of Commons should
be abolished.*—In our House of Commons, much
valuable public time, in the committee stage, might
be saved by dividing the whole of its members into
committees of suitable size; and by a due regard to
fitness and qualifications; and, generally speaking, by
abandoning the present rules as to committees of the
whole House. Such committees exist in theory, and
not in fact. In other words, much time of the House
of Commons might be saved by bringing the committee stage of a bill into harmony with common
sense and the importance of the subject. For
example, in a great number of cases, the bill is
supposed to be discussed in and by a committee of the
whole House. This is the theory. As a matter of fact,
it is nothing of the kind. Unless when a great orator
or statesmen is addressing the popular assembly of
the nation, the House of Commons is all but deserted,
and only an insignificant number of the members are
present at the discussion of a bill, or even on a motion
for a vote of no-confidence against a ministry; and the
great majority of the members are dispersed into all
sorts of places within and without the precincts of

the House, and waiting to vote when called upon according to their own opinions or party inclinations. Instead of having absurd and mock committees of 670 members, there should never be more than 30 or 40 members in any committee, and 20 or 25 should be a quorum, and power should be given to a majority of the quorum to act with the whole powers of the committee. Thus, instead of a huge committee wasting the time of the public and also of private persons, there should be ten or twelve committees of the most experienced members of the House; or, in other words, a large and influential committee in every important branch of administration and legislation, engaged in real and useful work for the state. Every committee should have power to elect its own chairman and vice-chairman, and have all the usual powers of the full House in the conduct of the business before it.

Private bill legislation.—Legislation on private bills comprehends a large number of subjects, and includes railway and harbour bills, water and gas bills, and a few miscellaneous matters of private interest. Private bills are, in general, subjected to the same laborious and dilatory treatment as public bills in all their stages. The exceptions to this general rule are that the committee is usually composed of about six members; and that the third reading is almost invariably of a purely formal character. I think that the exigencies of the nation demand an entire change in regard to those private bills. Legislation on private bills monopolises the best part of the day in both Houses of Parliament for about a half of the usual parliamentary session. This condition of things ought not to be allowed to continue any longer. There is no need for all those stages being taken before separate and distinct committees of the House of Commons and of the House of Lords, and also before the two Houses in full assembly. Such stages are merely useful to lawyers, professional witnesses, and local witnesses, in the way of large fees for their services in London. When private bills pass the ordeal of one House, they may, of course, just as much as public bills are, be opposed or defeated in the other House of Parliament. This double investigation and discussion of private bills before committees of the House of Lords and the House of Commons, and before the two Houses themselves, lead to a great waste of public and private time and money, and do not lead to any adequate return. The present condition of matters has long been condemned, and yet no effectual remedy has been provided for the grievance. Some years ago, a slight improvement was made on private bill procedure by the appointment of a standing committee for both Houses to inquire into and decide on the compliance or non-compliance with the standing orders of Parliament as to private bills.

Five alternative remedies have been proposed for the grievances as to private bill legislation. They are—(1) the present procedure; (2) a joint committee of both Houses; (3) National Committees in the Imperial Parliament at Westminster for England, Scotland, and Ireland; (4) independent quasi-judicial courts for each country; and (5) judicial and national inquiries for each country. The first alternative is almost universally condemned, and the second is not likely to be attempted in the present state of political opinion in this country. The third alternative is liable to the fatal objection of being as expensive as the present procedure; and the fourth alternative is liable to the serious objection that Parliament would not agree to part with all control over private bill legislation, which, in many cases, is as important to the public as the most general public bill. The fifth alternative is the one which seems to me to be the most suitable in all the circumstances. All inquiries before committees of each House of Parliament should be abolished, and independent committees of inquiry for all private bills should be established for England, for Scotland, and for Ireland.

The devolution of private bill legislation.—The devolution of private bill legislation on a national, or on an imperial, basis is a modified form of Home Rule, and has been urged as a perfect solution, or, at all events, as an intermediate stage between the present and some future and permanent form, of Home Rule. If this devolution takes place, it must be complete, or it will be useless. Parliament must not be allowed to interfere. The new tribunal must take the whole of the responsibility. Local inquiries, and then national or imperial inquiries, would destroy all sense of responsibility, and make things worse than they are. The decisions of any new tribunals to be established as to private bill legislation, ought to be treated in the same way as the resolutions of the judges as to contested elections in the House of Commons. Where there was no opposition, the local inquiry might, *e.g.*, be in the presence of the sheriffs of the counties in Scotland, or of the judges of the county courts in England.

But, on the whole, I am in favour of a separate tribunal for private bill legislation, and also of keeping up the distinction between legislative and judicial functions.

Proposal for courts in England, Scotland, and Ireland for private bills.—Each national court ought to conduct the whole of the preliminary inquiries before itself, and then send to the two Houses of Parliament reports, which should take the place of the present Provisional Orders, and thus become law, or be rejected, or amended, by either House in full assembly, and after due notice to the parties interested, or before the court, on the preliminary inquiry. Unless rejected or amended by either House of Parliament, such Provisional Orders should, after a certain definite interval, be passed into law. These courts of inquiry should have power to grant costs to, or against, the promoters and opponents of private bills, and in all questions as to compliance with the standing orders of parliament as to private bills, or of such orders as shall be substituted in their place. Such parliamentary private bill courts might have London, or the capital city of each country, as their head-quarters. Where objections were lodged to any bill, they ought to hold a preliminary inquiry to dispose of all technical objections against the bill, and to fix on the most convenient modes and places for inquiries, and ought to be obliged to go about each country to hear and decide on all private bills brought before them, and as much as possible hold their courts where the private bills originated, or were meant to apply. The judges or commissioners of such courts ought to occupy the position of judges of the supreme courts in each country, and ought to occupy a position which would place them above suspicion of bribery, corruption, or unfair or dishonourable conduct in any or the slightest particular. The cardinal and indispensibly necessary modification of private bill legislation is, that the examination of the respective bills should be made by properly qualified persons in the locality and on the spot. To set up tribunals in London, Edinburgh, and Dublin, would not remove the present grievances to any great or appreciable extent. Where there was no opposition to a bill, there should be ample provision made for a cheap and speedy investigation of their general principles and details by some public official department, and the present rules as to provisional orders might be largely adopted.

2.—NATIONAL SELF-GOVERNMENT.

What is local self-government?—Local self-government means national self-government, or county and municipal government. According to the first idea, England, Scotland, and Ireland, and even Wales, ought to be endowed with all the legislative, judicial, and executive powers of each country, and have an independent legislative assembly, and an independent executive government; and, in its fullest extent, have an independent exchequer for each country. According to the second idea, the county districts of England, Scotland, Ireland, and Wales should possess the same powers of government within their orbits as the large towns and cities under their charters of Incorporation or Acts of Parliament now hold and possess; and further, the towns and counties of Ireland should have the same powers of government as the large towns and cities of England and Scotland already possess. I venture to say that national self-government and county self-government are required for England, Scotland, and Ireland.

Extent of national parliamentary devolution required.—Devolution by the imperial Parliament of local and national business of a public kind has now become an imperative necessity. There is, in truth, too much to be done in the British Parliament, and too little time to do it. Great and fitful attempts are still made in Parliament to grant relief to grievances; but, on all hands, there is a universal consensus of opinion that this work cannot be done by the present agencies. The consequences are —(1) that the work of Parliament and of ministers of the crown is largely done by permanent officials; (2) that no effective parliamentary supervision of the great spending and executive department of the government exists; (3) that officialism and favouritism have largely and uselessly increased the public expenditure, without increasing the effectiveness of the public service; and (4) that millions of money have been squandered by government officials in consequence of an inadequate and imperfect supervision and responsibility in the different governmental offices of the state. Than a thorough departmental reform of the naval, military, and civil offices of the imperial government, there is nothing more necessary at the present moment. Power and responsibility are divorced; and when anything goes wrong, no one is responsible. We should have responsibility placed on each head of a department, on each workshop, on each office, on the heads and officers of each ship or fortress, on the head and officers of every army corps, of every regiment, of every company. This necessary devolution by the imperial parliament should, at least, comprehend poor laws, education, police, highways, public health, water and gas supply, and public enjoyments and amusements. In all these matters, the sphere of action has been either originated or extended since the Union of the kingdoms of England, Scotland, and Ireland. In the Unions between England and Scotland, and between Great Britain and Ireland, the distinction of public policy and private rights is clearly indicated, and should rigidly be restored and upheld. How far devolution should extend to the ordinary national laws as to person and property, inheritance and contracts, is not easy to decide. But, provided the extension of these last-enumerated subjects was made so as to comprehend all the three United Kingdoms, I do believe, as I have already publicly indicated, that no harm, but much good, would arise from establishing national legislative assemblies with full power to discuss and finally settle all matters and things, taxes and rates, within and for the separate geographical areas of England, Scotland, and Ireland. Let us have no half measures on this great subject of national and imperial policy. If national assemblies and national executives should hereafter be established for the three kingdoms, these national assemblies and executives must be supreme within the spheres assigned to them. To establish national assemblies and executives, and to allow them to be over-ruled by the imperial parliament or the imperial executive, by force, fraud, corruption, or any other means, would be impolitic and intolerable. Before parliamentary and executive governments can be settled in this country on a permanent basis, the matters entrusted to them must be clearly and explicitly defined, and should err, if at all, on the size of limitation than of extension. When we are told that the imperial parliament must be supreme, we ought to understand thereby that the imperial parliament, or some other body, such as the high court of the United States, must exist to see that the conditions of devolution are maintained; that the essential rights of civilized society are enforced; and that the rights of person and property are secure in every part of the empire. That such conditions could be laid down, I do not doubt for a single moment; and, as some of you are no doubt aware, I have attempted to show how these conditions can be laid down. Along with a national devolution of duties, there must be also a re-distribution of funds for the purposes of carrying on national self-government and local county and burgh administrative government. In regard to the establishment of national assemblies and executives, I hold, as a cardinal doctrine, that the devolution must be for all the three kingdoms, and must and cannot be for one, *e.g.* for Ireland alone. Neither provincial nor district county councils can do the work required so well as national assemblies and executives.

Subjects.—National self-government, in an adequate form, should include all legislation and control over the poor law; the elementary and secondary and university education; the roads, highways, and police; and the liquor traffic. It should also include the supervision of the administration of justice, and the maintenance and control of the national establishments, and the national and public works and buildings. In its widest sense, it would comprehend the passing and enforcement of all general laws within each country, but not of any laws which affected the general policy or administration of the empire, or of any matters which were retained by the imperial parliament. The local provincial judges, but not the supreme judges, should be placed directly under the supreme executive government of each country. There should also be an imperial court of appeal and an imperial court of parliament in London for the whole empire. In a rational system of imperial and national self-government, there ought to be imperial and national administrative officials, and imperial and national courts of law for the empire, and for all the nations of England, Scotland, and Ireland. All the imperial administrative, judicial, and other officials, whether in England, Scotland, or Ireland, should be appointed by the Sovereign, under the sanction of the ministers as at present; and all the national administrative, judicial, and other officials, whether in England, Scotland, or Ireland, should be appointed by the Sovereign, under the sanction of the ministers for each nation.

Federative Union required.—A Federative Union, after the plan of the American States constitution, as regards state rights, has become an imperative necessity for our Empire. Such a form of union may be postponed for a time. It cannot permanently be laid aside. By means of federation on a wide and comprehensive basis, the British empire might become the most powerful, as well as be the richest and most populous, empire in the world. We must have an imperial senate, and we must also have national senates. Each senate should be thoroughly representative of its constituency. These are the great and fundamental principles of federative union. Whether each senate

should be composed of one house or two houses is
of minor importance. I myself am in favour of
two houses in a democratic country such as ours,
in order to provide safeguards against thoughtless,
dangerous, or sudden modifications in our constitutional
form of government. In the British constitution, there
exist no precautions against constitutional changes,
unless by means of the House of Lords, or the now
obsolete veto of the Crown. Vast changes might
be made on the constitution by wirepullers, for
party purposes, for power or office, without ever con-
sulting the parliamentary electors of the country; and
yet we are told by the Radical party that we are
governed by the people. Take the late Irish Home
Rule Bill as introduced into the House of Commons,
or even as proposed to be modified in its passage
through that House. About this bill the country
was never consulted ; and, when consulted, the people
rejected it by their votes at the polls. In this, and
such like measures, the House of Lords may be
of invaluable use to the country. In the American
constitution, special and careful precautions are taken
against sudden constitutional changes. National independence for Scotland or Ireland should be strenuously opposed by every good, sensible, and patriotic citizen.
Devolution of legislation to national assemblies is
not, and need not be, and should not be, opposed to
imperial union and integrity, which should, and must
be, upheld at all costs and against all hazards.

*National self-government must be finally settled by
the people.*—As I have already indicated, I am myself
in favour of three separate and independant national
Parliaments for England, Scotland, and Ireland,

and of an imperial Parliament over all, and of each
Parliament being composed of two Houses rather than
of one House. I would, in fact, desire to assimilate
our Houses of Parliament and our executive government as nearly as possible to the American constitution, with its various independent state legislatures
and administrations, and its supreme legislative assembly and senate at Washington for the whole of the
states. The imperial senate for this country should be
representative of every kingdom, colony, and dependency in the empire. At some future time, I may be
called upon here, or elsewhere in your neighbourhood,
to enlarge upon this great and vital problem of national
and imperial government. For the present, I must not
consider it at any greater length than I have now
done. In the meantime, I pray and beseech you to
give the matter your most serious and anxious consideration. Mr Gladstone has told us that a nation
is at the back of the Irish members in supporting them
in their demand for national self-government. Even
although these words were true, what then? Are we
to allow the Irish people to overthrow the rules of
morality and justice and law, and to endanger the
British empire? Never—never—never! so long as
we are an imperial race, and endowed with imperial
instincts. As regards Home Rule in a safe and
reasonable form, the question must now be decided
by the constituencies and should not be allowed
to impede important and necessary reforms in the
present Parliament. Mr Burke was in favour of Home
Rule for Ireland and also of imperial government, and
of a firm and eternal Union between Great Britain and
Ireland. So also, for a time, was Mr Pitt, who carried

the present legislative Union between Great Britain and Ireland in 1800. It is deeply to be regretted that the views of those two great statesmen were not carried into execution in such a way as to give Ireland a national government, and to establish an imperial senate for England, Scotland, and Ireland, as well as national governments for all three. I believe that, if federation had been as well understood then as now, England, Scotland, and Ireland, and the British empire would have been further advanced than they are. We should be in no hurry to solve this great question, which ought to be most carefully thought out in all its grave and complicated relations.

3.—SCOTCH NATIONAL AFFAIRS.

Scotch local business.—The duties and importance of the Secretary for Scotland have gone on increasing, and will be still further enlarged ere long. As originally settled in 1885, the Scotch Secretary became an independent official personage, with very extensive powers, except as to law and justice, over the administration and state patronage of Scotland. By an Act passed last year, 1887, law and justice, including the royal prerogative of pardoning crimes, have been placed under the jurisdiction and control of the Scotch Secretary. No long period of time will, I hope, elapse before the Secretary for Scotland shall be formally and completely acknowledged as the Secretary of State for Scotland, and be entitled to a seat in the imperial cabinet. Before long, I hope, the Scotch Secretary's office will be fully equipped for the duties which naturally devolve upon it. The Secretary himself, whether a peer or a commoner, shall, I also hope, be as independent as the head of any other state department. As a cabinet minister, the Scotch Secretary would be more effectively heard as to all Scotch matters than he is at present. Therefore, he would be able to do more good work for Scotland than he can do now. He should, in fact, become the head and centre of the local administrative government of Scotland. Further, in the event of national self-government being, at some future time, established in Scotland, he would naturally become the chief minister of the crown in the national government of Scotland.

Scotch national assemblies and executive.—After most anxious and careful consideration of the subject, I, as an independent Liberal Conservative, can find no valid objection to Home Rule, or national self-government, comprehending all legislation and administration as to real and personal property, as well as to the church, poor law, education, police, and the like subjects, being granted to Scotland. Nay more, not a few Radical unionists are of opinion that the Scotch people could be entrusted with a large and comprehensive scheme of national self-government. For example, Mr Chamberlain has said that they might be so entrusted. But I venture to say that they do not wish to be entrusted with such a scheme of national self-government as was proposed by Mr Gladstone in 1885 for Ireland. Still, in all matters of real and personal rights, of poor law, education, religion, police, commercial law, and bankruptcy, the laws of Scotland and their administration are essentially different from the laws and administration of similar matters in England. While, then, I feel perfectly confident that a Scotch parliament or legislative assembly could manage Scotch local affairs far better, in every respect, than the imperial Parliament, I am also perfectly certain that the Scotch people would not willingly give up their inheritance and rights and privileges in the imperial Parliament as to imperial affairs, and that, rather than give up their imperial inheritance, they would prefer to leave matters to stand as they are. Many Scotch Radical representatives, and especially of the English legal profession, do not wish a Scotch parliament or legislative assembly, because they would lose their present seats, or be obliged to give up the practice of their profession in England. Moreover, we must never forget that the Scotch Radical members of Parliament do not wish to be separated from their English and Irish Radical colleagues in the imperial Parliament; nor do the English and Irish Radical members of the House of Commons wish to be separated from their Scotch political allies and friends. I put this question to you. How can, or why should, the Scotch people be satisfied with the imperial Parliament at Westminster, when, year after year, and for a long series of years, and with no prospect of any improvement, their affairs are, and probably will be, neglected and ignored; and when, year after year, their representatives in the House of Commons have to be satisfied with a few hours in a session being devoted to Scotch affairs? If so little time is necessary for these matters, what is the use of a parliament at Westminster as to Scotland or to Scotch affairs? Not only is Scotch legislation neglected, but Scotch legislation is blundered. For example, can any reasonable person imagine that the Scotch Titles Act of 1868 and the Scotch Conveyancing Act of 1874 could have been passed in a Scotch parliament, in which persons skilled in Scotch law were fully and properly represented ? Again, why are Scotch affairs so much neglected by all political parties at Westminster ? Because, in the first place, any liberal government can always depend on the majority of the Scotch members in almost every emergency ; and secondly, because the conservative government do not require to consider their Scotch conservative friends and supporters as they are obliged to consider their English. In the imperial Parliament at present, and for sometime past, but especially in recent years, there have been, and are, too many English lawyers, unskilled in our laws and institutions, who represent Scotch constituencies. But, so long as the present arrangements exist, this evil cannot be remedied; because, as a general rule, the Scotch advocates cannot afford, or do not wish, to leave the practice of their profession in Edinburgh, and to reside in London at the very time when their professional duties compel them to be in Edinburgh. When, if ever, the people of this country have a parliament of their own, in Edinburgh, for their own national and local affairs, as I have no doubt they will have, and perhaps sooner than most people believe, the proper and natural legal representatives of the Scotch people will be represented in the Scotch national legislative assembly. For the present, the establishment of a Scotch Secretary was a necessary and useful reform in the conduct of Scotch public business, and the further development and extension of this office will do much to facilitate the management of such business, and is the forerunner of better things yet to come.

National grand committees as temporary expedients for national legislatures.—Till national legislatures, consisting of two Houses, or of one House, and entrusted with purely and well-defined national matters, and not for imperial affairs, are established for England, Scotland, and Ireland, I think it would be a great advantage, in the conduct of public business, to have all public bills referred to national grand committees of England, Scotland, and Ireland, for the committee stage of all such bills introduced, at once, as a tentative measure, into the Imperial Parliament at Westminster. When a proposal was lately brought before the House of Commons for national grand committees, the Unionists opposed it on the ground that it was a provincial demand—Provincial demand, forsooth? If this provincial demand is not conceded, it will rise to the high dignity of a national demand, which must be conceded. But further, we have the authority of Mr Gladstone himself for saying that he himself opposed the principle of grand national committees, and that he had been unsuccessful in stemming the demand. Why, for example, should the religion, and education, and law of Scotland be determined by persons ignorant of these peculiarly Scotch subjects? I am not in favour of grand committees as a final, but as a tentative measure. National Home Rule on a general basis is inevitable. A national council should be representative of the nation. I hold that the Imperial Parliament is not representative of the people of Scotland, or of their laws, manners, and customs; and I even go further, and say the present Scotch representatives are not thoroughly representative of the Scotch nation, and that they are largely ignorant of our laws, government, and constitution; and, by a sort of invasion, our poor country has lately become the refuge and home of carpet-baggers and the politically destitute. Mr Bright was in favour of grand national committees; but he has always been opposed to an imperial parliament and executive. The Irish nationalists scout the idea of grand national committees as a full satisfaction of their demands.

National self-government indispensible to do parliamentary work.—We must soon attempt to solve the problem of local self-government in its wide as well as limited signification. This problem involves the subsidiary, and yet all-important questions as to whether the electors are to be the same as the present municipal and parliamentary electors, or different from them; and also whether the present municipal and county boards are to continue, or different municipal and county boards are to be established; and whether the representatives are to be the same as the representatives of the Imperial Parliament, or different persons. National self-government, or Home Rule, may be bad or regrettable; but, in some form or another, it must be tried before long. The treatment of Scotch business and Scotch legislation in the Imperial Parliament is, and has long been, disgraceful. As regards Scotch business it is greatly improved, but it is still far from perfect. Moreover, why the Scotch Departments of the State should be centralized in London is more than I can understand or defend. All the Scotch Departments of State should be centralized in Edinburgh as the metropolis of Scotland. As regards Scotch legislation, the condition of affairs is scandalous; and is such that the Scotch people, as I believe, will, and ought, not to tolerate it much longer. All the time which Scotland got last year for its necessary legislation in the Imperial Parliament consisted of a few hours on two or three Wednesdays of the whole session, and of an occasional few hours after midnight, when people, even legislators and politicians, should be asleep in their beds. Mr Parnell has said that Ireland could not return representatives to an Irish parliament in Dublin, and to an imperial parliament in London. I do not think that he is correct in his estimate of the capacities of the Irish people. But, although he ought to know, I suspect the inability arises from an unwillingness to be hampered in Ireland by an imperial parliament, and not from any national incapacity on the part of the Irish people to return representatives—why not the same persons ?—to an Irish parliament in Dublin, and also to an imperial parliament in London. Be this as it may, I am perfectly certain that no difficulty would be experienced in this matter in Scotland. I must now consider county local administrative government.

3.—COUNTY ADMINISTRATIVE GOVERNMENT.

County government should be administrative.— Amongst the political parties in this country, there is no serious question about the desirability of extending local administrative government to the rural or county districts upon the same, or a somewhat similar basis, as the municipal government of the urban districts. If there is any difference of opinion amongst them, it is about the extent of the powers to be entrusted to the new local authorities, the basis of taxation, and the extent to which the principle of direct and indirect representation should be adopted. Speaking generally, I have no hesitation in saying that the present urban self government should be extended to the rural districts, and that all the powers which may hereafter be conferred upon the urban districts should be extended to the rural districts. Taxation should involve representation. Whence taxation sprung, there should be the power of spending, or of giving powers to spend; and that either by the persons who are taxed, or by their representatives. As soon as possible, we should establish a wise and popular system of local administrative government, which should stand firmly, and without evasion, on the basis of our popular system of representative and parliamentary government. To be permanent, local county or rural self-government must be wholly elective, and to the same degree as local urban self-government. Further, personal as well as real property should be directly taxed for local purposes. In 1850, Mr Gladstone said that all private property, and not one class of property, should be liable for the Poor Rate. I would go further, and say, that all property, personal as well as real, should be liable, and directly liable, for all local rates as well as for all imperial taxes, and to the same degree and in the same proportion. As I have already indicated, local administrative government should extend to all matters concerning roads, water supply, gas, lighting, drainage, police, education, and the poor. Such a scheme of local government as I am now discussing should be purely administrative, and not legislative. To me it appears that County Boards, and even Provincial Councils, if endowed with legislative powers, would be expensive and inconvenient. Such legislative powers would involve the erection of local parliaments in every county or province, and a large number of

useless and expensive officials.   The Imperial, or, if
need be, a national legislature, should lay down the
general rules for local self-government; and the local
authorities should carry out these general rules, or, in
other words, should administer them.   Important
points require to be settled as to how far the local
administration of our educational system, our licensing
system, and our Poor Law system can be placed under
the new local authorities to be created, and how far such
systems can, or ought to be dealt with, by the local
authorities.   I shall discuss all these matters in detail
on some future occasion.   For the present, I am
inclined to go by steps, and to wait for a little time to
see how the new local rural authorities conduct themselves in the management of the business which must
soon be entrusted to them in England, Scotland, and
Ireland.   My principle in politics, as in personal conduct, is, *Festina lente*, hasten slowly.   The world is
not yet coming to an end; nor need we attempt to do
too much to be theoretically perfect in our schemes of
political improvement.   Let us leave, I say, something
for our successors to do in the time which is yet to
come.

*The English Local Government Bill and observations
thereon.*—The Local Government Bill for England is a
great, wide, and liberal measure of government on a
popular basis, and contains a wise and prudent separation of judicial and administrative powers.   After a
discussion of forty years on local county government, the
Bill introduced this session, 1888, by Mr Ritchie,
proposes to place County Government in England on
a thoroughly popular and democratic basis.   It does not
propose to destroy the valuable aid which can be given

in Local County Government by the country gentry. Indeed, if the present holders of power in the county administration of England lose the powers they possess, they will have themselves to blame. In a Government such as ours, and with the Parliamentary Franchise based on Household Suffrage, it is absolutely impossible to continue Boards consisting of nominated and non-elective members in the administration of the local government in this country. But, in our local administrative government, we should keep up the old, well-known landmarks as much as possible. As now introduced into Parliament, this scheme is stupendous in its proportions and far-reaching consequences, and it has been admirably worked out in its details by its author, of whom, on local grounds, we have all reason to be proud. Even although it may be greatly modified and curtailed, it will probably be a great scheme of administrative Re-organization of English County Government, and will stand forth as the greatest effort of any Government in this country for the solution of all-important and vital problems. As, I daresay, most of you know, this Bill takes the Poor Law Unions, consisting of two or more Parishes, in England, as its unit, and does not start with the Parish as the unit. But the same basis need not be adopted in Scotland or Ireland in the local county administration for either of these countries, to which local county government, on the same or a similar basis, must be extended as in England. I hold that the Parish, or something like it, must eventually become the unit for Local Government in Great Britain and Ireland. Further, I am inclined to think that the English Bill is too complicated for simple adoption, or even adaptation, to

Scotland; and that, in the Scotch Local County Government Bill, the Parish, and not a Union, should be
taken as the unit; and that the Parochial Board, the
School Board, the Police Commission, and the Road
Trustees should form a consolidated Council for a
Parish, or District, with power to levy one consolidated
Rate.   I do not much believe in the efficacy or useful-
ness of Provincial Legislative Councils.   I am against
their establishment as useless and expensive.   The only
grounds upon which I feel inclined to make any objections
to the provisions of the English Local Government Bill
are based on the clauses for granting compensation to
the Licensed Publicans and Hotel Keepers in England.
In reference to these clauses, I have to say that they are
unjust and inequitable, and that I hope that they will be
abandoned by the Government, or rejected by Parliament; and that, whether they are abandoned or not,
they ought not to be taken as the basis of compensation,
in consequence of the withdrawal of licenses, by the
Local County or other authorities in Scotland, on
moral or other grounds.   A publican's license is in the
nature of an authority to do certain acts for a certain
period; and in itself it involves no right to do those
acts beyond the period specified in the license.   To
raise a yearly license to the quality of an estate in fee,
or even for life, at the expense of the Local Ratepayers,
is unjust and inequitable.   All that a Licensed
Publican can reasonably claim on his license being withdrawn at the end of his license, is an equitable compensation for the loss of his goodwill in his trade at a
particular place, and injury to his stock-in-trade
therein.   Medical men usually get a year's income in
name of goodwill on the sale of their business.   Why

should a Licensed Publican get more from the Local
Ratepayers ?   If Local County Councils be wise, they
will not exercise any wild and fantastic and sweeping
changes in the Licensing system till the morals and
habits of the people are improved.

*There should be no indirect representation in Local
County Government.*—There is no reason why there
should be any indirect representation of corporations
or individuals in a perfect scheme of local and rural
self-government.   All the citizens of a free state should
be encouraged to take an active interest in the public
administration of its local affairs.   No duplication
of representation should exist in counties or rural
districts, unless as a temporary expedient, any more
than in cities, towns, and large populous districts in
Scotland.   The present system of local county government is based on the landed or aristocratic interest, and
is injurious to all parties, and is alien to the popular
spirit of our existing constitution.   If the landed
interest must needs be conciliated for the present, a
new agitation for more extensive and popular powers
than those to be conferred will soon be commenced,
and carried to a successful issue.   The landed aristocracy in this country should be wise in time, and avail
themselves of their ample means and opportunities to
guide the popular instincts and the aspirations of the
nation, and do all in their power to use their great and
exalted position in the world for the benefit of our
free, constitutional, and popular government, which
is a mixture of all the three great principles of political
life, namely, of the monarchical, aristocratic, and
democratic elements.   What I have now said must
suffice for Home Affairs in general.   I have now to

ask your attention to what I have to say on the present occasion as to Irish Affairs.

III.—IRISH AFFAIRS.

1.—PRELIMINARY OBSERVATIONS.

The practical question of the hour.—The greatest practical home-question of the hour is this : How are we to govern Ireland ?   How are we to make the Irish people peaceful and loyal towards the government of the United Kingdom of England, Scotland, and Ireland? How are we to make them contented, prosperous, and happy ?   Some people say, let us give the Irish people Home Rule according to the demands of the Irish National League.   Some say, let us give them a grand new scheme of Irish Land Reform.   Some say, let us give them neither the one nor the other of these things. Lastly, some say, let us give them a large and comprehensive scheme of local administrative government, and a thorough reform of their land laws, based on the establishment of a peasant proprietary.   I venture to say, let us give them both local administrative government, and national self-government, and land reform on such a basis as will have the elements of permanency, and as will be advantageous to all parts of the United Kingdom, and injurious to none of them.   To talk of the Irish people as unfit for local administrative government is downright nonsense and sheer hypocrisy. How can they be unfit for such government when they are considered fit for Parliamentary Government ?   A despot may hold the opinion of a few Liberal Unionists on this subject ; but a believer in free constitutional government is precluded from agreeing with them. I myself have no hesitation in saying that the Irish people are quite capable of wisely and prudently exercising all the civil rights conferred, or to be conferred, on the English or Scotch people.   Even if they were not so, we must act as if they were, and leave them to learn wisdom by experience, in the same way as we have done ourselves, and our forefathers before us, and after many and grievous blunders.   We have too long acted towards the native, Celtic people of Ireland as a conquered and inferior race.

Equality of rights to England, Scotland, and Ireland.—All the leaders of the great parties in the State, Liberals as well as Conservatives, have advocated certain great principles of local and national self government for Ireland, and they cannot now escape from carrying these principles to their legitimate and logical conclusions.   These principles are based on equality of rights to all the citizens of England, Scotland, and Ireland.   On the basis of equal rights, how can we effectually resist the Policy of Repeal of the Legislative Union between Great Britain and Ireland ?   At present, there is no such thing as a real, genuine system of local administrative government for Ireland.   The Baronial and Municipal Government of Ireland is a farce, a snare, and a delusion.   This Baronial Government is in the hands of the landlords and their agents ; and the Municipal Government is in the hands of the National Leaguers.   Since 1840, an agitation has been going on in Ireland for the Reform of Local Government in Ireland, and the necessary reforms in this matter have not yet been made.

The aims of the Irish Nationalists.—The Irish Representatives in Parliament have declared that they will never be satisfied with the concession of mere local administrative government, and that they ask national self government as a right. For several years past, Mr Parnell has been the most powerful man in Ireland, and has even been called, not without reason, the uncrowned king of the Green Isle. He himself may not be a Fenian and a Separatist. But the majority of his Irish and American supporters are Fenians, Separatists, and Republicans pure and simple, and they wish to set up a Republican form of Government in Ireland in imitation of the Government of the United States or of the French Republic. They and their leaders and allies in the British Empire may rest assured that the British and Irish people will tolerate no such form of Government in Ireland, or anywhere else within their dominions. Hence Mr Parnell's position is a grave danger to our country in the present and in the future. Mr O'Connell, the great Irish agitator, began his career as a Nationalist and an Imperialist, and was compelled, by the force of his surrounding circumstances, to become an advocate of Repeal pure and simple. Is Mr Parnell doomed to a similar fate?—Men who enter upon wicked and dangerous conspiracies are not complete masters of their own fates. Be this as it may, Mr Parnell's followers are, to a large extent, dangerous, fanatical, and mercenary agitators and demagogues. So far as I can follow the policy and aims of the majority of Mr Parnell's American and Irish allies, I have no hesitation in saying that these are, by assassination, murder, dynamite, insurrection, and civil war, to drive the present Irish landlords and the English party out of Ireland;

to break up the political connection of Great Britain
and Ireland ; and to set up Ireland as a free and
independent Republican State, and as completely
separated from Great Britain as the United States of
America now are.

They will be defeated.—That they will never accomplish
these nefarious and detestable purposes, I venture to
predict with the most perfect confidence.   The Irish
question is not a Protestant, nor a Roman Catholic,
nor an agrarian question only, but a great national
and imperial question of the highest importance.
As such, and as nothing less, can it be settled on
a comprehensive and permanent basis.   Now, for
the practical solution of this great domestic question,
the Conservatives have great advantages on their side,
and a splendid opportunity of conferring an eternal
service to the British Empire, and of covering themselves with everlasting glory and renown.   They must
put down the tyranny of the Irish National League ;
extinguish sedition and agrarian outrages and murders ;
and build up the broken-down social system of Ireland
on the basis of established law and order.   They must
quell the half socialistic and half political civil wars
which have so long been waged in Ireland, and which
are eating out the vitals of the country.   The Irish
National League must not any longer be allowed to
usurp any of the functions of the Queen's Government
in Ireland ; or terrorize over the people of Ireland at
the parliamentary or municipal elections ; or over-
rule private contracts ; or overthrow the judgments of
the ordinary tribunals of Ireland.   The despotism of
the League must be remorselessly put down ; and the
reign of law must be completely re-established.   Many

of the leaders of the League have urged the Irish people to hold fast by their farms, which are held, as they say, by the tenants at impossible rack-rents. Let them, at once, begin to teach them the excellent virtues of industry, honesty, and temperance, and they will show themselves, and actually become, real bene-factors of their age and country.

We must have National and Imperial Government.—We must have one supreme Parliament, one supreme law, and one supreme administration for the government of the United Kingdom and all its different parts and portions, countries, and nationalities. The Union between Great Britain and Ireland for imperial purposes must be upheld as permanent and irrevocable, and the repeal of the Union as regards Imperial affairs must be regarded as ruinous to individuals and dangerous to the State. On this point I have never wavered, and hope and believe I never shall waver. Mr Gladstone says, that he has now devoted the remainder of his long life to the satisfaction of the national aspirations of the Irish people. I decline to satisfy the aspirations of the Irish people, or any portion of them, unless in so far as may be advantageous to the United Kingdom as well as Ireland. Let us make no mistake as to the tendency of his recent teaching, and of the necessary consequences of his Irish Policy. His Irish Home Rule Policy might possibly serve his day, but it would not last much longer than that time. Home Rule, as he has expounded it, would, I fear, end, as in Canada and Australia, in our having no power, no influence, and no control over Irish affairs. It would lead to further and further demands, which would end in anarchy, confusion, and civil war.   It would therefore end in the virtual independence of Ireland, or in a despotic government being established in Ireland on its re-conquest.   If a nation has sovereign rights, she has a right to a separate national existence.   We should never, and I believe we shall never, concede a separate national existence to Ireland, unless as the price of peace on the termination of a successful war against us.   No such war is or can be within the scope of the wildest dream of the most hair-brained Nationalist, or of any other person than a downright madman.   This country is, or will soon be, prepared for a large and comprehensive scheme of national self government for Ireland ; because, as I think, such a scheme must sooner or later be granted to England and Scotland.   But it will never, I hope and believe, accept any scheme for the actual or virtual separation of Great Britain and Ireland, or one necessarily and inevitably leading to that result.   The legislative Union of Great Britain and Ireland as an imperial measure, and for imperial purposes, is the best and surest foundation of liberty in Ireland.   It therefore ought to be upheld and defended by all patriotic citizens in Ireland as well as in England and Scotland. Therefore, taking into consideration the views entertained by the Liberal Unionists as well as the Irish and Gladstonian Nationalists, the Irish problem which has now to be solved is, not whether there shall be National and local self government in Ireland, but to what extent National and local self government can be safely and wisely granted to Ireland as well as to England and Scotland ; and to what persons, associations or departments, cities, counties or provinces, National and self government, is to be conceded in the United Kingdoms of England, Scotland, and Ireland. Generally speaking, National self government must comprehend all public and local matters within each kingdom. Again, Imperial Government must comprehend all imperial matters within each kingdom, province, colony, or dominion, and it must have the power of directing and superintending law and order, and enforcing, in the last resort, private rights and duties, civil and criminal, in every part of the British Empire.

National and Ecclesiastical differences in Ireland.— Ireland has never been a nationality; for its races have never been fused into one homogeneous body. As a kingdom, it is not much more than a geographical area. Before the English conquest in the reign of Henry II. in 1172, Ireland had Home Rule, and with it anarchy, confusion, and bloodshed, and a perpetual state of war. So far as an Irish nationality can be said to be in Ireland, it was based on English laws and English government. The Norman invasion took the guise of a crusade in defence of the orthodox Faith of the Church of Rome. The English were colonists, and were mostly confined to a limited area called the English Pale. About two centuries ago, Ulster was peopled by English and Scotch colonists, and the native inhabitants were driven to the wilds of Kerry and Connemara. The Reformation of the Church in the Sixteenth Century intensified and perpetuated the original race discords and hatreds. It intensified the differences between the Celtic and Saxon populations before and after its introduction, and its seeds of discord blossom in our own times. In Ireland, feudalism, with all its harshness to the poor, superseded the old Celtic forms of law. It was allowed to have its full swing on the

great mass of the people without the restraining hand
of the royal authority, which, instead of being inter-
posed to modify the rapacity of the nobles and colonists,
fell with heavy hand on the native cultivators of the
soil as aliens in race and religion.   Coercion and war,
conciliation and peace, have followed each other in
Ireland by fitful starts, as one religious or political
party in England held the reins of power.   In the end,
and as the ultimate result, the people of Ireland have
had to pay the penalty, and, like the nether millstone,
have been crushed between the political factions on
this side of the Channel.   Nay more, the agriculture,
trade, and commerce of Ireland were not allowed to hurt,
or interfere with, those of England; and, when necessary,
were remorselessly extinguished.   We now reap the
fruits of English misgovernment in Ireland.   God is
just, and will punish the evil-doers to the third and
fourth generations.   Famine and starvation, and misery
and ignorance, have been the natural and inevitable
consequences of English and of British misgovernment.

The hatred of the Irish exiles.—Further, the revolt of
the American colonies, and the setting up of an independent and separate Government on the other side of
the Atlantic, have had great and important influence on
Ireland, and on Irishmen at home and abroad, not only at
the time, but also in 1782 and also at the present moment.   Thus, a hundred years ago, thousands of Irish
Presbyterians were driven to America by the stupid and
senseless Episcopalians entrusted with the government
of Ireland.   Moreover, since then, tens of thousands
of Irish Roman Catholics have been driven, by the
rapacity and cruelty of the Irish landlords, from their
ancient homes to the United States of America,

Canada, South Africa, and Australasia. All of them hated England then, and most of their descendants, Protestant and Roman Catholic, in America and elsewhere, hate her now with an undying hatred. In 1798, the English loyalists were massacred in great numbers by the Irish Roman Catholics. The French Revolution was the efficient cause of the independent Parliament of Ireland in 1782. The same mighty upheaval was one of the great causes which induced Mr Pitt to carry the Legislative Union of Great Britain and Ireland in 1801. Ireland cannot now be treated as a dependency or a colony, but must be treated by us as an equal.

We must maintain the legislative Union.—Now, I wish you to observe that the Nationalist demand for an Irish Parliament is not based, as you might expect, on the inability of the Imperial Parliament at Westminster to pass laws for Ireland. Much might and can be truthfully said on that score; but rather on the incapacity of the Imperial Parliament to govern Ireland justly and equitably. Why do the Irish Nationalist Party adopt this attitude? Can there be any other reason than that the Parnellite and Revolutionary Irish Parties claim an Irish Parliament for Ireland on the ground of abstract justice, and because of the great powers which, as they suppose, such an Assembly would place in their hands; and on the grounds, as they say, of Ireland being a nation, and of her power and influence in the Imperial Parliament being a snare and a delusion? Undoubtedly these are the reasons, or the chief reasons, which influence them. This being so, we must boldly and resolutely maintain the absolute supremacy of the legislative Union between Great Britain and Ireland as a great and fundamental principle in our government, and hold fast by our traditional policy for the last 100 years, to the effect that the separate political independence of Ireland is incompatible with the independence of the British Empire. Self-defence is allowed by all men to be a sufficient argument for defending one's self from attack, and even for restraining and attacking those who would endanger our liberty, our life, or our property. Let us, by all means, give the fullest justice to Ireland. But let us also refuse to be coerced by the dangerous or unjust demands, or actions, of revolutionary agitators, or the enemies of our country. We must not—we shall not—break up the British Empire to gratify any person, or party, in the state. As the Americans in 1861, so we must maintain that the integrity of the British Empire is not to be broken up. As they, so we have said, and mean to maintain to the end, that the separation of Ireland from Great Britain is not for the interest of the Empire. I am not now dealing with a question of justice, but of political prudence. Yet even, on the basis of justice, in the sense of giving every man his due, I am prepared to say that the separation of Ireland from Great Britain cannot, and never will, be permitted by this country.

The Unionist policy.—The policy of the Conservative and Liberal Unionist party is to restore law and order to their rightful supremacy in Ireland, and to put down and punish ruffianism, disorder, and crime, in every shape and form. Therefore, all breaches of the law and good policy, and especially all incitement to violence and oppression, and obstruction of the officers of the law, must be punished. The steady execution of the laws will put down the despotism and ruffianism of the Irish National Leaguers and their allies. The Crimes Act of 1887 has been, and still is, attacked with the utmost virulence by the Irish Nationalist Party and their allies in England and Scotland. But this Act is not, and cannot in any way be hurtful or injurious to good, but only to bad citizens; not to the loyal, but to the disloyal; and not to the well-behaved, but to the scoundrels. Such an Act of Parliament is coercive, but only in the sense in which all Acts of Parliament are coercive. All laws are, and must be coercive, and directed against crimes and violence, or for the enforcement of contracts and the judgments of the Courts of the country. This policy must and will be successful, and triumph in the end. The Conservative and Liberal Unionist parties are opposed to trading for place, power, or popularity, for their own sakes, and are determined to pursue a Democratic policy at home, and a national or Imperial policy abroad. But the present union of the Conservatives and Liberal Unionists cannot last for ever. It might easily and early be broken up by divergent views actually now existing amongst them to a considerable extent as to home and foreign affairs. We must be prepared for a contingency which might break the present Ministry to pieces, and make the advent of a Radical Gladstonian Government an absolute necessity. In such event, what are we to do? Why, as I think, the Conservative party must stand by their principles, and appeal to the People to support them. The present Irish policy is not an invention of the Liberal Unionists. All we can say about it is, that the Liberal Unionists support the Conservative policy at

I

present.   The reform of administrative or legislative
local self government must be granted to Ireland as to
the other two integral parts of the United Kingdom.
But this local government must be one and the same for
each and all of them, and must be consistent with the
legislative Union of Great Britain and Ireland for all
Imperial purposes. We must govern Ireland as we govern
England and Scotland.   We must make Ireland as free
as England or Scotland, in every respect.   We must
not put or keep Ireland under subjection to exceptional
laws any longer than is absolutely necessary, or than we
would maintain such laws in peculiar circumstances for
England or Scotland, even although, for the present, in
consequence of the exceptional state of public affairs in
that unhappy and unfortunate country, we must, perhaps, for the present, adopt different methods of enforcing law and order, and even make exceptional laws
for her unhappy and divided people and hostile factions.

Law, order, and reform needed.—Whatever we
do, we must not abandon the principle of maintaining the supremacy of the Imperial Parliament
over every part of the British Dominions, and
of enforcing law and order against all persons.   Home
Rule may be a good thing, or a bad thing; but it must be
obtained or rejected by argument, and not by force.
Standing on this firm and indubitable ground, the
supporters of the Imperial supremacy must inevitably
be victorious, and vanquish all their opponents.   In
political matters, as in all great questions of public
policy, the motives of individuals are of less consequence than the effects and tendencies of their actions
and opinions.   I hold that a politician is to be condemned when his actions, or opinions, are dangerous to

the State, no matter how good or excellent his motives and intentions may be. Whatever the failures of our government of Ireland may have been, and these failures are largely due to national hatred and religious bigotry, all the great parties in the State have been anxious to promote good government and good laws in Ireland since the Union in 1801. Absolute legislative independence, or total separation, would never be tolerated by us in Ireland, and would, I believe, be the cause of a civil war in Ireland before a very long time had elapsed. Every civilized country must enforce contracts, and make the law obeyed by great and small, rich and poor. Above all things, and before all things, we must put down disorder, disloyalty, and disunion in Ireland. The struggle for Imperial supremacy may be long, but it must and will be carried to a successful end. We must maintain law and order, and press forward all useful legislation, and equal legislation for Ireland as elsewhere. In my opinion, no permanent condition of things—political, social, and economical—can be built on the present state of society in Ireland. To make an improvement in these matters, the Imperial Government must make large pecuniary sacrifices, to enable the Irish people to gain a living in the country, by increasing and developing the industrial resources of the country ; by good roads, harbours, land drainage, and the like ; and by a large increase in the owners of land ; and by ultimately conceding the same powers of local, and, if necessary, national self government to the Irish people, on the same basis as I have stated. I now have to ask your attention to what I consider necessary for Ireland in the way of Parliamentary and Executive Reforms.

The legislative Union between Great Britain and Ireland.—The legislative Union between Great Britain and Ireland took effect in 1801, or nearly an hundred years after the legislative Union between England and Scotland. This legislative Union of the three United Kingdoms received the Royal Assent on the second of July 1800, and it came into force on the first of January 1801. Since then, with some few aberrations, the Imperial Parliament at Westminster has been very largely engaged in removing the errors and crimes of former generations in the government and legislation of Ireland. This legislative Union was intended to be, and, in fact, was, a great act of justice to the Irish people. It ought not to be repealed, or modified, without the strongest evidence of advantage to the British Empire as well as to Ireland. The so-called Grattan's Parliament, which existed from 1782 till the Union, never was an independent Irish Parliament, and was wholly composed of Protestants. The Imperial Parliament since the Union, and pre-eminently since the Roman Catholic Emancipation Act of 1828, has been far more national and representative of the Irish people than the Irish Parliament from 1782 to 1800, and more inclined and capable than it to act justly towards the Irish people as a whole.

Federal Government required.—A Federal scheme of Government for the United Kingdom is a desirable thing in itself, and will come in due time; but it is not, by any means, the most pressing necessity for Ireland. In fact, it is not likely to be adopted for some years to come. England and Scotland have as much need of such a scheme of Government as Ireland. But, until it can be fully elaborated, and made suitable to our wants, it can easily stand over for the present. How the supremacy of the Imperial Government is to be maintained in the British Empire; whether, for example, by a Supreme Court as in the United States, or by Delegations as in the Austro-Hungarian Empire, or in some other way; requires the deepest and calmest consideration from the greatest statesmen of our age and country. But, of course, our Irish fellow citizens, with their natural impetuosity and brilliant imaginations, can understand none of these difficulties. All things will come in good time and in a proper way. No doubt, Mr Chamberlain holds that an Irish Parliament, set up in Dublin, would be expensive, ineffective, and dishonest. But I have to confess that I do not agree with him. I believe that an Irish Parliament would bring new elements of wealth, education, and social position into competition with the present representatives of the Irish people; and that the character and tone of the Irish Representatives in Parliament would be improved. I do not wonder at the hatred and opposition of the Irish people, and of their representatives, against the English Government of Ireland ever since the Irish Conquest, about 700 years ago, up to the present century. Now, as always, the Government of Ireland is concentrated in London; that is to say, in the hands of a strong English official class in Dublin, and subordinate to English officials in London. If the Government of Scotland had been carried on in the same way, Home Rule for Scotland would have been imperative long ago. What Ireland imperatively stands in need of are—(1) County and Town local government for administrative purposes; and (2) a strong, central, national Council in Dublin, whether in the name of a Parliament or a legislative Council, I care not.   Now, observe, that the Conservatives and Liberal Unionists are willing to grant a wide and comprehensive scheme of local government as soon as Ireland is properly and fully reduced to submission to the ordinary laws of the land.   But they say that they will not be responsible for any proposals involving, or tending to involve, separation.   In other words, they, in my opinion, declare that they will not be responsible for the restoration of Grattan's Parliament, or for the establishment of such an Irish Parliament as Mr Gladstone proposed under his Bill of 1885, or under his subsequently modified views.   I hold that they are quite right in assuming this attitude.   I also hope that they will stand to these principles, and will defend the unity of the Empire, and the supremacy of the Imperial Parliament, at all hazards.   In the scheme which I have propounded and published, I have clearly indicated that, in my opinion, the supremacy of the Imperial Parliament and the unity of the Empire must be maintained.

If repeal, then Domestic and Imperial Parliaments should be established.—If the Imperial Parliament at Westminster must be broken up, or rather, if certain duties now performed by the Imperial Parliament must, as I think they must very soon, be relegated to representative and national Assemblies, it ought not to be so by the fragmentary and dangerous scheme of the late Liberal Government.   That scheme would have ended in absolute Irish independence, and the separation

of Ireland from this country, or in civil war between
Great Britain and Ireland. If a new departure is to
be made, and a new constitution is to be created for
Great Britain and Ireland, it ought to be by a dissolution of the Imperial Parliament into its component
parts of Queen, Lords, and Commons in each kingdom
for the domestic affairs of each kingdom, and by the
creation of an Imperial Parliament for the three kingdoms for all matters of Imperial interest, and on such
a basis as would admit Representatives in the Imperial
Parliament to be chosen from all the legislatively
free, independent colonies and independencies of the
Empire. To such a confederation of the British
Empire we are rapidly advancing, and therefore, we
should take steps to provide for its consummation.
Before long, there must be Imperial Confederation or
Dissolution. We stand in need of an Imperial Parlia-
ment for our Imperial interests, duties, rights, and
obligations, and for these alone. We need National
Legislatures for our National interests, duties, rights,
and obligations, and for these alone. We have had the
Home Rule schemes of the Irish National League, of
Mr Parnell, and of Mr Gladstone. We have had the
Irish Provincial Council scheme of Mr Chamberlain.
We have had the Local Government schemes of the
Liberal Unionists and the Conservatives, of Lords
Salisbury and Hartington. We have had Colonial,
Austro-Hungarian, and American Home Rule pressed
upon our consideration and for our adoption. Let us
now apply our minds to discover the solution which
is best suited to our wants. Let us have a wise and
permanent settlement of this grave and vital subject
by a full and complete investigation of our complicated
and national and imperial interests.

Ireland is not entitled to any special privileges.—As the British Empire is unique in its government and position in the world, so must the solution of this grand problem be unique. Ireland has no right to a form of government which would be injurious or dangerous to the British Empire. Notwithstanding all the Irish National talk about Ireland having an indefeasible right to national self government, and apparently according to the wishes or demands of a majority of the Representatives, yet, the Irish National League, and the English and Scotch and Welsh Liberals, and all who support them in their absurd contentions, must be taught, beyond the shadow of a doubt, that Ireland, and every other part of the British Empire, must be satisfied with the government conferred by the Imperial Parliament at Westminster, and that any violent steps taken to usurp the functions of the Imperial Parliament must be treated as unconstitutional, and as treasonable. So long as the laws of a civilized state continue, they must be obeyed, or the whole government will soon become anarchical, and be destroyed. Free discussion in Parliament, or in presence of the People, for the removal of alleged grievances belongs to every British citizen, and ought to be as a sacred and inviolable birthright. It stands in a very different category from violent efforts to change the government of a state. In my opinion, the present condition of Parliamentary and Executive Government in this country cannot last much longer. But whatever is done, or whatever change takes place in our Government, the supremacy, unity, and integrity of the Imperial Parliament at Westminster as to all Imperial affairs, and matters so considered by the Imperial Parliament, must be maintained and defended. Whatever is done, or whatever change is made, we must maintain and defend the fundamental principles of society, namely, freedom of industry, the security of property, and personal freedom. As a first and necessary step towards these things, disloyalty and the Irish National League must be, at once, put down. We must hold fast by the Union of Great Britain and Ireland in all its chief and essential features as established in 1800, or the state of affairs will become the same as in 1641, 1690, and 1798, and, alas! as bloody and disastrous.

Home Rule Manifestoes of 1881 *and* 1882.—An Irish Home Rule manifesto was issued in 1881. It declared that the Land Act of 1880 was insufficient; that a native Irish Parliament was necessary for Ireland; that the Irish struggle of 700 years for independence would not be abandoned; and that, as in 1873, the Irish people claimed the right and power to manage those affairs which appertained to themselves alone, and that Imperial matters should be left to the Imperial Senate. On the extinction of the Irish Land League, as an unlawful Association, by the Liberal Government, the Irish National League was established in October 1882. The new and transformed Association then issued a manifesto announcing that its aims were—(1) National self government; (2) the extension of the Parliamentary and Municipal franchise in Ireland; and (3) the development of Irish industries: that is to say, as we were authoritatively told, Ireland was to manage its own affairs; establish an Irish peasant proprietary; create Local Boards to be elected by the People, and not to be nominated by the Government; abolish the Irish Lord-Lieutenancy; and control the Irish

police, poor law, and education.   In these two docu-
ments, there is a complete enunciation of Federal Home
Rule.   Until about November or December 1885, the
Irish National League substantially adhered to their
scheme of National Government for Ireland and Imperial Government for the Empire.   But the Leaguers
enlarged it as soon as they found that the Liberals
could not be restored to power without their aid and
assistance.

Mr Sexton criticised and condemned.—In October
1887, Mr Sexton, in the Dublin Town Council,
gave expression to this opinion: "No act," he
said, "passed by the British legislature for
Ireland against the will of the Representatives of
Ireland has any moral sanction or moral force on the
will and conscience of the Irish people."   Here, of
course, he speaks of moral, and not legal obligation.
But what does his opinion really mean?   Does he mean to
say that, when a majority of the Irish Representatives
vote against an Irish Bill in the House of Commons,
this Bill, after it receives the sanction of the Imperial
Parliament, is not obligatory on all the people of Ireland,
or that they, or any of them, are at liberty to disobey
it as null and void?   Unless he meant this, he was
talking utter nonsense, and, what is worse, dangerous
nonsense.   The spheres of moral and legal obligation
are perfectly well-known and recognised as essentially
different in many respects.   But in regard to binding
force, a legal obligation is binding within its own
sphere independently of the moral law.   His
doctrine, as a political doctrine, is wrong, unconstitutional, and absurd.   Suppose, for example, that an
Irish Parliament for the whole of Ireland were to be

established by the Imperial Parliament, and passed some law against the wishes of Ulster as to education, land, commerce, or taxation, and that Ulster were to set up this doctrine as a ground for non-obedience, would he or his leader, Mr Parnell, allow the people of Ulster to set such a law at defiance? Of course, he would not. And yet Ulster does not wish or ask for Home Rule. Nay more, a majority of its Representatives are against the Imperial Parliament at Westminster granting Parnellite or Gladstonian Home Rule. How can he draw a distinction between the two cases, which are exactly parallel? No man is necessarily under a moral obligation, although he may be under a legal obligation, to obey a law he dislikes; and, in a sense, every man has a moral right to disobey the law he dislikes. But if he disobeys the law, he does so at his peril, and he makes himself liable to punishment. Any other doctrine is subversive of constitutional freedom. The constitutional doctrine is that all laws should be enforced until altered or abrogated. The Sextonian doctrine was naturally followed by defiance of the Queen's Government acting under the Crimes Act of 1887 ; but it has not upset the Queen's Government in Ireland, as it was intended to do.

The Irish Nationalists are dangerous revolutionaries.—The truth of the matter is, that the aims and methods of the National League are revolutionary and unconstitutional, inasmuch as they are based on force and violence, and not on argument and justice, and that the Leaguers have no regard for the honour of the Empire. While the Nationalist agitation is legitimate on the surface, it is impregnated with revolution and disorder. It is in violation of the ordinary laws of morality and honesty. It is aimed at the destruction of the basis of all law, social order, and civilization. If Home Rule in the shape of Irish independence were granted to Ireland, no long time would elapse before the flood-gates of revolution and anarchy would be opened wide; and we would be obliged, in self-defence, to interfere between the rival and contending factions of Roman Catholics and Protestants, farmers and labourers, capitalists and workmen. Mr Dillon says that he will never be content until the Irish people have power over their own affairs by means of an Irish Legislature and an Irish Executive. What does he mean by Irish affairs? Suppose the Irish people refused to pay Imperial Taxes, or to allow recruiting for the Imperial Army, or agreed to join our enemies, as Scotland and Ireland, long ago, have done before, what would the people of the United Kingdom do? The Irish people say, and have long said by their Representatives in the Imperial Parliament, that British Laws are not binding on their conscience; that they are not made by their consent; and that we act wrongfully and unlawfully by enforcing these laws. Suppose an Irish Parliament and Executive supported these opinions, we must enforce our rights at the point of the sword, or allow the United Kingdom to be dismembered. The struggle between the Constitutional and Revolutionary Parties in this country is a great and memorable one, and will not be completely fought out for some years to come, and then, I hope, the Constitutional Party will obtain a great and signal victory over the Party of Revolution. If the Irish Nationalist Parliamentary Party were not combined with the Irish Republican Brotherhood, the Fenians, and other like Associations in Ireland and America, why do they not

denounce the crimes that can be and have been traced
to such Associations ?   Surely the denunciation of
crime is not contrary to their schemes of government
and national regeneration ?   Why did they never lift
up their voices in condemnation of the horrid, bloody,
and shameful murders committed in Phœnix Park in
May 1882 ?   If we have had no actual war or insurrection in Ireland, the Irish revolutionaries have not
been slow to tell us that the means, not the will, were
wanting.   The secret of the success of the Revolutionary Parties in Ireland is, that they have persuaded
the Irish tenants that an Irish Parliament will give
them their farms for little or nothing.

Gladstone's proposals submitted to Parliament.—In
March 1886, Mr Gladstone's Irish Bills were communicated to the Liberal Cabinet.   They contained provisions
for the following purposes, namely—(1) the establishment of an Irish Parliament of one Chamber ; (2) the
buying out of the Irish landlords at an estimated cost of
£150,000,000 or £200,000,000 ; (3) the interest on
the Irish Land Purchase to be paid to an Irish Land
Court ; (4) no contribution to be made by the Imperial
Exchequer to local Irish Taxes ; (5) the Irish Parliament not to have power to establish religion, nor a
hostile tariff against British Trade ; (6) the representation of Ireland in the Imperial Parliament to be in the
proportion of thirty Members for £3,000,000 yearly ;
and (7) the Royal Constabulary were to be disarmed,
and placed under the control of the Irish Parliament.
In April 1886, the Irish Home Rule Bill was printed,
and publicly made known, and the Conservative party
determined not to oppose the first reading of the Bill in
the House of Commons.   But Lord Salisbury as Leader

of the Conservative party, and Lord Hartington as the Leader of the Liberal Unionist party, resolved to do all they could to oppose the Bill on the second reading in the House of Commons. The second reading of the Irish Home Rule Bill was rejected, and the Gladstonian Government retired from office. Then Lord Salisbury, with the approbation and support of the Liberal Unionists, took the helm of affairs, and he and his Government, notwithstanding the Dissolution in the autumn of 1886, remain in office still.

Observations on the Gladstonian proposals of 1886. —The Irish Land and Home Rule Bills settled nothing finally, and created new difficulties by the pecuniary obligations indicated in the Land Bill, and by the political and religious restrictions suggested by the Home Rule Bill. The Parnellites hardly concealed their dislike to the political restrictions and pecuniary obligations imposed. They merely accepted them as satisfactory and final for the time being. With their allies in this country, they would soon have found reasons for objecting to the proposals, and agitating till they got them modified. The loyal minority were not sufficiently protected by this Home Rule Bill. The landlords were fiercely denounced as harsh, cruel, and unjust rackrenters. Nay more, a Protestant Imperial Parliament was asked to concede the principle of National independence, and yet put restrictions on the power of an Irish Parliament in regard to establishing the religion of the majority of the Irish people in Ireland. This Gladstonian Home Rule scheme was, therefore, dangerous and reckless. It was based on gambling, and not on true statesmanship. It is now acknowledged by its own authors as imperfect. We

are told that the Home Rule Bill and the Land
Bill of 1886 are dead and gone. I do not doubt that
they are. In their place, a better and more rational
and enduring scheme will yet be devised, and will be
passed by the Imperial legislature amidst the applause
and to the satisfaction of all parties in the state.
National self government for England, Scotland, and
Ireland is the solution to which we must turn in the
end, and in the course of a few years. It must be
based on well-defined and equal laws for all, and it
must clearly lay down and explicitly define the
rights and duties of the National Legislatures and the
Imperial Parliament. The Parnellites asked that there
should be an Executive Government in Ireland, free and
independent, and corresponding to the national
aspirations. They were offered a Parliament and an
Executive, shackled and manacled by inconsistent and
impossible conditions, and totally different from what
the Parnellites asked and demanded as a national
right. The National claims as asserted by the Parnellites were not granted by Mr Gladstone's Home
Rule Bill. Therefore, even although passed into law,
it would have been merely the stepping-stone for
further demands and further agitation. According to
some people, Irish Home Rule is simply another name
for the expropriation of the Irish landlords without rent,
and without compensation. Such a scheme of Irish
Home Rule, if followed by such results, would be
nothing less than confiscation and theft.

We must treat Ireland, in every respect, on the
same terms as England and Scotland, so far as the
condition of that country will allow. We must introduce local county and urban government into Ireland

on the same basis as we have it, or will have it, ourselves, and with as much despatch as the circumstances of our parliamentary procedure will allow. As yet, we have scarcely begun the work of local government in Ireland ; and not much can be said in its favour so far as already introduced.   I have further to say that the indefinite postponement of local administrative government in Ireland cannot be admitted as a general principle.   To Ireland a great debt is due by this country for the wrongs inflicted upon her, during centuries of oppression and misgovernment, in the interests of the English commercial classes, as well as of the great English landed proprietors.   Indeed, I am not at all sure that the English commercial policy of last century was not more injurious to Ireland than the English landlord laws in Ireland.   Having given parliamentary representation to the Irish people, on the same basis as to ourselves, we cannot refuse to extend to them the same local government we do now, or will yet in future, possess.

Reform needed in the Irish executive.—Till recently, and since the Reformation, the cardinal principle of English government in Ireland has been to foster and maintain the supremacy of the English landed interest, and of the English Episcopal Church, and generally, yet not always, of the Presbyterian Church, or, generally speaking, of Protestantism in Ireland as against the Church of Rome.   Gradually this form of supremacy has been weakened, and has now been overthrown.   We must now legislate for and govern the Irish people under constitutional and democratic principles.   The old doctrines of the English government were a snare and a delusion, and had to be abandoned as untenable. Still, we must enforce law and order as they exist under the Constitution, and extend the principles of justice and righteousness into every department of the Empire, and amongst all classes of the People. We must make all these great principles of government supreme throughout the length and breadth of the Empire. We must be just in all our ways in dealing with Ireland, and fear not what may be the consequences. What is just and righteous is Godlike. What is Godlike ought to be made to prevail in a civilized community.

There are three possible solutions.—There are three ways of ending the present embroglio in Ireland, namely, separation, conciliation, and repression. Which principle, or principles, should be adopted? We must oppose separation by every means in our power. We should punish all breaches of the existing law. We should proceed on our way in bringing the laws of Ireland into harmony with the eternal principles of truth and justice. We should exert our utmost strength to remove the bitter feelings which have been engendered in the minds of the Celtic and Roman Catholic people in Ireland by past cruelty and oppression, and strive to attain to a real and firm Union between all classes of the people in Ireland, and between all and every one of the three kingdoms of England, Scotland, and Ireland. United, we can defy all our enemies. Divided, we are in danger of falling a prey to their envy and dislike. By all means, let us have the widest possible extension of self government in Ireland as well as in England and Scotland. But this extension must be consistent with the maintenance of the integrity of the Empire. What is good for one

K

kingdom is good for all the three United Kingdoms. What is not good for one of them is not good for the others. True, all the three kingdoms are, in many respects, differently situated and constituted. But what I wish to see utterly abandoned is the idea that the Irish are not so capable of enjoying and working constitutional government on a popular basis just as much as England or Scotland. What I wish to see is the repudiation of the doctrine that Ireland is to be deprived of popular government in consequence of the disloyalty of some of the Irish people. I say, perish such a thought in a great and free country such as ours. Let us firmly and persistently carry out these principles, and, I believe, the dawn of a real and happy Union between the three United Kingdoms is at hand.

Radical, Whig, and Conservative Theories.—The Radical Unionist theory of government for Ireland proceeds on the basis that Ireland should be governed by Irish ideas, and expands its doctrines into the establishment of peasant proprietary and local administrative government for Ireland. The Whig based his theory of Irish government on a Protestant Church and State. The Conservative based his theory of Irish government on a national Church and a national State. Let us stand by the integrity of the British Empire, and give a national solution to this great question. We have had Protestant ascendancy and Roman Catholic ascendancy in Ireland, and know and feel that neither the one nor the other has ever worked well in that country. We have established justice and equality in Ireland for upwards of half a century; and we must uphold and maintain these principles in future. Thus we shall conquer the enemies of the

Union, maintain the integrity of the United Kingdom of Great Britain and Ireland, and also give peace, happiness, and prosperity to a distracted and unhappy country. We should not allow political injustice, or religious ascendancy of any kind, Protestant or Roman Catholic, to be re-established in Ireland under the aegis of the State. By steadily and fearlessly acting on these principles, I hope, and believe, that we will conquer a noble and long down-trodden and oppressed people, not by arms, not by injustice, but by the universal diffusion of the principles of justice and equity throughout their country. The laws which now exist, or may exist at any future time, must be enforced by the whole strength of the United Kingdom. This rule is a fundamental principle of every civilized government, and must not be departed from on any consideration. We must allow no man however popular, and no association however powerful, in any part of the British Empire, to be substituted for the supreme executive power of the Queen and her Ministers, or for the legislative supremacy of the Imperial Parliament at Westminster. The supremacy of the law and the constitution is the best and surest guarantee for justice and freedom in every country and in every age.

Opinion is ripening for great constitutional changes. —In December 1887, Mr W. H. Smith said that the Irish Nationalist party would not accept State rights, as in the United States, Sweden, Norway, and Austro-Hungary. He says that they aimed at Independence, and, aided by the Fenians, were aiming at the Independence sought in 1798, 1846, and 1867. About the same time, Lord Randolph Churchill said at Stockport that he was determined to oppose legislative re-

peal and separation. These statements throw a flood of
light upon what took place between the Conservatives
and the Parnellites in 1885 ; but they do not affect
the general question which has now to be settled.
Also about the same time Lord Roseberry said that
the Liberal Party wished Home Rule as in the United
States. I, therefore, infer that he is an Imperialist
Home Ruler, and not a Parnellite Home Ruler; and
that the Conservatives and Liberal Unionists and
Radical Unionists will yet settle this great question by
a compromise, and on a firm and permanent basis. At
all events, I do not despair of this result. Lord Beaconsfield himself was in favour of a policy of conciliation
towards the Irish, and of giving them as much power
as the Scotch people had in Scotland, and of granting
to the Irish power over local, but not over Imperial
affairs. So said Sir Michael Beach in January 1888.
As regards the Irish National demand for Independence, it must be refused peremptorily and for ever.
Do not let us close our eyes to the realities of things.
If the Irish people were hostile to us while we were
engaged in a great European war, the position of affairs
would be very serious to us; for we would be compelled
to maintain a large army in Ireland to keep them
from rising in rebellion, or we would be obliged to concede their demands ungraciously and disastrously and
by force, just as happened in 1782. Now, as then,
the Irish Nationalists ask the powers conceded to them
by Grattan's Parliament in 1782 ; and they, therefore,
ask complete and practical independence. This demand
cannot and will not be granted by the present Parliament ; and, as I hope, by no Imperial British Parliament at any time. Irish Nationalism is a real fact in

British politics; but British Imperial Unity is a greater fact, and a more powerful one in this country and in the world.

3.—AGRARIAN REFORM.

Irish Land Problem.—In my opinion, the Irish Land agitation is essentially the greatest Irish question. This question is social, economical, and political. This is also the opinion of the leaders of the Conservative party and of the Liberal Unionist party; and, in accordance with this view, the Conservative Government are, as I hope, soon to introduce a Bill into the Imperial Parliament for the final settlement of this question. The great mass of the Irish people are poor and miserable. They depend almost solely on a scanty agriculture for their means of living, and usually have farms much too small to enable them to gain a livelihood therefrom for themselves and their families. Unless these two great facts are recognised by us in the solution of the Irish Land problem, no Land Act of any kind will ever confer peace on Ireland, or happiness and prosperity on its people. The truth is that, in the most disturbed districts of Ireland, in those of Clare, Connemara, and Kerry, the farms are so small, and the tenants are so poor, that farms, without any rents, would not, and could not, make the tenants and their families contented, happy, and prosperous. There are 100,000 Irish peasant farmers who each pay £4 of yearly rent for their farms. Till a large emigration of the Irish people takes place from Ireland, and many thousands of these small farms are enlarged, voluntarily or compulsorily, we never will, nor can, have peace and prosperity in Ireland.

A drastic Land Act required.—The Liberals, as well as the Conservatives, are agreed that a drastic Irish Land Bill is indispensible. The old territorial or feudal system, which has done an immense deal of harm to Ireland during its existence there for the last three or four centuries, has utterly broken down in Ireland, and has left nothing in its place except the greedy and harsh commercial system of land ownership. The agricultural people of Ireland are consequently, to a large extent, in abject poverty and destitution. The introduction of the feudal system into Ireland arrested the natural development and civilization of Ireland, and ultimately left the people under a huge load of debt, and a large number of harpies in the shape of bailiffs, land agents, and rapacious money-lenders. Ireland is almost a purely agricultural country. So far as it is industrial in the northern districts, it is so chiefly by the energy and activity of an alien race and an alien religious denomination. Most unfortunately, the selfishness of the English commercial classes, aided and abetted by the British Parliament, caused everything to to done, during the last century, to restrict and even destroy the Irish industries, for the advantage of the English manufacturers of linen and woollen goods. Unless the reign of law and order is upheld in Ireland there is a danger that the Irish people will sink deeper and deeper in misery, and that the land there will largely go out of cultivation, or be greatly deteriorated in value. The settlement of this grave land problem, of this cankerous sore, is a great national question, and demands the best thoughts and actions of the wisest and most patriotic men in the country and of all the political parties in the State. As far back as 1866, Mill, the great political economist, urged the establishment of peasant proprietorship in Ireland at any cost, and as a great national policy. All the efforts to solve the Irish agrarian problem have been merely approximations to his advice. His views must ultimately be adopted, or there will be no peace for Ireland or ourselves.

Is not yet solved.—The recent Irish Land Acts of 1870 and 1881, which were to give peace and happiness to an unhappy and long misgoverned country, have intensified the deplorable state of affairs in Ireland, and we are now forced to undertake further reforms on the Irish Land Laws. The justification, if any, of our past efforts to solve the Irish agrarian problem, and of our continuing our efforts in the same direction, is to be found in the facts, that the system of great landlords and also of dual ownership has failed in Ireland; and that it is necessary, to a large extent, to establish the occupiers as owners of their farms, in order to maintain the law and government of the country, and to prevent the landlords from being deprived of their property. The attempts hitherto made by Mr Gladstone to solve the Irish land problem in harmony with Irish sentiments have utterly failed. The Act of 1870 was intended to legalize the rights which the Irish tenants had, or were supposed to have, in their tenancies. But the Act of 1881 was a clear unjustifiable interference with the rights of private property. We are embarked on a sea of troubles from the irreconcilable and contradictory views of legislators as to arrears for rent in Ireland. We should never have tried to fix the rents to be paid by Irish agricultural tenants to their landlords, because we have not the necessary appliances to satisfy all parties ; and because efforts to do justice were doomed to failure from the first, on the grounds of history and experience, and were bound to be expensive to the State and to individuals. The intervention of the State between private persons and free and capable citizens in private affairs is, as a general rule, a stupid blunder. In Ireland we have three differ-ent tribunals dealing with the land question, at an expense to the country of £130,000 a year. We must also recollect that the costs incurred to the lawyers must have been enormous, and have had to be paid out of the pockets of the suitors before the tribunals. I think that every one of those Courts should be abolished, and that the parties should appeal to the ordinary tribunals for justice, on a fixed basis to be settled by Parliament. The Imperial Parliament would, I think, have acted wisely by adopting Griffith's valuation, or something like it, higher or lower, as would, on investiga-tion, have been just and fair, and made it the basis of all Irish rents and all purchases of farms by the Irish tenants, and made a grant to the Irish landlords and their mortgagees, by way of compensation for their being deprived of the full ownership of their lands and securities.

Working of the Irish Land Acts.—The working of the Irish Land Acts has, therefore, been clumsy and expen-sive, and has caused great delay and much litigation. In June 1884, the Duke of Argyle, in reviewing the working of the Land Act of 1881, and the Report of the Committee of the House of Lords on the subject, demonstrated (1) that the expectations of the Liberal party had been falsified; (2) that the decisions of the Commissioners under the Land Act had not been judicial; (3) that the ownership of Irish land had been rendered unsaleable; and (4) that the tenant right had become more valuable than ever.

Dual ownership must be abolished.—Dual ownership has been created or legalized by the Land Acts of 1870 and 1881. But the Land purchase clauses of the Act of 1881 have been an absolute failure. Judicial rents have been a farce, and have ended in a rough-and-round reduction of about one-fourth of the rent. The long tenancy of fifteen years, intended for the protection of the Irish tenants, has also been abandoned as harsh and unjust. What grand, what splendid land reformers, we have lately had amongst our Liberal statesmen! In February 1887, we were told by Lord Cadogan, speaking on behalf of the present Conservative Government, that "dual ownership is to be abolished." But how? That is the question. I say by some plain, simple, and self-acting process, which, with the aid of Irish local government, backed by the Imperial government, will confer the ownership of the land in Ireland on all occupiers, or as many as possible, who wish to buy their farms, at a fair and reasonable price. The occupiers of the soil in Ireland have, by statute, been made joint-owners with the old proprietors; and, to a large extent, at least, they must be made the sole owners.

Essentials of a good Irish Land Purchase Bill.—The essential conditions of a good Irish Land purchase scheme must be based on buying out all the agricultural tenants under £10 of yearly rent; on giving inducements to all tenants under £50 of yearly rent to surrender their holdings for combination of holdings, and subsequent distribution on an enlarged scale of suitable size; by giving absolute rights of purchase to all tenants above £10 of yearly rent; and by prohibiting subdivision of farms under twenty, thirty, or fifty acres as may hereafter be determined as fit and proper. To make the small tenants in Ireland the owners of their land under a general land purchase scheme would not materially improve the condition of the very small occupiers, and would cause a considerable loss to the Imperial Exchequer. If a small tenant can buy his tenancy, he should have full power to do so, but he should not be allowed to do so at the expense of the Imperial Exchequer. Where the land cannot give a livelihood to the occupier, either by reason of its small size, or of the sterility of the soil, the State might, and ought to advance money to the landlords to enable them to buy out incapable or useless or impoverished tenants. A comprehensive scheme of Irish Agrarian Land Reform must do a great deal more than buy out the landlords. In some districts in Ireland, the present occupiers could not earn a moderate livelihood even although they got their farms for nothing. We must be on our guard against a general refusal in Ireland to pay instalments due to the State. The Plan of Campaign of the Irish Land League might be exercised with enormous force against a compulsory State Land purchase scheme carried out at the risk of the Imperial Exchequer. On social and economical grounds, the compulsory expropriation of the private owners of land would be a great loss to Ireland. In every case, precautions should be taken that the price should not be increased to the detriment of the tenant or the State.

The Land Act of 1887.—The Conservative Government introduced their Irish Land Bill for 1887 into the House of Lords, and explained that it was temporary, and was intended to fill up a gap till they were prepared with an Irish Land purchase scheme, which they hoped to introduce into Parliament in 1888, and on a wider and more comprehensive basis. This Bill proposed to deal with the harsh and unjust evictions of a few harsh and unjust landlords, and to promote the creation of a peasant proprietary in Ireland. It was sent to the House of Commons pretty nearly in its original state, except as to its bankruptcy and peasant-proprietary clauses. It was subsequently amended in the House of Commons to the effect of allowing leaseholders, who were deliberately excluded under the Land Act of 1881, to have the full privileges of yearly tenants. The Bill was returned to the House of Lords, and the extension of the Bill to leaseholders was agreed to. It was then amended by enabling the County Court Judges to deal with applications as to a re-valuation for three years by and according to a scale of prices to be fixed for different districts. As thus amended, the Bill passed the House of Commons and the House of Lords, and received the Royal Assent. We must never forget that this piecemeal legislation cannot go on much longer. A general scheme of peasant proprietorship must be introduced, and we must, beforehand, clearly understand on what principles it is to be founded : *e.g.* whether it is to be voluntary or compulsory; whether general or partial; and whether by the Imperial Exchequer or some commercial agency of Land Banks, or the like. Of this Act of 1887, we have been told by Mr Chamberlain and by Lord

Randolph Churchill that there must be no great extension. But, all the same, a still greater extension must take place, or the Irish agrarian problem will never be settled. Of course, we must not forget that the Irish agrarian agitators hold that the Irish landlords are not entitled to more than prairie value. We must prevent an Irish Home Rule Parliament trying to carry out this valuation in settling the Irish agrarian problem.

4.—GENERALLY.

The general policy needed.—Ireland must be governed on the principles of law and order, honesty and equality, justice and firmness, but, above all things, on the principles of justice. We must never forget that justice consists of two things, namely, of good laws and of their enforcement; and that no good Government can exist in any country where these two things are not combined. We must maintain social order, religious liberty, and personal freedom in Ireland, and fearlessly pass and enforce good laws for that country. We will then find that the Irish people can as easily be governed, in the same way, as other peoples, namely, by reason, by principles of justice, by sentiment, and by interest. The Irish people are thoroughly demoralized by the lawlessness of the last few years, and by the teachings of dishonest political leaders. Lawless gatherings should be checked at the outset, and illegal organizations broken down. Incitements to crime and violence should be punished, and the supremacy of the law vindicated by the simplest and most effective means. Let us, then, first of all, as first in the order of merit and necessity, solve, once and for ever, the

agrarian problem in Ireland; and then the problem of
Irish rural and urban local administrative government:
and then the great political problem in Ireland will be
as easily settled there as in England and Scotland.
Mere concessions to agitation will never gain over the
Irish agitators to us, or conciliate them towards us.   To
try to conciliate madness and wickedness is to connive
and inflame both.   Dispassionate justice can alone
save Ireland and ourselves from terrible evils at
present, and also in the near future and in distant ages.
The principles of government for Ireland can no longer
be those of the Protestants, or of the landlords, in Ireland;
but they must be those of a democratic State working
on the basis of monarchical, aristocratic, and democratic
ideas, and on the basis of a free Christian State, and of
liberty and toleration and legal and moral rights.
Some people hold that the restoration of law and order
is indispensible before any more remedial legislation is
attempted.   I do not agree with them.   I am fully
convinced of the necessity of restoring law and order;
but I do not see why remedial legislation, so far as seen
and acknowledged to be just and necessary, should not
move forward at one and the same time.   A doctor
may put his patient under restraint, and yet work for
his patient's recovery by remedial measures.

We must improve the material condition of Ireland.—
If we could convert a large number of the present farmers
in Ireland into freeholders, the whole character of
Ireland would be changed for the better.   The sense
of property has many elevating and conservative
tendencies on people. · We must, however, be on
our guard against making the Irish landlords the scape-
goats of our sins.   They have already suffered a good deal

at the hands of the Imperial Government. If we do not take care we may find that the Irish landlords will come to the conclusion that they can make better terms for themselves with the Irish National Party than with us. Do not let us forget that the Irish question is an Imperial as well as an Irish problem. For the Imperial Government to expropriate the Irish landlords, and to give them nothing more than the guarantee, or security, of an Irish Board of guardians, or the local rates, would be a gross piece of injustice, and would be unworthy of our traditions as a great, honest, and upright people. Ireland has a great stake at issue in her land, houses, banks, railways, and the like; and numerous persons, loyally devoted to the interests of Great Britain, are interested therein. These persons and things must not be left in Ireland without ample protection by Great Britain against the rapacity or wickedness of Irish agitators. In the regeneration of Ireland, nothing is more necessary than that these should be protected by us now and in all time to come; and, in the next place, that new roads, new railways, new harbours, and new fishing-boats, should be increased, and, generally, that a State development of Ireland, for a time, in all industrial, commercial, and agricultural enterprises should be promoted.

Ireland is far behind us in law, order, and industry.—Ireland is several centuries behind England or Scotland in all that pertains to life, civilization, and good government. Unfortunately for her and for us, she was never conquered by the Roman Empire, and was never thoroughly brought within the sphere of perfect submission to law and order. The Brehon or ancient Irish judges, were empowered to decide differences in Ireland in ancient times ; but they had no force behind them to enforce their decrees. They were arbitrators rather than judges. This state of matters has given rise to great weakness and disorder in Ireland in ancient and modern times. Lord Salisbury has truly said that poverty was the disease of Ireland, and lawlessness the curse of Ireland. A great source of income to the Irish labourers and small farmers has been lost in England and Scotland by the invention and introduction of reaping machines at the harvest time. It is gone permanently and for ever. A new condition of things has sprung up on this side of the Channel, and the Irish labourers and small farmers must now starve in Ireland, or get their farms enlarged, or emigrate. The small farmers in Ireland are poor, and cannot earn enough for a moderate, even a scanty, livelihood for themselves and their families. When people are always on the border-edges of starvation, they become reckless, and the easy prey of wicked and designing demagogues. Improve their material condition, and they improve in their lives and conduct. We must also put an end to harsh evictions in Ireland, and all their dramatic incidents. We must proceed on our way to convert the Irish tenants into owners of their farms. We must study this question long and deeply, and be guided by the wisdom and experience to be gained from Switzerland, Belgium, Prussia, and other countries in which the State has been obliged to do what we must do in Ireland. We have already gained some experience in the working of the Land Purchase clauses in the Acts of 1870, 1881, and 1887. Further, we ought not to be surprised at the reluctance and opposition of the Irish tenants to be evicted from their farms ; for,

if evicted, they may naturally enough suppose that
their successors as tenants will become the owners of
their farms.   Hence the opposition to eviction, and the
hatred against extraneous caretakers, emergency men,
and the like.   Of course, they know that the new
comers, in most instances, would have as good a chance
of getting the land as themselves.

Time arrived for solution.—It is high time that
Ireland should cease to be the battle-field of rival
British politicians, struggling for office and power in
the State.   It is high time that Ireland should be
governed by the great and unchangeable laws of justice,
truth, and honesty.   It is high time that British
statesmen should propound, and should not conceal, an
Irish policy which would bring as great contentment
and tranquillity, and as solid a Union as has long
existed between England and Scotland.   It is high
time that Ireland should cease to be a land of evictions
as no other country is in this world; and that the
poverty, squalor, and famine which have been produced, in a large measure, by Feudal laws and English
injustice and oppressions, should cease.   The greatest
evil in Ireland, as was said, nearly fifty years ago, by
Lord Beaconsfield, is an Absentee Aristocracy.   This
evil must now be removed by the establishment of
a numerous and widely diffused peasant proprietary in
Ireland, and by building up society in Ireland on a new
foundation.   Let us put an end to every form of
misgovernment and oppression in Ireland, and crown
the glorious reign of our beloved Queen by a grand
act of justice, generosity, and peace.   The separation
of Ireland from Great Britain would be intolerable in
Great Britain and Ireland ; and as none of the nations

concerned can really wish it, let us dismiss this solution from our minds.   Let us now direct our attention to a scheme by which the national and imperial aspirations and necessities of the times in which we live shall be realized.   Let us proceed, as speedily as possible, to arrange public matters in such a way as to establish the Imperial Parliament at Westminster for Imperial affairs, and National Legislatures for England, Scotland, and Ireland for purely national or domestic affairs.   When we apply the principles of justice to this great Imperial problem, let us be on our guard not to establish a new form of religious ascendancy in any part of Ireland, or over any of our Irish fellow citizens.   The Protestant ascendancy in Ireland has been an unmitigated curse to the Irish people and to ourselves as well.   A Roman Catholic ascendancy in Ireland would be nothing less, and would become unendurable, and would speedily bring about a war between Ireland and Great Britain.   The Irish problem must be solved independently of all class, of all race, and of all religious interests, and on a broad, national, and imperial basis.   Any man who would now propose to solve it on an Irish National basis is an enemy of this country, and is guilty of high treason to his sovereign.   On the basis of general principles, capable of general application to the three kingdoms, and as indispensible for the working of our Parliamentary Government, I hope concessions will be made on this great question of Home Rule and Imperial Government.   I attach great importance to the distinction of State and Union rights as developed in the American Constitution, and look upon them as equivalent to national and imperial rights.   I also attach great

importance to the stipulation in the American Constitution as to imposing difficulties in the way of making
constitutional amendments.

IV.—THE COLONIES.

1.—INTRODUCTORY.

*General principle of our foreign policy and relative
Colonial responsibility.*—The general objects of our
foreign policy are, (1) our safety at home, and (2) our
security abroad. Peace at home and abroad is our
greatest and most permanent interest as to our foreign
policy. In order to have this peace, our own sea-girt
isles must be safe from attack within and without, and
British India and all our colonies and dependencies
must be equally safe, and our highways on the ocean
must be safe for our commerce and shipping in every
part of the world. We are no longer an agricultural
community, as we were at the beginning of this century.
We are a commercial people, and without enormous
and costly importations of food, we could not exist for
any length of time. Our fleet should be invincible as
against any probable hostile combination opposed to us.
If we are not invincible to this extent, our wealth, our
greatness, and our power are not worth an hour's
purchase. One great centre of our commerce is the
Mediterranean, in which we are supreme by our fleet
and fortresses. But we must remember that the
Mediterranean is merely a highway for our commerce,
and not our home ; and that, if some Radical politicians
had their own way, the Mediterranean would be
abandoned by us, and we should fall back on the Cape

route to our Australasian and Eastern colonies and our
Indian Empire. Those who hold such Radical views do
not know the loss to our commerce entailed upon us by
such a policy. Still, we ought to keep our Cape route
clear for all emergencies, and, if necessary, open to us
at all times as an alternative route instead of the Suez-
Canal route, by means of a large number of war ships
and swift cruisers. For our Indian Empire and our
colonies, we have waged great wars, and spent huge
sums of money. We have also lent to them large sums
of money for their development. Our contests with
Spain and France in the New World have invariably
ended in our annexation of new colonies. Our Colonial
Empire is the result of slow, deliberate, and persistent
efforts on our part against our enemies, or on the
trackless ocean and the desert shore. Now, barren
deserts have become smiling fields and orchards, and
the solitary haunts of the wild sea-birds have become
the busy haunts of men engaged in carrying on profitable and successful commerce between the different
parts of the British Colonial Empire. Our people
increase by thousands and tens of thousands in all
parts of the world. For the protection of this great
Colonial Empire, we depend on our Imperial Navy on
the High Seas, and on local efforts by our richest and
most important colonies ; *e.g.* our Canadian Dominion
and the Australasian Colonies. To maintain our commercial and Colonial supremacy, we need, above all
things, intelligence, integrity, honesty, and ability, and
should cultivate these virtues by all means in our
power in our early education and daily life.

Duties of our Colonies as to local defence.—Now, to
defend one's own territories is the duty of every self-

governing people, and not less so of a self-governing colony than of an imperial state. Of course, the mother country is ultimately responsible for the defence of our self-governing colonies, in the event of their not being able to protect themselves. But, as a general rule, every self-governing colony, by its very nature, is responsible for the good government of the territories placed under its control. Till lately, this duty was wholly performed by the mother country for our colonies; but it is now partially discharged by the rich colonies themselves. As regards the defence of the Colonial and Indian Mercantile Marine on the high seas, it is wholly discharged by the mother country at her own expense. On the ground of justice, it appears to me that India and our rich and populous Colonies should contribute towards the general expense of the Imperial Navy in proportion to the benefit and protection which they receive from our Navy. India and all the British Colonies are free to carry on their trade where, and with whom, they please. They are not now restricted, as they once were, to the British ports for their trade and commerce. Any injury done to our Colonies, or to the shipping and commerce of the Colonies, by a foreign State, is an injury done to the parent State as well as to the Colonies, and demands reparation according to the law of nations,—by peaceful means if possible, and, if a peaceful settlement is impossible, by war. To defend India and the colonies, and our commercial ports at home, and to provide the necessary coaling stations abroad, is an absolute duty on our part, and a great national question for politicians and statesmen in the near future. We have hitherto depended chiefly on our naval supremacy for our power; and we should always do so in future. So long as we are supreme at sea no power on earth can successfully attack, or injure, us. In laying down the basis of Imperial, Indian, and Colonial Defences, we must be very cautious, and scrupulously just in all our dealings, or proposals. The British Colonies, which have been endowed with the powers of self government,—*i.e.* the Canadian Dominions, the Cape Government, and all the Australasian Governments except one,—have full powers of legislative and judicial and executive governments. Although the Imperial governors are the representatives of the State, they are practically as impotent as the crown now is in matters of government at home.

We must uphold the principles of political and religious freedom throughout the Empire.—Whilst allowing the great boon of civil, political, and religious freedom to Europeans in every part of our dominions, we must never allow them to subjugate the natives placed under their control to injustice or cruelty. All who repose under the British flag must have their rights protected in every part of our Empire. All our fellow citizens of whatever clime, or colour, or religion, must be entitled, and permitted, to enjoy the blessings of civilized government.

2.—CANADIAN GROUP.

Dominion existed twenty-one years.—This year, in July 1888, the Canadian Dominions will have been confederated for twenty-one years. They have displayed great activity and great success during the

whole of that period.   The Dominions are of immense
extent, and of great wealth present and future; and
their people are strong, vigorous, and full of life.
Canada has virtual independence, and wishes to
keep it.   Generally speaking, she has no desire to
separate herself from the mother country, or to enter
into a political or commercial union with the United
States.   The ports of Halifax, St. John, and St.
Andrews can be made as convenient for her commerce
as Boston, New York, and the other American ports
on the Atlantic.   A Union between Canada and
the United States is an old question.   At all events,
it is as old as the Munroe doctrine of 1837, or fifty
years ago, and nothing has been done on either side to
carry it a step in advance.   No doubt, when an energetic
Canadian leaves his mother country and sets up in
business in the United States, and becomes successful
in his new home, he is anxious that his mother country
should be annexed to his new domicile as much as
he is himself.   But the majority of Canadians have never
seen, and do not now see, this matter in the same light.
They wish to stick to us.   They are proud of us, and
we are proud of them.   But if forsaken by us, and
left in the lurch, what could they do?   An appeal to
justice would be of no use against any resolute
determination on the part of the United States to
annex the Canadian Dominions.   Even the Canadians
of French origin are in favour of the British connection,
and against political union with the United States.

*External raids and internal disturbances put down
by Canada.*—Frequent rumours have arisen of
voluntary and forcible annexations of the Canadian
Dominions to the United States of America.   But they

have never come to anything of any importance. Occasional raids by Irishmen, or their descendants, and sympathisers with Irish independence, have been made from the United States upon the Canadian territories. Nay more, some few years ago, the French colonists, who, for the most part, reside in Lower Canada, stirred up temporary and insignificant disturbances in the prosecution of Home Rule or Local Government for themselves. But all these raids and disturbances have merely shown, (1) that the Canadians do not wish to be annexed to the United States of America; and (2) that they can easily oppose and put down isolated, occasional, and temporary efforts in North America to change the political relations now existing between the United Kingdom of Great Britain and Ireland, or between the mother country and the Canadian Dominions. They are content with, and glory in the rights which they have obtained from this country, by their constitutional charter ; and also with the rights, privileges, and immunities held and possessed by them as integral portions of the United British Empire,— which comprehends not only Great Britain and Ireland, but also all our possessions in South Africa, Australasia, and India, and territories in almost every part of the habitable globe. Such rights confer upon them all the rights of citizenship of our free and glorious Empire.

Negotiations for Union between the Dominion and Nova Scotia and Newfoundland.—At present, negotiations are proceeding between the authorities of the Canadian Dominion and of Nova Scotia and Newfoundland, for their being all united under one and the same government. Just now, Nova Scotia and Newfoundland are governed as independent colonies.

After this Union takes place, as I hope and believe it may, we shall probably see an important extension of the Canadian railway system, and a consequent improvement in the transit of goods and passengers between this country and America, by means of an extension of the Canadian railway system to Newfoundland. I also hope to see progress made for a closer Union than now exists between the Canadian Dominions and our West Indian Islands. This group of islands may, before long, be joined to the Canadian Dominions in a political and commercial Union; for they are all next-door neighbours, and might be highly useful to each other in their natural and artificial products and manufactures. But such a Union would not be for our interest in the event of a commercial and political Union between the Canadian Dominions and the United States.

Canadian colonization.—Canada offers advantageous terms to all who will take up their residence within the Dominion. To every colonist she offers 160 acres of land for £120, payable in twelve years, with the first payment beginning in the fifth year. Why should thousands of our population live in the back streets and slums of our cities, when health and wealth are to be obtained by an active and happy life, at no greater distance than a sea voyage of eight or ten days? All are not qualified to be farmers. But thousands who are will not go where they could vastly improve their condition in every respect.

The Pacific Railway finished.—In carrying out some of the greatest undertakings of the Canadian Government for the present and future development of the Dominion, the Canadian Government of the day has occasionally been thwarted, and even defeated for a time. It was so in the construction of the Pacific Railway, now, at last, completed at great expense. The Pacific Railway connects the Atlantic Ocean with the Pacific, and passes through Canadian territory alone, and opens up an important highway for the commerce of Canada, Britain, and the whole world. The Canadian Pacific Railway cost £26,000,000, and provides us with an alternative route to Australasia and India by land and sea, and, with the exception of the Atlantic and Pacific Oceans, passes over territory which is part and parcel of the British Empire. It passes over our own land territories from east to west, from the Atlantic to the Pacific Ocean, and it gives us the basis for a future Pacific Electric Telegraph Company. This route affords us an invaluable alternative route instead of the Suez and the Cape routes to the East. In this aspect it is, to us, as a great maritime power in the Atlantic and the Pacific Oceans, a route of incalculable value. This new route is the shortest route to all places in the Pacific to the east of Hong-Kong. How far the Pacific Railway alters our military or naval relations to Canada remains yet to be seen. What we do know is, that the completion of the Pacific Railway is strong evidence of the energy and persever-ance of the Canadian people under many difficulties, and that it adds one more highway to the commerce of the world, and open up one more road for our trade to the East, and especially with India and Australasia. This new route opens the vista to a great development in the trade between Canada and Australasia. It may also help forward the great principle of Imperial Federation, by drawing the remotest parts of our

Empire into closer proximity. Canada is now placed on the highway of an important route between Europe and China and the Eastern world.

Fisheries Treaty.—An important treaty was lately negotiated between Commissioners appointed by the Queen, and Commissioners appointed by the President of the United States, as to the Canadian Fisheries; but it will probably be rejected by the United States Senate, with whom, by a majority of two-thirds, the final approval of foreign treaties in the United States ultimately rests. [This Treaty was rejected in the summer of 1888.] The Canadian Fisheries have long been the subject of violent and dangerous quarrels between us and the Canadians on the one hand, and the United States on the other. These disputes go back as far as the date of the Declaration of American Independence, about a hundred years ago, and have been the subject of various treaties. The arrangements made have sometimes been based on strict international law, sometimes on commercial freedom, and sometimes on the basis of compensation to be paid by the United States to the Canadians. But the Americans, in their negotiations with us, have always set up untenable claims to the Canadian fisheries, which are very valuable, on the ground that the fisheries belonged to the Americans of the United States after their Declaration of Independence as much as before it. These claims are without the slightest foundation in fact or law; and have always, and rightly, been ignored or repudiated by this country. On the whole, this unratified Treaty is a fair and reasonable settlement of this fisheries dispute, on a permanent basis. For the present, and quite independently of the treaty, there can easily be brought into existence a sub-convention or proposed *modus vivendi*, voluntarily offered by the British Commissioners, for two years, in the hope of a ratification of the treaty. This may be made the basis of our present friendly relations until some permanent arrangement is reached. But, if the Treaty be rejected [as it has been], the Canadians are not bound by the *modus vivendi*. In this matter, we must not flinch from a firm and just assertion, and, if necessary, enforcement of our just rights according to the law of nations and international treaties. We have justice on our side. Let us stand by it firmly and resolutely. Bluster will not do. We can afford to despise the bounce and bluster of those who say that the United States would have the Arctic Ocean as their northern boundary, or war would be inevitable. Let us hope that no event will break in upon the harmony existing between us and the United States, and that the friendly and commercial intercourse between us and Canada and the United States will go on enlarging itself without bounds. As for a commercial Union between Canada and the United States, we must make all parties clearly understand that we cannot, and never will, agree to it. Against a commercial treaty in the ordinary sense, and in no involving, or tending to involve, political union, we ought to have no objections whatever. That we should be responsible for the Canadian Dominions, and not be placed on an equality with the United States, which is a foreign power, is absurd and ridiculous. Last April, 1888, Canada decided against unrestricted reciprocity with the United States, and preferred unrestricted reciprocity with this country. Shall we not so decide likewise ?

3.—AUSTRALASIAN GROUP.

A great nation has arisen.—The Australasian colonies
are making great strides in population, in wealth, and
in everything which makes a great people. There can
be no doubt that, in the Southern Pacific Ocean, a
great nation, capable of exerting a great civilizing
influence in that quarter of the globe, and not merely
of exerting its civilizing influence on the group of
Australasian colonies, but of extending its civilizing
influence on the far-distant and populous Empire of
China, has, within the last few years, arisen from the
womb of the Mother of Oceanic States. Aye, and it
is determined to act with magnanimity, and to have
a careful regard, and an anxious forethought, for everything which concerns the future of a powerful and
mighty people. A British Australasian Empire is no
longer a dream, or a prophecy. This great idea was
dimly apprehended by navigators and colonists in
former times. It was imperfectly and slowly adopted
by this country, or rather, for a time, was neglected or
regarded in this country with suspicion and dislike.
It has now been boldly formulated by the Manifesto
of the Sydney Convention in 1884, and has now
become an axiomatic truth for the Old and the New
World.

*Our Australasian colonists aim at supremacy in the
Southern Pacific.*—The ultimate aim of the Australasian colonial policy is the annexation of the Polynesian
group of islands, including New Guinea and all the
South Sea Islands. In 1883, resolutions were passed
in Victoria that the mother country ought to annex

all the islands in the Southern Pacific from New
Guinea to Fiji. Without going so far as this Victorian
resolution, we ought to remember that this supremacy
of our Australasian colonists in the Southern Pacific has
been cherished by them for the last thirty years ; and
that, inasmuch as Imperial as well as Australasian
interests are thus involved, we must protect and uphold
the supremacy of the British flag in the Southern
Pacific Ocean, where the trade is substantially in our
own hands. Portugal and France, as our competitors
and rivals there, have fallen out of the race. Holland,
which has large and populous colonies in the Southern
Pacific Ocean, alone remains. At the same time, we
must recollect that Germany as well as France are now
both competing with us as civilizing powers in the
Southern Pacific. As yet, we are merely at the first
stages of the transformation scenes which may change
the whole aspect of affairs—political, commercial, and
social—of our Australasian colonies.

A great career awaits the Australasian colonies.—
Our Australasian colonies have all the materials to
make them great and powerful. They have intelligence,
wealth, industry, and population, and, at a rapid rate,
are increasing in all these elements of national greatness.
No doubt, jealousies exist as to the leadership, and as
to the site of the future Australasian capital city, and
the like. But these are minor circumstances, which,
before long, or at all events, in due time, will be sure
to give way, and be thrown aside, in view of the common interests of all. The burst of Australasian
enthusiasm recently displayed when our Australasian
brethren and fellow citizens voluntarily offered, and
sent, us some of their stalwart sons to Egypt, at a

moment of pressing danger, went straight to our
hearts, and will ever be remembered by the mother
country with pride and gratitude. The old country
has a deep sense of interest in all our colonial fellow
citizens, who know and highly appreciate and recipro-
cate the feeling. As time marches onward, and our
colonies become stronger and stronger, and richer and
richer, in all the things which adorn and fortify human
life, I have the utmost confidence that the interests of
one and all of us and them will call forth reciprocal good
wishes, and acts of brotherly kindness to a greater
extent than has ever happened in our past history.

4.—SOUTH AFRICAN GROUP.

*Condition of South Africa complicated and danger-
ous.*—In our South African possessions, we have a
great, complicated, dangerous, and unsolved problem.
There we have the Cape Colony, which is governed as
a constitutional country, under ministerial responsibility, and in the midst of a population descended
largely from a kindred, but still from a different, stock
of the Anglo-Saxon race, and having undergone very
different experiences, from our own, and now ruling
over a large native black population. There also, we
have the Natal Colony, governed as a crown dependency, with a limited amount of popular government,
and with an essentially English and Scotch population,
small yet compact, ruling over vast numbers of
ignorant and barbarous and unindustrious natives.
Still further, there also, we have two independent
States, namely, the Transvaal Republic and the Orange

Free State, with their European populations, almost as entirely Dutch in origin as at the Cape, and bearing us, for many reasons, no great love or friendship, acting and re-acting upon our own colonies in South Africa, and also upon the natives, in such a way as to be dangerous both to us and to themselves. Just now, 1888, the prospects of South Africa are not very bright. But the development of the Diamond and Gold Mines of South Africa will, as happened in Australasia, possibly help us to solve various South African problems, which now appear to be insoluble. South Africa is a garden of Eden. It is rich in minerals, and in boundless fields for corn and pasture. We have committed grave blunders in South Africa as elsewhere. *Humanum est errare.* But in South Africa, and elsewhere, a Divine Providence guides and shapes our ends. Just now, negotiations are proceeding for a commercial union between the Cape, the Transvaal, and the Free Orange State, and based on contributions being made out of customs duties collected by the Maritime Provinces on goods destined for the Inland States. Such a commercial union would be just and fair in all the circumstances, and would probably lead to a more intimate union on a political basis. Therefore, I wish it success with all my heart.

Our South African interests are great and increasing. —Our interests in South Africa are great, and are largely on the increase. When India fell into our hands in the end of last century, the Cape was invaluable for our communications between the East and the West. It had been the same to the Dutch before our Indian Empire was established on the ruins of the Dutch and the French and the Native powers in India.

The Cape was, in fact, our half-way house, where sailing-ships, in the olden times, invariably stopped on their voyages between this country and India. Thereafter, when steam was introduced into mercantile and war ships, the Cape became more necessary to us than ever ; because a coaling station for our steam-ships, when they were mid-way between our Eastern and Western Empires, became indispensibly necessary. Although the Cape route is not now so essential to us as it formerly was, and was even till quite lately,—that is to say, till the Suez Canal opened up a new route from the Mediterranean to the Persian Gulf,—and although it can never again be so important to us as before, at least, so long as we have the control or the use of the Suez Canal, and of the new Canadian Pacific Railway ; yet, the duties of our position, and the interests of our Empire, compel us to defend and protect the Cape route as a great Imperial interest, and, consequently, to protect and advance the interests of our South African possessions against internal discords and external aggression. Nay more, through Central Africa civilization may yet join Khartoum, Dongola, Berber, Cairo, and our South African possessions.

The Native question the greatest question.—In South Africa, the problem as to the future position and civilization of the Natives is the greatest of all. On this problem, diverse opinions, and opposing and destructive theories are held by many here at home, and by our own colonists in South Africa. Worse still, opinions and theories have been different and antagonistic at different periods of time, and under different British Governors in South Africa, and also under different Colonial Secretaries here at home. Constant friction and opposition have been the results ; and long, harassing, and expensive wars have been the usual concomitants. Whatever our political party, we must never forget that force, gently but firmly used, is the only means by which savages and barbarians, such as the Native Africans are, can be ruled and brought under subjection to civilized government. Amongst the Black Natives of South Africa, constitutional government and parliamentary institutions are, at present, utterly impossible and absurd. No man should have the power to govern another in the slightest, or most insignificant, affair, unless he is able to govern himself with a reasonable degree of justice and good policy. Some people think that every man as a human being is entitled to vote for laws for his country, or, at least, to give his vote for representatives to do so in the great council of the nation. I certainly do not believe anything of the sort, and feel some confidence in your agreeing with me in my opinion on this matter. I have no great confidence in Mr Stanhope's settlement of Zululand. It is no settlement at all, and it must be modified or entirely changed. The Natives of Zululand attacked our Stations, and thought that we were going to retire from South Africa. They were astonished when they found out their mistake. They must be taught that British sovereignty has to be maintained in South Africa. Savages everywhere must be ruled by a combination of love and fear. For sometime, intrigues have been going on in South Africa, north of the Orange River, with the South African Republic, with the view of promoting the predominance of Germany in that region, and of stopping our progress northwards

N

towards the equator and also towards the sea. Both aims must be frustrated.

A general native policy indispensible.—The native local disorders of South Africa can never be remedied until a large, native local scheme of peace and civilization has been established for Bechuanaland, Basutoland, Pondoland, and Zululand. For all these tracts of country, we require a firm and stable government, capable of maintaining order, collecting revenue, and protecting life and property. We also need to establish a general scheme of education for the natives in the first principles of industry, morality, and virtue. In such a scheme, we should allow native customs, and amongst others polygamy, to die out. An administration such as we have in Ceylon, and with a just, experienced, and prudent Governor at its head, is required for the native districts of South Africa. We have the requisite knowledge, experience, and means at our disposal to civilize the South African natives. Let us begin the grand work at once, and thus put an end to our frequently recurring native wars in South Africa. In such a scheme, we, and we alone, must be supreme in South Africa. We must clearly and unmistakably make all and sundry know, beyond doubt, that we are to remain in South Africa, and rule and govern South Africa, as the sovereign and paramount power there. We have incurred great responsibility in South Africa by undertaking to civilize that part of the vast Black Continent. We must, therefore, perform the duty we have undertaken. We must not abandon it, as some faint-hearted people would have us to do. Amongst not a few Liberal and Radical politicians of some public reputation, there is a profound feeling of weariness and discontent as to our government in South Africa. We must, therefore, be on our guard against being surprised into an abandonment of South Africa by a Liberal or Radical Government in the event of serious native or other disturbances arising in South Africa, if a Liberal or Radical Government happened to be in office at the time. We have shrunk long enough from performing our duties in South Africa. Our policy of retreating and then going forward has not been successful. Let us fearlessly advance in the interests of trade and civilization; and we will get far better results than we have got in South Africa for a long time. The Boers and the Africanders may dislike our policy of Imperial supremacy; but they must submit to it. At present, great caution and courage are needed in South Africa, or we will be involved in grave disorder and great expense in our South African Empire.

The necessary Policy as to Confederation and the Natives.—What, then, is our duty in South Africa? It is to bind this part of our territories more closely to us than ever by the establishment of a strong and firm Policy, based on our mutual and common interests of defence and commerce, and of mutual aid and assistance in all that concerns the happiness and welfare of our fellow-citizens in South Africa, and under one Governor-General or Viceroy, and under one Parliament, or Federal Council for the whole of our South African Empire, and with local legislatures for the different European States or Provinces, and with Diplomatic Agents for all the different Native States. Nothing, I believe, will contribute more to the progress of civilization in South Africa than the

appointment of a Viceroy for the whole of South
Africa, unconnected with the politics of any one
Colony, and acting as the Sovereign's Viceroy, with
the supreme executive control of public affairs, under a
constitutional government, sanctioned and established
there by this country. Till the most important branches
of administration are under one supreme government,
the progress, even the peace, of South Africa is
insecure. We may have given, perhaps too soon, yet we
have given, and we cannot take away, the free constitutional government conferred on Cape Colony.
Let us help this Colony to make a good use of her
liberty, and encourage her to take the lead in the
civilization of South Africa in all that concerns the
happiness and the welfare of the White and the Black,
the European and the Native African peoples. Let
us help her as the largest and the richest, and, at
present, the most capable South African Colony to
begin, and to begin at once, to lay the foundations of
a South African Confederacy of Free European States,
including the Natal Colony, and the Transvaal, or
South African Republic, and the Orange Free State;
and also to make wise and prudent arrangements
amongst themselves, with our sanction, for the government of the Natives and the Native territories, with
the view of raising the Natives in the scale of civilization, and of ultimately absorbing the Natives into the
South African Confederacy, with all the rights and
privileges of freemen, and of full citizens of the British
Empire. Thus, and only thus, can we hope to lay a
firm and permanent foundation for this vast and fertile
territory in South Africa. Under a wise and
beneficent government, nowhere else in the wide

world might a numerous and happy people live
prosperously and contentedly than in the fertile lands
of the Cape and the Natal Colonies, or in the extensive
pasture lands of the Transvaal and the Orange Free
States. In South Africa, there are millions of acres
of land awaiting the future European immigrants who
will yet flock thither, and live in peace, happiness, and
prosperity.

5.—IMPERIAL AND LOCAL LEGISLATURES.

*Desirable to have an Imperial Parliament, and all
our Colonies directly represented.*—As you are perhaps
aware, the Colonies of France have representatives in
the Great National Assembly in Paris. Why, then,
should not the British Colonies have the same, or
similar privileges? When we are at war, the British
Colonies are liable to be attacked by our enemies.
When we are at peace, they enjoy all the advantages
of our peaceful relations with our allies and friends.
Besides, our trade with the British Colonies is yearly
increasing at such a rate that great advantage to us
and to them would arise were they to be directly
represented in the Imperial Parliament at Westminster.
Still, such a representation would almost be impossible,
and perhaps worse than useless, in the present condition
of political parties in this country, and of the existing
political relations of England, Scotland, and Ireland
in the Imperial Parliament at Westminister, in the
House of Commons and in the House of Lords. True,
such an Imperial Parliament as I have suggested is
not yet practicable ; but it will soon be, and sooner

than many suspect.   As I have lately published a
brief outline of such an Imperial Parliament, I will
not weary you at present with recapitulating what I
have already written on this subject.

The advantages of Imperial and Local Legislatures.
—By such an arrangement, or scheme as I have
sketched, we would enormously improve our
present Government by conceding self government where, and when, necessary, and by
strengthening the Empire in its imperial interests
and duties.   At one stroke, we would settle
the Irish political question on a broad and
enduring basis; strengthen the Imperial relations of
the whole Empire on deep and sound foundations;
and put an end to trivial dissensions and disputes
in the present Imperial Parliament at Westminster.
Just now, there is a danger of our present Parliament
degenerating into an incapable parish vestry.
Further, new constitutional arrangements would enable
us to found our Government in every part of our Empire
on just principles and mutual interests.   For example,
on the one hand, we can defend the British Colonies
far more effectually than any other power in the world.
On the other hand, neither our Australasian, nor South
African, nor Canadian Colonies can defend themselves
effectually against any of the first powers of Europe.
Moreover, we should now aim at establishing an Imperial
Commercial Bund throughout the length and breadth
of our Empire.   This aim can only be imperfectly
realized by Conventions or Understandings or Agree-
ments.   Free Trade is our long-established ideal system
of commercial relations; and our Colonies are indispensible to us for the maintenance of our Imperial

power. Let us apply Free Trade within the territories
of the British Empire, and we will do much to promote
the establishment of Free Trade, with all its beneficent
advantages, throughout the world. Nay more, the
Colonies are yearning towards us for sympathy and
encouragement in their aspirations for a closer union
of political, defensive, and commercial interests. In
every part of our Empire we need a closer union of
all its parts. So says Lord Tennyson; and so
say I. Lord Rosebery says, that Imperial Federation
is necessary for our commercial supremacy, and also
for our very existence. But this Imperial Confederation must be voluntary, and not compulsory. It must
begin with our Free, Constitutional Governments, and
go on till it comprehends every Colony and Dependency
of the British Empire. Imperial Federation is condemned by Mr John Bright as a vain dream. It is
no dream. It is a great reality, destined to revolutionize the imperial relations of the British Empire,
and bring it into harmony with the actually existing
condition of things within its wide-spread and gigantic
dominions and territories. Shall we turn a deaf ear
to the imperial aspirations of our brethren in the
colonies? I say no, never.

*The Conservative Party should undertake the great
and necessary work of Imperial Confederation.*—The
Conservative Government should at once set about to
work out a practical scheme of Government for the
whole Empire, and applicable to England, Scotland,
and Ireland, and capable of being extended to every
part of our wide-spread and gigantic dominions.
This work can best be undertaken by the Conservative
Party, or by a combination and common understanding

between the Leaders of the great Liberal and Conservative Parties; for the Radicals, who are now the efficient and ruling members of the old Liberal party in this country, bemoan and lament over the burdens of an Empire which they are incapable of governing. I am sorry to add that I am very much afraid that the Radicals are more bent on social revolution at home than good government at home or abroad. Of late, for example, since 1880, the Foreign and Colonial Policy of Liberal Governments has been a disgraceful combination of self-effacement and retirement from dangers. Yet, forsooth, we are now urged to put another Liberal or Radical Government into office, and allow it to rule and decide on the political action of this great Empire. Are we mad? As I have still a good deal to say in future on this theme, and as I have already detained you too long, I must now bring my present discourse to an end.

V.—CONCLUSION.

The greatness of the British Empire.—We shall soon be 100,000,000 of English-speaking people, with a population of 250,000,000 of Native Indians under our charge. What a gigantic responsibility we have incurred to act honourably and govern well! Rome in all her greatness and power was nothing to the British Empire. Greece in the height of her maritime supremacy cannot be compared to us in power and greatness. No nation in modern times ever has, or does now, approach us in all the elements of national greatness and power. Are we capable of wielding such immense power for the advantage of our fellow citizens, and the honour of our country? The Monarchy and the Aristocracy of our country, as political institutions, backed and supported by the prowess of the nation at large, have built up a mighty Empire for us and our descendants. Can the Democracy rule and govern this great inheritance in wisdom? Some wise men say that the Democracy cannot. But, for myself, I have not lost confidence in my fellow citizens to perform the mighty task imposed upon them. My object has been to impress you with the magnitude of the work before you. May you act worthily in the part allotted to you by destiny and by the constitution of your country !

[N.B.—The last proof sheets of this Lecture or Discourse revised on the 14th of March 1889.]

ADDRESS

INDIAN, EGYPTIAN, AND FOREIGN AFFAIRS

(DELIVERED AT DUNDEE ON 30TH MAY 1888).

I.—PRELIMINARY.

GENTLEMEN,—I have to bespeak your kind and patient attention to a Political Address on Indian, Egyptian, and Foreign Affairs. As last night, at Broughty Ferry, when speaking on Home, Irish, and Colonial Affairs, so to-night, I shall urge upon you seriously and anxiously to listen to what I am to submit to you as the truest, the most prudent, and the most honest policy which can be adopted by this country at the present time. I may be somewhat, or even wholly, wrong in what I said last night as to our National Home Policy, and in what I am to say to-night as to our Imperial Foreign Policy. But, whether I am or not, I have done my best to arrive at the truth ; and as to this evening's discourse, I have to ask you to be the fair and impartial judges.

Introduction.—In consequence of the state of affairs in Europe and Asia, we ought to provide against great and sudden changes, which might seriously endanger our position as the citizens of the greatest power in the world. As there is a considerable degree of ignorance and indifference amongst us as to our Imperial interests, I hope the subjects I have chosen for discussion this evening may not be indifferent to you. With our popular government, there is a necessity for carrying the people along the road of wise policy. In a despotic country, no such necessity exists. From an enlightened standpoint, Indian, Egyptian, and Foreign Affairs are very closely related to each other. As I hope to show you, there are, in foreign policy, wheels within wheels, which are not commonly well understood. In fact, the foreign policy of all the great European powers is the result of geographical, ethnical, religious, and historical influences, which would require a lifetime to understand and explain. All I shall attempt to do, on the present occasion, will be to lay before you some of the leading truths in regard to the three great subjects upon which I am to speak to-night. I may say, however, that my original intention was to deliver a separate address on each of the heads of my address. For the present, I must confine my observations to a less elaborate illustration than this intention would have necessitated.

II.—INDIAN AFFAIRS.

1.—INTERNAL.

(1)—GENERAL.

The British-Indian Government is paternal and despotic.—To all intents and purposes, our Indian

Government is despotic. Properly speaking, it is a paternal-despotic Government, or rather, perhaps, a constitutional-despotic Government. It is certainly not a popular or constitutional Government pure and simple; for there is no representation of the people in the Legislative Councils of the Indian Empire. Our mighty Indian Empire of 250,000,000 souls is, in reality, governed by the Indian Viceroy as the Representative of the British Sovereign in India, and by the Indian Secretary as the Minister of the Crown in this country. Both of these great State officials are under the control of the Imperial Parliament at Westminster.

Official Classes, Commerce, and Exchange.—Inasmuch as all the chief appointments in the civil and military departments of the Indian Government are mostly held by highly-educated and capable Europeans, who are sent out to India as the most able rulers, governors, generals, judges, and administrators whom our country at home can produce, there is no wonder that the cost of our Indian Empire is great, and tends largely to increase. How far this cost can and ought to diminish is a question which has often been discussed, and will again be often discussed. There cannot be a doubt, I think, that the financial condition of India demands the most serious and anxious attention of all who take a deep and intelligent interest in the prosperity of the Indian Empire. That the Indian rupee, with a value of two shillings in India, is reduced by one-fourth of its nominal value in this country, has wide and far-reaching political and commercial consequences which cannot be ignored. Commercially, in the ordinary course of trade, the fall in the value of Indian money, which is mostly silver, —as it is in nearly all Eastern countries,—does not involve our merchants in a loss on a sale of their goods for the Indian market; because they calculate upon the diminution in value, and raise the price of their goods to such an extent as will cover the expected fall at the time of payment in gold. This increased price, often one-third, has to be paid by the people of India, and may often increase the mercantile profit; but it may also diminish the total value and bulk of our commercial dealings with India. Again, on incomes and profits made in India, and remitted to this country to be paid in gold, the loss by exchange falls on certain, not all, classes of the Civil Indian service. In the discharge of obligations contracted before the fall in the value of the Indian rupee, and which have to be paid in gold in this country, the loss by exchange is very great. For example, the Indian Government have lost, on an average, about £3,000,000 sterling every year for nearly fifteen years past by this cause alone.

Political, military, and social changes.—In the minds of the natives of British India, there have been implanted ideas which will bring about gigantic changes in India, and which will revolutionize the entire scheme of our present Government there. No doubt, all the countries of the East tend to be conservative and unchanging in their general political tendencies. But, although Brahminism is mouldering away, Islamism is proselytising. Although the Hindoos have changed very little in the last half century, the Mahomedans of India have become more powerful and energetic than ever before. The Mahomedans hate the Christians. They despise the Hindoos, over whom they formerly ruled, and think that they ought to rule the whole of India even now. The Hindoos do not wish to enjoy the forms of Western civilization and government. They wish good government, and they also wish the Government of India to remain in our hands as at present. The Mahomedans would like to see the downfall of the Christian Governors of India, and even to expel them from India, and to regain their former position of supremacy. The Hindoos are peaceful; but the Mahomedans are warlike. We hold the sword of power and the balance of justice between the great rival races and creeds of India; and we compel all our Indian fellow-citizens, irrespective of race or creed, to obey the laws. Still, we must keep our eyes open to the social and political changes which are rapidly taking place in India, and prepare ourselves to meet them with justice and firmness. To establish a popular and representative form of Government in India, at present, or at any time, would be one of the greatest revolutions ever effected in the history of the world; for we must never forget that the Indian people are more diverse in origin, in race, in laws, and in language than the whole of the peoples in Europe. At present, and for a long time to come, Popular Representative Government, such as we ourselves possess at home, is an utter impossibility in India. Although created, it could not be worked, or even maintained. In India we have great feudatory Princes, with large armies under their own control, and with independent, internal governments of their own. These Princes are unquestionably controlled, and are liable to be overruled, by the British Residents at their several courts, in their foreign relations with each other, and with foreign States and the British Indian Government. But they themselves are possessed of great power for good or evil. If they were all to combine against us, they could do India and themselves and us an immense deal of harm. As a matter of fact, however, they are, as a rule, on the very best terms with the Paramount power in India, and they look to us to defend their rights and privileges against every foreign or domestic foe. For some considerable time past, the large native and semi-independent armies, composed mostly of imperfectly trained soldiers, have been looked upon by us as a serious danger to the general peace, and as an expensive and useless luxury to the Princes themselves. Doubtless a happy and peaceful solution of this matter will be reached in the course of time. In the meantime, let us hope that the existing friendly relations between the Indian Government and the Indian Feudatory Princes will grow in strength, and that the example of the Maharajah Holkar of Indore, who recently offered to place his troops at our disposal, will be generally and loyally followed by all others of his high rank. Let us hope that, before long, and with the sanction of all concerned, the armies of the semi-independent Princes of India will be placed on a cheaper and more effective basis than at present, and will be indissolubly linked to our Imperial Indian forces in the protection and defence of the highest and best interests of the people of India and of this country, from which India has obtained so much peace and prosperity, and from which it can obtain much more of both than from any other country. Nothing would more advance our own and native Indian interests than a perfect union of the diverse races of India; and nothing will more contribute to that desirable consummation than a strong, central British Government, ruling over all, high and low, in truth and justice, and all manly and national virtues. I repeat that India's greatest need is the union and amalgamation of the Indian Princes, Leaders, Peoples, and Races in a Patriotic Nationality under the aegis of the British Crown, and by a slowly-extended and well-considered development of local and national government. Through the influence of the Natives, of the Chiefs, and of the Princes on the Imperial Government, and wisely directed in the interests of the Indian people, the native people of India can be raised to a higher position in the scale of nations than we ourselves, unaided by them, can raise them, —e.g. by the abolition of child marriages and the like. To concede Home Rule to India, in accordance with the demands of Bengalee agitations, would be unjust, criminal, and disastrous to us and the Indian people themselves. In our Indian Government, great changes are inevitable before long. But Home Rule on the basis of India for the Indians is the panacea of traitors, fools, or madmen. Perhaps, Provincial Legislative Councils, composed of the great Native Chiefs and Princes and of elected Representatives of the great cities, would be the best solution which could, at first, be adopted. Whatever we do, let us go by steps, and with caution.

British Supremacy in India.—British supremacy has been firmly established in India for the last hundred years. During that period, large territorial acquisitions have been made by us. But our conquests in India are now virtually ended. Whatever additions may be made to our Indian Empire will be forced upon us by revolt, or by the necessities of defence. On three sides of India, the ocean surrounds our vast Indian dominions with their teeming and industrious populations; and all the other European powers are practically excluded from the whole Indian peninsula. True, the French and the Dutch have some territory in India, but their influence there is really insignificant.

Our general Indian Policy.—With all our unwearied activity, we are naturally phlegmatic. Voluntarily we scarcely ever do anything to alter our national policy at home or abroad. For example, the Indian Mutiny swept away the old East India Company, which, notwithstanding its many virtues, had long become obsolete, incapable, and corrupt as the governing power over a great Empire. But a new and wiser policy was, at last, seen to be necessary. Generally speaking, our Indian policy is plain and simple. It aims at the security and peace of India. Further, we must improve and develop the Indian railways and canals and commercial relations. We must teach the Indian people to learn to govern themselves, and manage their own internal affairs. In the meantime, we must help them to rise in the scale of civilized nations, and in the arts of peace and happiness. We must also defend our Indian possessions from external attacks by land and sea. Hence, we must keep our eyes open to the proceedings of Russia in the Steppes of Central Asia, and also in Persia and Afghanistan. We must also be alive to the proceedings of Russia and France, and, perhaps, of other powers, in the Mediterranean Sea

from the Gulf of Venice to Egypt, and also in the Suez
Canal, the Red Sea, and the Indian Ocean. What
gigantic duties, therefore, rest primarily on a population of 35,000,000 ! and yet, they are performed easily
and magnificently. Beyond all doubt, we have reason
to be proud of our country, and of its glorious achieve-
ments in the present as well as in the past, and in the
interests of civilization and universal peace, as well as
of our own national aggrandisement.

Civil Progress in India must be slow.—The problem
we have to solve in India is stupendous, and must be
carefully and slowly worked out, it may be, for the
next two or three generations. Impatient haste would
bring the whole fabric of Indian society to ruins; and,
then, there would inevitably follow many generations
of despotic government, with all its evils intensified to
the highest degree. If the problem is gigantic, we
are not without encouragement to go on with the
work. In 1833, Lord Macaulay said that he would
give constitutional government to the Indian people
when they were fit for it. In 1882, Sir Richard
Temple said that Western ideas should be promoted
amongst our fellow citizens in the East; and that,
although blunders would be made in so doing, there
could be no serious objection made to this course being
adopted. Whatever has been done in this direction
by the establishment of legislative councils in India
has justified the wise and benevolent intentions of the
originators. Thus, for example, in 1885, a legislative
council for Poona was opened by the governor of
Bombay; and, as I believe, with excellent results. In
this great policy of liberty, we must carry with us the
rich and educated classes of India; and gradually intro-

duce all the people of India to a share in the legislation
and government of their country. Slowly and gradually
we must raise the people of India to our own level in
civilization and government.

The Indian Council useless, and the British Parlia-
ment incompetent to deal with ordinary Indian Affairs.
—On the whole, the present mode of governing British
India has worked fairly well. But the London Indian
Council, created to assist the Indian Secretary in
the performance of his duties, and also the Imperial
Parliament, with its power of control over Indian
affairs, have both turned out to be utter failures.
This Indian Council has no effective power of control
over the Indian Secretary, and can give advice only
when asked. Worse still, the Imperial Parliament
has no practical or effective control over Indian affairs,
legislative, administrative, or financial. Indian affairs
are utterly ignored by the Imperial Parliament, or left
to a few Indian experts, civil, military, and commercial,
who have obtained seats in the House of Commons,
but who exert no influence on the laws or administration of India. The way in which the Indian Budget
is annually discussed at Westminster is utterly useless,
and is a disgrace to a legislative assembly claiming
any control or influence in the government of a
mighty Empire of 250,000,000 of people. This evil
has been long acknowledged ; but the remedy is not
easily found. India is practically governed by the
Indian Secretary, or Under Secretary. The British
Parliament has virtually no influence in moulding the
laws, government, or administration of our Indian
Empire, although, by the constitution, India is supposed
to be under the government of the British Parliament.

This is a condition of affairs which bears condemnation
on its face, and cannot, and ought not, to be tolerated
any longer. To pass laws for India is not within the
province of the British Parliament. But to supervise
the general government of India, to remove injustice,
grievances, cruelty, and oppression, is within its
province, and ought never to be abandoned, but should
be more steadily and strenuously performed than
hitherto. Under the existing obstructive deadlock at
Westminster this is impossible.

*The British Parliament is not fulfilling its duty to
India.*—As a matter of fact, the British House of
Commons exercises, and can exercise, no more effective
control over the Indian Budget than over the Budget
of the Canadian Dominion. The evening, or part of
an evening, devoted, once a year, to Indian finance, is
to all intents and purposes thrown away. Our Indian
Government is a patchwork, and the result of the
exigencies which arose in the progress of our Indian
conquests and of our Indian administration.
Gradually, however, the fact is dawning upon the
minds of the Imperial Parliament, and of the people
at large, that the dual government, consisting (1) of
the Viceroy and his legislative council in India, and
(2) of the Indian Secretary, with or without his
council, in London, is most objectionable, and tends
greatly to excessive expenditure and bad management.
We are not discharging our Parliamentary and Imperial
duties to India. Indeed, in the present condition of
political parties, and parliamentary procedure in the
House of Commons, and of our existing constitution,
we can never hope to do so. This is a dangerous
condition of matters, which cannot much longer be

allowed to continue with safety; because the demand
for a popular form of government in India is becoming
stronger and stronger every day amongst the educated
natives, whose interests and inclinations all lie in the
direction of having greater native influence and control
over the Indian Government. My anticipation as
to the future government of India is, that we will
soon find that a Viceroy, and half a dozen Commissioners, more or less under the Viceroy, cannot rule
India; and that we will have to create, at least, half
a dozen virtually independent governments in India,
and make each of them practically responsible to the
Indian Secretary at home in London.

*A Commission of Inquiry as to Finance and
Administration imperative.*—Although we may reasonably hope that the huge blunders as to the cost of
any future Indian war will not again occur as it did
in reference to the Afghan war in 1880, we cannot be
at all sure that something similar, or as bad, may not
occur. By way of illustrating what I mean, take a
few recent examples of what have occurred. Thus,
the Home Government, as far back as in 1873, wished
to abolish the import duties on Manchester cottons;
but the Indian Government at Calcutta would not
consent to their abolition for ten years. Even then, the
Indian officials wished the duty on Indian tea and
coffee to be removed in this country; but the British
Chancellor of the Exchequer would not consent to its
removal, and has not yet consented. In this matter,
as I think, we have taken advantage of our position
as the supreme power over India. We should act justly,
without loss of time, towards India. Free Trade should
not be all on one side. Again, all efforts in the House of

Commons to reduce the yearly and increasing home charges for civil and military pensions, and the like, and to reduce the enormously increasing general expenditure of India, have utterly failed. The great increase in the home charges in the course of the last ten years, during which period they have been nearly doubled, calls for a searching and thorough inquiry. Such an inquiry was promised by the Liberal Government in March 1886, and had been determined on by the Conservative Government which immediately preceded it. Difficulties, however, have since arisen as to the scope of the inquiry ; and in June 1886, the order, in the House of Lords, for an Indian Royal Commission of Inquiry was discharged, and Lord Kimberley informed the House of Lords on that occasion that he did not agree with the nature of the Commission proposed by Lord Randolph Churchill in the House of Commons. Lord Salisbury defended Lord Randolph's proposals. Nothing has been done in this matter, and things have gone on, and are likely to go on for sometime to come, as before. As far back as 1879, Mr Fawcett called the attention of the House of Commons to the inadequate supervision of the Indian finance in the British Parliament, and he moved for a Committee to report on the working of the Indian Act of 1858, and subsequent Indian Acts as to the Indian Government. The then Chancellor of the Exchequer, Sir Stafford Northcote, said that he would not object to the proposed inquiry, if the Committee were allowed to inquire into the general administration of India. Like the proposal of 1886, the inquiry proposed in 1879 was abandoned. But it must be made before long, and so as to cover the whole ground suggested by the Chancellor of the Exchequer in 1879.

Upper Burmah conquered and annexed.—The war waged in Upper Burmah in 1885-86 was not of long duration, and was admirably and successfully conducted. The King's military preparations were insignificant and futile, and his troops fled at the approach of the British forces. Almost without any loss of blood, his capital fell into our hands. The stockade and walls of Mandalay, the capital of Upper Burmah, could not withstand the destructive power of our artillery, or the bravery of our soldiers. After the capital was given up to the British forces, the King, and all his queens and family, and royal household, surrendered. The King has since been confined in India as a prisoner of war, and is most honourably treated. His country has been annexed to the British Indian Empire by the Viceroy. Thus, the four great rivers of Eastern Asia, the Indus, the Ganges, the Burrampootra, and the Irrawaddy are within the Queen's dominions, and have to be guarded against all the enemies of the British Indian Empire. The total population of Upper Burmah, and of Lower Burmah, which was annexed in 1826, is about 7,000,000, or nearly twice the population of Scotland, and one-half greater than the population of Ireland.

We must reduce Burmah to good order.—We must still continue our efforts, in real earnest, to reduce the various hostile districts to law and order, and force the marauding bands of robbers, called dacoits, into thorough subjection to law. Although these things can be done very slowly, and only after much trouble, there can be no doubt whatever about the result in the end, for, by the Viceroy's proclamation in 1886, sanctioned by the Home Government, Upper Burmah, which was an outlying buffer state against Afghanistan, Tonquin and France, and was also interjected between us and Russia, is permanently, and for ever, annexed to the British Indian Empire, and is to be administered by such officers as the Viceroy of India may appoint. To carry out this policy, nothing will help us more than to be on the most friendly terms with China, which has awakened to the advantages of Western commerce and civilization, and which may become a source of great commercial advantage to our Indian Empire, and ourselves, and also to the vast, populous, and industrious Empire of China.   I believe that our latest annexation to the British Empire affords us a magnificent basis for a vast increase in our trade with China, in its south-west provinces.   But railways will require to be constructed to enable us to take full advantage of our good fortune in this part of the world,—*i.e.* in Eastern Asia. [Since these words were uttered, a commercial Treaty has been entered into between China and British India to develop trade in this neighbourhood.]

2.—EXTERNAL.

(1)—GENERAL.

Our external Indian frontier policy.—As regards our external policy in connection with our Indian Empire, the most pressing matter is to place our frontier defences and alliances on a firm basis. This involves a consideration of our Afghan, Persian, Russian, and Chinese policy. Allow me, therefore, on the present occasion, to direct and confine your chief attention to our Afghan and Russian policies, which are undoubtedly the most important.

Russian assurances as to Afghanistan.—In 1869, Prince Gortschakoff made a communication to the British Foreign Minister that Russia considered that Afghanistan was beyond the sphere of Russian influence.   Accordingly, in January of that year, assurances were given by this country to Shere Ali to that effect, and were gratefully acknowledged by him.   Another communication was made by Russia to Britain in 1872 to the same effect as in 1869.   This was clearly defined in a despatch by Lord Granville of the 17th of October 1872.   Whatever doubts may now exist as to the meaning of this second communication, our interpretation of it is clearly defined in the British despatch of 1872.   As Russia continued to advance in Central Asia, and conquered and annexed every State with which she came into contact, Shere Ali became alarmed.   But, as the British Government would do nothing to remove his fears, Shere Ali began to think of leaning upon Russia, rather than Britain, for support and protection.   The progress and success of Russia in Central Asia, and the changes in Russian and Afghan policy, and the war between Russia and Turkey in 1877-78, gave rise to the Afghan war of 1878 between Shere Ali and the British Indian Government. This war was brought about by our own stupidity. I pass over the last Afghan wars, and the re-constitution and re-union of Northern and Southern Afghanistan under Abdul Rahman, and must now

speak of the assurances given by the British Government to the present Ameer.

*British assurances given to the Ameer against unjust
aggression.*—No difference of opinion existed between
the Liberal and the Conservative policy of 1880 as to
the desirability of our evacuating Cabul; for the
Conservative Government had, in the spring of 1880,
ordered that the British troops should leave that city
by the month of October following, and the Liberal
Government, which came into office in 1880, followed
in the footsteps of their predecessors as to Cabul.
But a divergence of opinion did exist between the
two great political parties of this country as to
Candahar being left in the possession of the British
army. On this point, General Roberts differed from
General Stewart; and other high military authorities
differed from each other. Moreover, Lord Cranbrook,
the Conservative Indian Secretary, was in favour of
Candahar being in the possession, or under the military
control, of British India. In November 1880, however, Lord Hartington, the Liberal Indian Secretary,
finally decided that Candahar should be restored to
Afghanistan, and his policy as to Candahar and Herat
has been carried out, and has worked admirably well.
Further, in the following month of December, the
Ameer received assurances from the British Indian
Government that, if he should be interfered with in
his own country by any foreign power whatsoever, he
might absolutely rely on the British Government for
help and assistance; and that, if he were attacked,
Britain would repel the aggressor. Nearly a year
afterwards, in August 1881, Lord Hartington stated,
in the House of Commons, that the independence of

Afghanistan was a matter of vital interest to us, and
that we would not allow any country to interfere in
the external or internal affairs of Afghanistan.   Thus,
at last, we tardily assumed a fair, just, and honourable
attitude towards the people of Afghanistan and their
ruler.   If such assurances had been given by any
Indian Secretary, Liberal or Conservative, to Shere
Ali a few years before his death, we would have had
a faithful ally in the then Ameer of Afghanistan, and we
would never have been obliged to go to war with
Shere Ali in 1878.   Shirking duty in any case does
not pay in the long run.   The policy of shirking
national duties brings calamity and disgrace,—not
peace and honour.   Our Afghan war against Shere Ali
was the natural result of cruel selfishness, or downright
stupidity, on the part of the Liberal Government of
1873 and the Conservative Government of 1878.   We
wished to bind the Ameer to defend our interests on
our north-western frontier ; and yet, strange to say,
not be obliged to defend his interests, or comply with
his natural and reasonable wishes.   Neither private
persons, nor nations, can act in that way towards their
inferiors, equals, or superiors.   Superiors must be
treated with deference, equals with equality, and
inferiors with consideration.

*Arrangement at Rawl Pindi between the Viceroy
and Ameer.*—While the serious matters connected
with the recent delimitation of the Afghan frontier were
unsettled, and were even dangerous to the peace of
Central] Asia, a conference took place, in 1885,
at Rawl Pindi, between Lord Dufferin, the Viceroy of
British India, and Abdul Rahman, the present Ameer of
Afghanistan.   At this conference, it was finally settled

that the Ameer should be the ally of this country; that he should defend Afghanistan against all our enemies; that the defences of the Afghan frontier should be enlarged and strengthened; that British military officers should be stationed at Herat; and that a British viceregal diplomatic representative should be sent from Calcutta to Cabul. Accordingly, in August 1885, a Native Indian Representative from the Indian Viceroy was received, with great ceremony, at Cabul as British Indian Ambassador at the court of the Ameer. Since then, our Afghan policy has prospered at Cabul. The fixing of the frontiers lying between Russia and Afghanistan has now been completed, and ought to contribute towards the maintenance of peace. By the surrender and internment, in India, of Ayoub Khan, in November 1887, we have strengthened Abdul Rahman's possession of the Afghan throne, and our own position in Afghanistan, by one and the same stroke of good fortune and good policy.

Our future Afghan policy.—In the circumstances which have lately emerged in Central Asia, we must take care that Cabul, Herat, and Candahar are placed beyond the reach of Russian ambition. Afghanistan is our first line of defence for India against Russia, and must be guarded, and, if necessary, strenuously defended by us. Russia should not be allowed to take up a position south of the river Oxus; and yet, to take up such a position is one of the supreme aims of the Russian military party. Beyond the Suleiman range of mountains lies our first line of Indian defence. This great fact is now acknowledged by all competent and unprejudiced authorities. Thus, at last, we, to all intents and purposes, have arrived at the much condemned scientific frontier for India. Calmly and resolutely, and as an essential part of our Indian frontier policy, we must defend Afghanistan against all external foes, or grave internal disturbances.

Our North-Western Frontier defences.—Quettah, on our north-western frontier of India, was taken possession of by the Viceroy, in May 1877, as a place of arms, and was intended to be made, as it certainly ought to be, an important link in the chain of offensive and defensive operations contemplated by the then Conservative Government, in order to hold, or to dominate Candahar, by the completion of a railway between Sibi and Pisheen. We must always be prepared to convey an Indian army to take possession of Candahar; for the death of the present Ameer, Abdul Rahman, might develop a dangerous condition of affairs in Afghanistan. Moreover, we ought not to allow this great and important city to fall into the hands of Russian generals, or Russian allies. But, strange to say, and in violation of what ought to have been done, and in subordination to the demands of party exigencies, and as soon as the Liberal Government obtained office in May 1880, the railway between Sibi and Quettah was abandoned, and the necessary materials which had been conveyed to the north-western frontier were taken back across the Indus. But, in November 1882, the Liberal Government was obliged, by the force of events, to change their policy as to this railway, and they accordingly ordered these materials to be again taken back for its construction. Year by year, proof had been accumulating as to the wisdom of the Conservative policy to connect Candahar and Quettah by means of a railway, and no

opposing voice of any importance is now heard against
this railway, which was finished in the spring of 1887.
The railway to Candahar is also being rapidly pushed
forward towards completion.   When this railway to
Candahar is finished, and as long as the present
frontiers of Russia and Afghanistan stand good and
are maintained, we will be able to take and hold Herat
before Russia can seize upon it.   This is the *raison
d'être* of our Afghan railway policy on the Indian north-
western frontiers.   As to Quettah, I have to add that
all the great military authorities are unanimous as to
our duty to hold it by a strong force.   As a military
station, its importance is unquestionable ; but like all
other such places, its expense is considerable.   This
place of arms, as it has now become, covers our Indian
frontiers, and would, at least, for a time, stop any
sudden invasion carried on against India, and would
enable us to concentrate our Indian armies in the
north-western provinces, where our greatest Indian
military forces are stationed, and also to concentrate all
our forces within the Indus.   Lastly, it would enable us to
get reinforcements from England, or other parts of the
British Empire, to meet any formidable or expected foe.
Quettah and the Pisheen Valley were, in November
1887, proclaimed by the Viceroy of India to be part
of British India, and within our territories known as
British Beloochistan.   In the following month, the
Pisheen Valley railway over the Khojak Pass was completed, and was the copestone of our Indian frontier
policy.   At the further end of this Pass is Chaman,
which is a British outpost, and gives us the practical
command of the Hilmund.   We must enlarge and
follow up our policy of being on friendly terms with

the native Afghan frontier tribes, the Afreedees and
Kuzerees. We must also be fully acquainted with
every important event which takes place in Persia;
and extend our railway communications into
Afghanistan, and complete the Sind bridge over the
Indus to Candahar and Girisk; and be always ready
to seize Herat, which is the most important city in
Central Asia. We must prevent Russia getting down
to the Persian Gulf.

The Indus is our most vulnerable point in India.—
From the Bolan Pass to the river Indus, there is a
plain of 150 miles long by 100 miles broad. This
region is our most vulnerable point in India. Therefore, as I have already said, we have our greatest
military forces in the north-western provinces.
General Hamley and Professor Vambery both say that
we should defend India by means of Candahar, and stop
any hostile forces at that point, and also concentrate
our military forces within the Indus. Candahar blocks
the way to India from the north. It is near Kurrachee,
which is almost sure to be the centre of any war which
may be waged between us and Afghanistan on the
one hand and Russia on the other. Yarkund, in
which a British Agent was stationed in 1875, is also
an important district in reference to the defence of
India from external foes; because it affords another
easy access through Cashmere to India. But the most
important points for the defence of India against attack
from the north-west are Quettah, Mooltan, and
Kurrachee, which three places form a trilateral line of
great strength against an invasion of India by land.
To complete our system of defensive works for India
a large outlay of money will be required. But, then,

we must remember that the defence of a great, rich, and populous country like India cannot be done on the cheap.   Some of our Radical politicians, at home, however, seem to think or act otherwise.   I confess, I do not believe in the economical or the sentimental policy of cosmopolitan theorists in government, or in their national or imperial policy.

(3)—RUSSIAN POLICY IN CENTRAL ASIA.

Russia steadily advances in Central Asia.—After the Russo-Turkish war of 1854 was ended by the Treaty of Paris, and after the Russian advance into Europe was, for a time, rendered impossible, Russia directed her steps towards Central Asia. Russia accordingly proceeded to overthrow the warlike and barbarous Khanates, or chiefs, of Central Asia, and to establish her own supremacy in that part of the world.   Her advance in this direction was sometimes accidental, and arose from external circumstances, disturbances, or attacks.   But it was as certain and inevitable as if it had been deliberate.   Every advance was made the stepping-stone, and basis of operations, for further advances.   Twenty years ago, Russia took two years to transport troops from the Kirghis Steepe to her southern borders on the north of our Indian Empire. How vast the change ! She is now coterminous with Afghanistan, and, therefore, at our very doors.   In 1882, the Russian Home Government was urging the construction of a railway from Orenburg to Tashkend, and thence to Bokhara, and thence to Afghanistan and Peshawar.   Russia has already constructed a railroad

P

through the desert of Central Asia.   In March 1887, she had arrived at a point within sixty miles of Sarakhs, and close to Meshed and Herat, whither branch lines were projected; and in May of the same year, this railway was within twenty miles of the Afghan frontiers.

When this railway, which is constructed from the Eastern shore of the Caspian to Chardjui on the Oxus, is extended to Bokhara, Samarkand, and Tashkend, the Russian advanced posts will be on the Chinese and Indian frontiers, and will be in un-interrupted railway communication with all parts of the Russian Empire.   Russia has aims directed against China as well as against British India, and she will probably find that, in any future contest between ourselves and her as to India or Afghanistan, that she will have to reckon with China as well as with us.

Central Asia and Russian Policy.—Central Asia covers three million square miles, and is about three-fourths of the size of Europe.   There, at one time, the population must have been enormous; for there, in ancient times, existed the populous cities of the Persian Empire of sacred and profane history.   In Central Asia, the population is now small and sparse, and cannot resist the shock of civilized warfare, and, consequently, the Asiatic hordes crumble to pieces at the touch of a great civilized military power fully equipped for modern warfare.   Therefore, the neutral zone, of immense extent, existing between us and Russia a very few years ago, and upon which we placed great confidence as a protection in 1873, has disappeared; and, at last, after much labour and great delay, and considerable danger, the territories of Russia and Afghanistan have been acknowledged by Britain and Russia as coterminous. How long the new Russo-Afghan frontier will stand depends entirely on the peaceful attitude of Russia, and on the firmness of our own government in upholding and defending it. According to the *Novosti*, a Pansclavonic or Russian journal of April 1887, circumstances will impel Russia to move forward on the river Oxus to Andkoi, Maimeneh, all still left to Afghanistan and on the south side of Russia's desert frontier, and towards India, and she will never stop till she attains her natural frontier on the Hindoo Küsh. When, if ever, Russia is again impelled to annex any Afghan territory, she will find that we are prepared to resist her, and also to reopen the Eastern question in a fashion which also will astonish her. When the British people are thoroughly aroused to a sense of danger, or of gross injustice, our fury is terrible, and is always disastrous to our enemies.

Bokhara the next Russian annexation in Central Asia.—The Russian advance in Central Asia being, for the present, stopped in the direction of Afghanistan, and being impossible in the direction of Persia, without serious danger of war between Britain and Russia, Russian activity in this part of the world will take the direction of Bokhara, which, beyond all question, will be annexed at the very first opportunity, by the force of circumstances, and then adopted as a *fait accompli*, as usual. Bokhara and Cabul are closely related politically and geographically to each other; for Kuhm, Balkh, and Kunduz in Afghanistan formerly belonged to Bokhara. Besides, the Maimeneh, Sivis-

Pul, and Andkoi districts are in dispute between Afghanistan and Bokhara. Therefore, to reduce Bokhara under Russian influence and control, and to become the heir of all the Bokharian claims and grievances against Afghanistan will admirably suit Russian policy and ambition as a basis for future operations against Afghanistan. In Bokhara, then, we may expect to see the next act in the central Asiatic drama.

Persia almost subjected to Russian influence.— Unless we change our policy at Teheran, Persia is ultimately doomed to be conquered in the march of the Russian armies; and then the Shah of Persia, like the Khans of Central Asia, will be reduced to a state of vassalage to the Czar. For some time past, we have abandoned our ancient policy of active diplomatic intervention at Teheran. Lately, however, by the wise and prudent conduct of our ambassador at the Court of Persia, efforts in the direction of increasing our political and commercial influence in Persia have been made, by the present Conservative Government, to regain the high position of influence which we once held at the Shah's Court; but these, I am sorry to say, will most probably be relaxed as soon as a Liberal Government returns to office. Between the policies of the Liberal and the Conservative parties there are essential and eternal differences, and the country must soon adopt and rigidly adhere to one Foreign policy or the other. For my own part, I stand by the Foreign policy which is just and advantageous to my own country, and not by that which is sentimental and advantageous to every country but my own.

Russian Policy in the Persian Gulf and Afghanistan.
—Russia has her eyes steadily fixed in two directions in
Central Asia. In one, she has her eyes fixed on
Afghanistan; and in another, she looks towards the
sea. Towards the sea, she is bent on getting an opening for her trade, and a station for her military and
naval forces in the Persian Gulf. Here, for a short
time, but only for a short time, we can treat Russian
policy with indifference. Still we must remember
that the realization of Russian ambition in Persia
would give Russia a great power of control over our
overland route to India by way of the Mediterranean,
the Suez Canal, and the Red Sea. So long as we
maintain our naval superiority over any two of the
great naval powers of the world, we can afford to look
with unconcern on Russia's eager gaze towards the
great Indian Ocean. At present, Russia cannot
seriously injure, or menace, us in Persia or the Persian
Gulf. Far more serious, however, is the point upon
which the Russian Generals and Governors in Central
Asia have fixed their eyes in a south-easterly direction,
namely, in the direction of Afghanistan. Beyond all
question, we should keep Russia out of Afghanistan
by every means in our power. Our plain and simple
duty as regards our Eastern policy is to see that our
position in Central Asia is made as strong as possible,
and especially in Afghanistan and Persia, and also in
Turkey and the Mediterranean, and especially in Asia
Minor and Armenia.

Russian Policy in Central Asia.—We must be
under no mistake as to our duty, or our prospects, in
this matter. We know, from past experience,
that Russia cannot restrain her military officers and

governors in Central Asia, and that she could not even although she would. Our own country is being driven out of the market of Central Asia for the prints and calicoes of Manchester. This result is being effected by Russian railway communication from the heart of Russia to the heart of Central Asia, and also by Russian hostile tariffs. Unless we exert ourselves by greater commercial activity and energy in Asia Minor, in Persia, and in Afghanistan, our country will suffer great commercial loss by Russian activity, energy, and policy. By regaining political influence in Persia, our commercial influence will follow; for commerce always follows the flag, and Russia is getting alarmed at the prospect of our recent diplomacy in Persia. We wish peace in Central Asia and in every part of our dominions. But we must not be afraid to assert our rights, or to defend them. Temporary peace, of course, we can have in Central Asia on Russian conditions; but a permanent peace in that part of the world, in the present condition of foreign affairs, is utterly impossible. Russia thinks that, as an Asiatic power, she has a great civilizing mission to carry out in Central Asia, and even in British India itself. She has pursued a great traditional policy, for, at least, a century and more, to get possession of Constantinople. We need not, therefore, be surprised at her conduct in Asia or in Europe, in which the deliverance of India from British slavery, and the most thorough-going and ambitious schemes of aggression against Turkey are mixed up, and inextricably combined.

Russian Policy in Asia and Europe.—The aggressive policy of Russia is directed towards the realization of of these two great and supreme objects, namely, (1) her Asiatic mission; and (2) her dreams of Pansclavonic unity in Europe. Both these objects have been pursued separately and simultaneously, without ceasing, for several generations. In the pursuit of these, her two greatest projects in foreign policy, she has marched her great armies East and West, and will not stop at any point till she is compelled by some European power, or powers, to do so. Austria and Germany are immediately and deeply concerned in the progress of the Russian advance into Europe. We are deeply and immediately concerned in her Eastern advance into Asia, and especially into Central Asia, in the direction of our Indian Empire, and also in her advance into Europe as tending to endanger our maritime highway between this country and India and Australasia by the Mediterranean Sea, the Suez Canal, and the Persian Gulf, and also between this country and India by the overland route through Armenia. Our European interests against Russia are, therefore, practically identical with Austrian and German interests against Russian aggression, and, I believe, will, if necessary, be treated on this basis of common interest. To keep Constantinople out of the clutches of Russia is a matter of common interest to Britain, Austria, Germany, and Italy. But to defend India by a hostile Foreign Policy against Russia in time of peace would be the greatest madness on our part. We must defend British India in India and in Central Asia. We must defend our interests in Europe by a European Policy. If we are true to ourselves, we can defend British India against the whole world. As we have always done hitherto, we, like brave men, with a noble history, and a grand future destiny, must look to, and rely upon, our own right arms to gain us the victory over all our enemies in every part of the world.   Acting thus, we have nothing to fear from Russia, or any other power in the world.

Britain and Russia should cease to be opponents in Central Asia.—We must make up our minds where Russia must stop in her progress in Central Asia, and firmly stand faithful to our resolution on this point.   Russian supremacy in Central Asia has been beneficial, is now indisputable, and is now indispensible.   In Central Asia there is ample room for both Russia and ourselves.   Nay more, I entirely agree with those who think that everywhere we should enter into an honourable rivalry with Russia in the arts of peace and commerce, and not in a deplorable contest with her in the arts of barbarism and war.   Still, we must not forget that the commercial policy of Russia in Asia as well as in Europe is based on protection, and is injurious to our trade to a very considerable extent.   Here again, we are met by the unquestionable fact that Trade follows the Flag.   All the same, let us remain at peace with Russia as long as she does not injure us or our allies.

III.—EGYPTIAN AFFAIRS.

Political condition.—Egypt is a province of the Ottoman Empire; but is practically independent of the Sultan.   It is a Turkish province, under special powers secured and sanctioned by Europe.   Yet it is naturally looked upon as a valuable part of the Turkish Empire ; for the Sultan receives a yearly tribute of £750,000 sterling from the Khedive, who receives nothing from him in return.   This tribute has been pledged by the Sultan in security of £17,000,000 sterling. Egypt is divided into Lower and Upper, and each division has distinct and well marked peculiarities in conformation, population, and customs.   Lower Egypt is flat ; its population are industrious peasants ; and its customs are peaceful.   Upper Egypt is hilly ; its population are wandering Bedouins, whose habits are warlike. Both divisions of the country have rich soils.   With good government, they would become prosperous and wealthy.   From the dawn of Egyptian history, the great mass of the people have been peasant farmers, who were indifferent about forms of government, and anxious, above all things, to get a livelihood in peace and comfort.   Again, from the earliest ages, foreigners have ruled over the people of Egypt ; and usually with a rod of iron.   In modern Egypt, as it now exists, the Pachas are the landowners, and hold the military and political power of the country. The people are composed of three distinct races, namely, Copts, Arabs, and Circassians.   The Copts are the aboriginal inhabitants of the country, and the tillers of the soil, and are called Felaheen.   The Pachas are either Arabs or Circassians.   The rulers are mostly Circassians.   The Copts were subdued by the Byzantine Emperors ; afterwards the Arabs conquered Egypt ; and then the Turks conquered Egypt. Before and after the conquest of the Arabs by the Turks, the Copts and Arabs, who had largely been Christians, became Mahomedans.   The Felaheen have been great sufferers by the rapacity of their Turkish and Circassian rulers.

What are our interests in Egypt?—What are our national interests in Egypt? Let us see how they are defined by Lord Granville in his despatch of the 11th of July 1882. His lordship stated (1) that there was a large British community in Egypt in need of protection for their lives and properties; (2) that we had large material interests in Egypt and that the Suez Canal Company was in need of protection; and (3) that we had an important special interest in Egypt, inasmuch as Egypt was on the direct maritime route between England and our Indian possessions, and our Australasian Colonies. Again, what said Mr Gladstone in the House of Commons on the 10th of August 1882? While he declined to define the objects of our military occupation of Egypt, he said that the military occupation would not be permanent, and that the final settlement of Egyptian affairs would be for Europe, and not for any power singly. On all these points Conservative as well as Liberal Statesmen are of one mind.

We wish a free and independent Egypt.—What we all wish, and what we should certainly wish, is to exclude the interference of all the European powers, except our own, from Egypt, and to educate the Egyptian people up to the duties and rights of responsible self government, and to make and keep the land free and independent for the Egyptians themselves. In this matter, we have, in the most solemn manner, pledged our good faith to the Great Powers; and we will serve our own interests, and the interests of the world, for the present and in all time to come, by faithfully and

honourably standing firmly to our engagements as of
old. The policy of Lords Clarendon and Palmerston
was to keep Egypt out of the clutches of Turkey, or
of any other great power. Our policy as to Egypt
ought to be on the same lines of policy, and also to
prepare the Egyptians for a full and practical independence, within the limits of existing Treaties, or
within the limits of such Treaties as may hereafter be
peacefully and amicably made between the Khedive,
the Sultan, and the great European powers.

We should re-organize and evacuate.—Our duty to
Egypt and ourselves is to perform the obligations we
have undertaken in Egypt, and then to leave it to
the Egyptians. But, as yet, it is quite clear that the
time for our evacuation has not arrived. For example,
the Soudan is not pacified, and we must see that
Suakim and Wady Halfa are amply defended against
all attacks by Osman Digna and all his allies.
Further, the Egyptians are at present as incapable of
governing themselves as they were six years ago.
The native Egyptian officials are under the control of
British officials, and they are as much in need of supervision as at the time we entered upon our laborious and
expensive task of re-organizing Egypt after the destruction of Alexandria, and the subsequent defeat of Arabi
Pacha, and the general smash of all Egyptian Government. Progress in re-organization has been made, but
not enough to justify us in withdrawing our support
from the edifice which we have raised on the ruins of the
old, corrupt, and dangerously inflammable material in
the Egyptian Government. We entered on this task
with reluctance. Unaided and alone we must bring
our task to a successful issue. France has no special

rights to interfere in Egypt beyond those of the
European continental powers.   She has acknowledged
that she has none; and we must keep her bound by
her recognition of our position, when she refused to
take any effective joint action.   Now all serious war in
Egypt has been at end for about four years.   The
horrid dogs of war are chained, and the sweet doves
of peace stretch out their wings.   We have put an
end to official corruption and arbitrary injustice in
Egypt.   We have improved the condition of the
Felaheen, and released them from many onerous and
slavish duties.   We have, in a word, substituted civil
order and rational government for military violence and
oppression.   Let us calmly and resolutely go on with
our work, and bring it to a successful end, and put an
end to our own military occupation at the earliest
possible moment.

Anglo-Turkish Convention.—In 1887, a Convention
was arranged at Constantinople between the British
Minister extraordinary sent to the Sultan and the
Turkish Ministers.   The chief articles of the Convention were (1) that the British military forces
should be withdrawn from Egypt in a year and a half
from the sanctioning of the Convention by the Sultan ;
(2) that we should have the power of re-occupying
Egypt in the event of an invasion ; and (3) that the
Khedive, if he could, might restore his own power in
the Soudan.   France and Russia combined to oppose
the ratification of this Convention by promises to and
threats against the Sultan ; and, in the end, they
succeeded in preventing the Convention from being
ratified by the Sultan.   Our occupation of Egypt has,
therefore, been indefinitely postponed ; and all efforts

on the part of the Sultan to induce the British Government to renew negotiations as to Egypt have been and ought to be futile. When it was too late, the Sultan discovered that his real and best interests had been sacrificed at the instigation of France and Russia, whose aims do not coincide with the permanent advantage of the Ottoman Empire. Some of our Continental critics assert that we will never give up Egypt altogether. Whether they are right or wrong in this view depends on circumstances. Most assuredly we ought never to give up Egypt to any other foreign power ; and consequently, we are involved in a virtual Protectorate of Egyptian independence. A very common idea in France is that, if we would retire from Egypt, France would then go in and occupy it. France, for example, would like us to abandon Egypt at once, and also to give up the Island of Perim, which is British territory, and is at the mouth of and commands the Red Sea. But we are not likely to surrender Perim, or absolutely to give up our interests or control over Egypt. We are also prepared, by our fleet, and all other means, to defend our highways to and from all parts of the British Empire at all hazards.

The Suez Canal Convention.—After much labour and negotiation between France and this country, and between them and Turkey, a convention has, at last, been agreed upon for the neutralization of the Suez Canal in peace and war. Without entering into the details of this Treaty, I have to mention that this Treaty has been sanctioned by all the Great European Powers, and may, therefore, be accepted as another step in advance of an old European policy to neutralize, as far as possible, the great highways of commerce for the general interests of the world. At one time, it was thought by foreigners that, being in Egypt, we would never lose our hold over it; and, at all events, would never do anything to preclude ourselves from the advantage of possessing the Suez Canal for ourselves, both in peace and in war. We have, however, practically conceded the general claims of universal commerce in the Suez Canal. Nay more, looking upon the interests of peace and of commerce as of much higher importance to us than our special interests at a time when we might be at war, we have agreed to the neutralization of the Suez Canal. We must therefore look to the Cape Route and the Pacific Canadian Route for our means of communication with our Indian Empire and our Australasian and other Colonies in the far East. Thus the Suez Canal becomes a great international highway for the commerce of the world, and realizes the great aim of its original promoter. The entire freedom of the Suez Canal at all times, and in all circumstances, for the world, is the great idea at the root of this Convention.

Slavery was to be, and should be, abolished.—In 1877, the Khedive entered into a convention with us for the abolition of Slavery in Lower Egypt in 1885, and in Upper Egypt in 1889. This arrangement aroused the slave-owners against the government of the Khedive; and in 1882 and subsequently against ourselves. Slavery is indigenous to the Soudan, and to most countries in the East; and its proposed abolition in Upper Egypt gave rise to a powerful movement amongst the Arab slave-owners and slave-hunters for its continuance. From the Soudan, numerous slaves are taken to Lower Egypt, and across the Red Sea to Arabia, amidst the most heart-rending scenes of cruelty and barbarity. Loaded with chains, the poor wretches, men and women, are driven like cattle by their masters through Upper Egypt. Every year, thousands fall dead on the way before they reached the Red Sea. Such abominations and traffickings in human life and misery, are, by all means, to be put down, and with all the power and influence at our disposal. This is a great question of civilization and justice for me and you, and also for this country, honourably connected as it has been in its efforts to extirpate slavery in British territory, and throughout the whole world. Slavery is a stigma on humanity, and a disgrace to the human race. The traffickers in human beings are the enemies of mankind, and are liable to the punishment of death by the laws of every civilized nation in the world. The slave-trading Moslem Arabs in Central Africa are depopulating Central Africa. Every year they are causing the death of thousands of their kidnapped victims. They should be put to death without remorse. They should and could be effectually prevented from carrying on their wicked trade by a few hundred soldiers stationed at posts all along the coasts of the Red Sea opposite Arabia.

The Soudan War.—In 1882, Zobehr, the great merchant slave-owner, and ruler of a large tract of territory in the Soudan, stirred up the Bedouins of the desert against us and the Khedive, and induced his son-in-law, the Mahdi, or Saviour, to stir up the Mahomedans in the Soudan against us as strangers

and Christians. Osman Digna took the command of
the forces thus arrayed against the government at
Cairo, and involved us in a costly war, and the loss of
many noble men and gallant soldiers. Amongst whom,
we must reckon the heroic Burnaby and the noble
Gordon Pacha. I hope that the hateful traffic in
human flesh and blood in the Soudan will be the fruit
of our sacrifices in that dark and benighted land. To
leave the Soudan to the slave-owners to carry on their
detestable commerce would be an eternal disgrace to
us. We should not be content with striking at
slavery on the Red Sea, or on the Red Sea coast.
We should strike at its basis and centre in the Dark
Continent of Africa, by establishing some kind of
civilized government in the Soudan, pledged, determined, and able to extirpate the hateful slave traffic,
root and branch. By doing this, we might make some
atonement for the miseries which we have inflicted on
the people in that quarter of the globe, and thereby
confer a lasting benefit on the world, and gain, it
may be, an imperishable crown of glory. Than the
abandonment of Gordon Pacha in Khartoum by the
Liberal Government nothing is more disgraceful in the
meanness and selfishness of any British Government,
ancient or modern. Mr Stanley has, however, gone,
with a small expeditionary force, fitted out by private
benevolence, to Bahr Gazeth to seal up, if possible,
the awful charnel-house of Africa; to place an
impassable barrier against the hateful trade of the
Arab slave-traders; to free Equatorial Africa from
the scourge of the slave-trade, and to open that
region of the world to trade and civilization. He has
gone forth on a grand work of justice and humanity.

Let us hope that he may be successful in his gigantic
and glorious enterprise ; and that he and his followers
may successfully and permanently carry the banners of
peace, trade, and civilization to the very heart of
Africa.   We once heard a great deal by some great
authorities in this country about the Soudanese
fighting for freedom.   We hear no more of such
nonsense by these great authorities, who had much to
learn about Egypt and most other foreign countries,
and their aims and policies.   Under the impulses of
religious Mahomedan fanaticism and hatred of the
Christians, and of the desire to conquer Lower Egypt,
and to establish a new dynasty at Cairo for Lower
and Upper Egypt, the Soudanese endangered our
position at Alexandria, Cairo, and the Suez Canal.
We have not gone to Egypt in vain !   We have done
something to the poor Felaheen in Lower Egypt by
obtaining the abolition of forced labour, called corvée.
Let us complete our philanthropic work of Egyptian
emancipation by gradually, yet utterly, abolishing
slavery in every part of Egypt.   As the abolition of
the corvée required the sanction of the Great Powers,
and especially of France and Russia, so will the
abolition of slavery in Egypt.   Can, or will, they
object to such a grand and glorious work ?   I do not
think so ; but, even if they did object, we should
wait till the necessary sanction was obtained.

IV.—FOREIGN AFFAIRS.

1.—THE EUROPEAN SITUATION.

Maritime Highways.—Here I could have wished to
point out and explain to you the importance to us of

Q

keeping open the great maritime highways of the world, and of increasing, and not diminishing, the means of communication to our Indian and Colonial possessions in the East and West; that is to say, the Mediterranean, in which we hold the islands of Gibraltar, Malta, and Cyprus; in the Suez Canal, which has now been neutralized, but which forms an important and connecting link between the Mediterranean and the Red Sea and the Persian Gulf, in which we have fortresses or war ships to protect our highway between the Mediterranean and our Australasian and other Eastern Colonies and our Indian Empire. In these great highways, our interests are fully secured by existing Treaties and present rights of possession; but, in the event of war in South-Eastern Europe, we would be obliged, by diplomacy, and, perhaps, by naval and military forces, to see to our defences in those great highways. On this policy, Austria and Italy and Britain have virtually agreed to defend their common interests; and, without any treaty, Italy and this country are almost certain to co-operate in their defence by their naval forces. No doubt, some craven-hearted or ignorant people in this country advise us to abandon the Mediterranean, and to abandon Gibraltar, Malta, Cyprus, the Suez Canal, the Red Sea, and the Persian Gulf. But I venture to assert that we will never give up one of those places until we are unable to defend it, or until we have abandoned India to Russia, or until we have shrunk into the insignificance of a second or third-rate power in the rank of European nations. Those calamities are not yet come upon us; nor are our hands so feeble, nor our hearts so week and cowardly, as to abandon our national greatness, or to ruin our national trade and commerce, upon which that greatness so greatly depends. But time and place forbid me to enter upon these and cognate matters, and make me feel that I have already attempted to discuss too many subjects, which would require hours, aye days, weeks, and months, for their complete elucidation. All I am able to do is to touch the *summa vestigia rerum*, and leave fuller explanations to be given on future occasions. For the present, I must make an effort to explain to you the leading features of the pending disputes in the Balkans, and the policies and attitudes of the Great European Powers in regard to this great problem, which, for some months past, has nearly involved the whole of Europe in all the horrors and miseries of a gigantic war. Alas! not even yet is, and I fear never before the God of war rides out amongst the hosts of Europe will be, the European Continent likely to settle down in peace.

2.—THE BALKANS.

Servia as an example of Austrian and Russian Policies.—In Servia, there are two great political parties. One of them has King Milan and Monsieur Garashannin at its head, and may be called the National Servian party, aiming at an independent Servian nationality, and resting on Austria for the realization of its aims. The other party has Monsieur Ristics at its head, and may be called the Pro-Russian and Anti-Servian national party, and aims at supplanting King Milan as an independent Prince, and at substituting the Prince Karageorgevics or Prince of Montenegro in the King's place. This party rests on Russia for the realization of its policy. At present, May 1888, Austria is supreme in the Councils of the Servian Kingdom, and even Monsieur Ristics and his party appear to have somewhat abandoned their old policy of hostility to Austria in the Balkans. Whether Austria or Russia predominated in Servia, Austria, backed up by Germany, will strenuously oppose any grave intrigues in Servia by the Pro-Russian party; and, if necessary, will occupy Servia in self-defence against the Russian party in the Balkans. Austria and Germany are well acquainted with the great problem which, ere long, will have to be solved in South-Eastern Europe. They know perfectly well that the problem is, whether Eastern or Western civilization is to prevail in Europe for the future, and they are determined to fight for Western civilization as against Eastern civilization. In the solution of this problem, we, like Italy, must take a share.

Russian policy of aggression.—The Russian policy of aggression is, and has always been, the same. A few Russian emigrants or philanthropists are sent forward into the coveted territory. They create disturbances, or take advantage of those troubles which already exist. A cause for Russian intervention soon arises in a real, or alleged, necessity to defend Russian subjects. Diplomatic complaints are made, and, sooner or later, the Russian armies march into the coveted territories, and, seldom or never, leave them. This has been the course of Russian policy in Georgia and Circassia, and so it has been in Central Asia; and so it will be in Europe and Asia until

Russia comes into contact with a power which boldly
and resolutely says to her in language not to be mis-
understood : "Thus far and no further."

Armenia, Bulgaria, and Roumelia nearly in the
clutches of Russia.—This game has already made rapid
progress in Armenia and Bulgaria and Roumelia ; and
the time appears to be at hand when the long-coveted
prizes are about to be seized and appropriated, or
attempted to be seized and appropriated, by Russia.
Armenia, Bulgaria, and Roumelia are thoroughly impregnated with the Russian system to which I have
alluded. Unless prevented by stronger forces than
their own, they will easily be subdued and annexed
by Russian intrigues and Russian arms. If Russia
should thereafter obtain Constantinople, and succeed
as the chief heir to the Ottoman Empire, she would
be absolutely supreme in the Black Sea, the
Dardanelles, and the Bosphorus, and speedily become
a great Mediterranean naval power, and she would
soon be supreme from the Indus to the Nile, and then
no power would be strong enough to stop her from
exercising a predominant influence over Europe. If
this is to be the course of events, let us, at all events,
do what we can to provide against it. In this aspect
of the Eastern question, we must keep in mind that
Austria and Germany are indifferent as to the leadership of the Bosphorus, but are not so of the
Dardanelles ; or, in other words, they are indifferent
to the sovereignty of Armenia, but not of the Balkans.
If Turkey cannot re-organize herself, and purge herself
of her official corruption and national bankruptcy, and
renew her lease of life by an approximation to Western
ideas, and Western forms of Government, no power on

earth can save her from utter destruction.   Roumania
was very badly treated by Russia in the last Russo-
Turkish war in 1877 ; for she was forced into the war
by Russia, and had to bear the brunt of the battle,
and got nothing in return, and she had to give up the
Dobrudsha district to Russia.   She is not likely to
fall into the same mistake again.   On the other hand,
we may expect the mountaineers of Montenegro, and
also all the proteges of Russia, to promote Russian
interests to the utmost of their power.   Further, if
Russia should get possession of Armenia, and the
bordering territory, Turkey will fall to pieces, and
Russia will become predominant on the Bosphorus.
Unless Armenia is better governed by Turkey than
hitherto, it will inevitably fall into the clutches of
Russia, who is already on the borders of Armenia.
Russia is believed to have made proposals to Turkey
to accept Armenia in payment, or part payment, of
the Turkish war indemnity due to Russia, and also to
give an undertaking to the Sultan to defend the
remainder of her territories against all external
or internal foes.   Whether made or not, the Sultan
has not been foolish enough to accept the offers of Russia
here supposed to have been made.   The Armenian
Christians, at least, who live on the shores of the
Black Sea, hate the prospect of being ruled by Russia.
On the Asiatic side of the Black Sea, Russia has long
been carefully planning an attack on Turkey; and, in
carrying out her plan, she has made Tiflis and
Batoum the bases of her future military operations
in this region.

Armenia.—The population of Asia Minor is composed of various races, religions, languages, and

shows no tendency to amalgamation. The broad religious distinctions are Mahomedan and Christian. In Asia Minor, small, indeed for ages little, advance has been made in civilization. After the fall of Schamyl, large numbers emigrated from Circassia into Asia Minor; and after the late Turko-Russian war, large numbers emigrated from Roumelia, Bulgaria, and Circassia into Armenia. The refugee emigrants in Asia Minor are estimated at a quarter of a million; and are migratory in their habits, wandering hither and thither, as the great nomad tribes did in the same regions in the days of the Jewish patriarchs. Anatolia, a district of Armenia, has a fine situation between the Black Sea and the Sea of Marmora, and has a magnificent seaboard. Here we have what is generally supposed to be the cradle of the human race, the garden of Eden, and the great Mount Ararat, where Noah's ark is supposed to have settled after the Flood. The mountains are high and rugged; the people, beautiful, industrious, and mostly Christians. Down to the fourteenth century, the people of Armenia had a great commerce and a great history. Armenia touches the Caspian, the Euxine, and the Mediterranean, and embraces the waters of the Tigris and the Euphrates. The estimated Christian population of Armenia is one million, and the Mahomedan about three quarters of a million. Armenia is part of Asiatic Turkey, and aims at semi-independent power.

Rivalries in the Balkans.—From the time of the last Russo-Turkish war, Servia and Bulgaria have been rivals, and both of them have been patronised by Austria and Russia as the interests of the one or the other of these great powers seemed to require.

In fact, they were the pawns in a game of chess, in which the kings and queens were to win the game, and carry off the winnings, and the pawns themselves were to get nothing from either of the great potentates.

Recent events in Armenia.—In 1880 and 1881, the condition of affairs was lamentable. Famine and starvation spread themselves widely over the land; and the wild and lawless refugees murdered, robbed, and violated the poor, defenceless natives. Life and property were unprotected, and famine and disorder reigned supreme in the most fertile lands in the world. Proposals were made to the Porte to put an end to these miseries; but they resulted in nothing. The great curse of Turkey is the centralization of all government at Stamboul. The Armenian reforms needed are local Administrative Reform, and honest and enlightened, and to all intents and purposes, permanent governors. Nothing, however, has been done to remove, or even diminish, the grievances of the Armenians, and official corruption and cruelty proceed in their course as before, and neither Britain, nor any of the great powers, will do anything to induce or compel the Sultan to improve the Government of Armenia. We have made representations to the Porte; but we have done nothing more. Why? Because force, or threats, would throw the Sultan into the arms of the Czar. Strange to say, improvement in the Turkish Government from without, or from within, would not be pleasing to the Russian Government. The end of the whole matter is that the Armenians are beginning to look forward with indifference, if not with equanimity, to Russia, their hereditary foe, as a liberator from Turkish oppression. As Russia is advancing her power and influence and forces in the direction of Asia Minor, and as the incorporation of Asia Minor by Russia would mean the establishment of Russia at Smyrna, and would make Russia a Mediterranean power, you will, at once, perceive the importance of Armenia in the present condition of European affairs.

Servian aims.—Servia was the ally of Russia in the last Russo-Turkish war, and fought bravely and well for her patron, and got little or nothing for her trouble. But all the same, she aims at the leadership of the Balkan States, and the restoration of the ancient Servian kingdom, which, at one time, included Bosnia, Macedonia, Bulgaria, Thrace, and Thessaly, and stretched from the Aegean to the Adriatic. In 1860, she had a population of half a million, and has now a population of two millions. She, in fact, aspired to be the head centre and rallying point of a projected kingdom of Southern Sclavs; but her recent encounter with Bulgaria showed that her ambition was greater than her power. At the end of the last Russo-Turkish war, she was pitched aside by Russia, and has since alternately become the tool or the toy of Austria or of Russia. As a greatly enlarged Servia is a hindrance to the realization of Russia's own dreams of conquest in South-Eastern Europe, Servia has lately been forced to lean upon Austrian support, and, for the present, Russia has lost all influence over Servia. Without Austria or Russia, Servia cannot do anything of any consequence in peace or war, or in the realization of her ambitious dreams of conquest; but she has never been satisfied with the virtual annexation of Bosnia and Herzegovina to Austria. Servia looks upon and claims these two provinces as part of her ancient inheritance. Russia was also dissatisfied with this virtual annexation, and can play on Servian hopes and fears in regard to them for her own special advantage.

Bulgarian aims.—Bulgaria, as a Turkish province in 1876, was not engaged in the last Russo-Turkish war, which was ostensibly, but falsely, alleged by Russia and her sympathisers in this country, to be waged against Turkey in consequence of the oppression, cruelty, and misgovernment of Turkey against the people of Bulgaria. It was, in reality, waged by Russia, with the sanction of Austria and Germany, and as a means of obtaining compensation to Russia for her neutrality in the last Franco-German war. However, I do not go back upon the lying pretences for this war. I shall take matters as they stand. Bulgaria was liberated from the Turkish Empire as the result of the last Russo-Turkish war. Therefore, naturally enough the Bulgarians are grateful to the Russian people for what they have done for them. Although by the Treaty of Berlin, the principality of Bulgaria was placed under tribute to the Sultan, it is practically independent. Nay more, although the principality of Bulgaria did not, at first, comprehend Eastern Roumelia, yet, if the wishes of Russia had been gratified at the end of the war, it would, under the Treaty of San Stephano, have comprehended all the Turkish territories from the Black Sea to the mountains in sight of the Adriatic; and, in addition to all this, 1000 miles of Servian territory, and an additional population of one million people. All this new territory and population, placed as was intended by the Czar of Russia under a Prince of his own selection, would have practically annexed the whole of them to the Russian Empire, and would have placed the Sultan of Turkey completely under the power of the Czar. Eastern Roumelia having a population of 1,000,000, and Bulgaria Proper, as placed under Prince Alexander, having a population of 2,000,000, United Bulgaria and Eastern Roumelia have a population approximating to that of Scotland. This large Principality, contemplated by the Treaty of San Stephano, was reduced to Bulgaria Proper under the Treaty of Berlin, but it was enlarged to a big united Bulgaria and Eastern Roumelia by Prince Alexander the original nominee of Russia, and against the express wishes of the Czar. Why, quite lately, did Russia object to the enlargement of Bulgaria to the dimensions contemplated under the Treaty of San Stephano, and to the total release of big Bulgaria from the oppression of Turkey? Simply because a United Bulgaria delayed, and perhaps thwarted for ever, the realization of the national policy of Russia as regards Constantinople. Servia, raised to the rank of a kingdom in 1882, with the sanction and approval of Austria and Germany; and Roumania, raised to the same rank in 1881, under the same sanction and approbation; and Montenegro, still a principality, have long been the diplomatic toys of Russia; and Bulgaria and Eastern Roumelia have also been placed in much the same position as the older sister principalities in the Balkans. For the present, however, the sovereigns of Servia, Roumania, Bulgaria, and Eastern Roumelia have gone over to the side of Austria, and are guarded in their rights and liberties by the Austro-German alliance, or the league of peace, for the maintenance of the *status quo* in Europe. But we do not know how long they will

remain so.   Again, the Prince of Montenegro clings to
Russia, with good reason ; for, with the aid of Russia,
he has hopes of adding Servia to his own dominions.

Prince Ferdinand chosen Prince of Bulgaria.—The
recent development of events in Bulgaria is most
important for us to understand.   In 1886, Prince
Alexander of Battenberg was dethroned by the
emissaries, machinations, and intrigues of Russia, and
his restoration was prevented by the Czar, and the
great European powers would not lift a finger on his
behalf.   Then, although the Prince returned to
Bulgaria for a few days to appoint a Regency to
govern the Principality, he finally retired from
Bulgaria, and could not be persuaded to return at the
urgent request of the Bulgarian people.   The Czar of
Russia looked upon Prince Alexander as a rebel against
Russia for uniting Bulgaria and Eastern Roumelia,
and for placing himself at the head of a United
Bulgarian people in contradiction to the wishes of the
Czar, and perhaps, as I am inclined to believe, contrary
to previous engagements of Prince Alexander himself.
Subsequent to his capture, deportation, and abdication,
he refused to be re-elected to the throne of Bulgaria.
Then, the Regents appointed by him began to look
out for a successor to the Bulgarian throne.   For a
considerable time, all their efforts to find a successor
were in vain, or were defeated by the Czar, who,
besides being incensed at the union of Bulgaria and
Eastern Roumelia, wished a nominee of his own to be
placed on the Bulgarian throne.   The Czar's favourite
nominee was the Prince of Mingrelia; but the
Bulgarian people would have nothing to do with him
as their Prince.   What Russia really wished was a

Protectorate or an annexation of Bulgaria; or, at all events, control over the Bulgarian army and finances. The Bulgarians rightly considered that the realization of Russian aims in regard to their country inevitably ended, sooner or later, in the extinction of their independence, and in the annexation of their country to Russia. The Regents, therefore proceeded to govern the Principality to the best of their ability, and they succeeded to a degree which surprised most people in Europe. While in office, the Regents governed the Principality with prudence and wisdom at home. Nay more, by a mission which they sent to the courts of Great Britain and of all the great European powers, they opened the eyes of a good many persons to the intrigues of Russia against Bulgarian freedom, and secured an effective, if not a general, adherence to their views and line of policy. In fact, as Dr. Falk said in November 1887, amidst the ringing cheers of the Hungarian Diet, "The Bulgarians by their prudence and wisdom have earned their independence and freedom."

Bulgaria and the Treaty of Berlin.—That the Union of Eastern Roumelia with Bulgaria was a breach of the Treaty of Berlin cannot be doubted. But that this Union has been permanently effected to all intents and purposes is beyond all question. That the Assembly of the Sobranje, or General Assembly, of Bulgaria and Eastern Roumelia for the election of a Prince in 1887, was contrary, or at least not conform to that Treaty cannot be denied. But, in consequence of the avowed hostility of Russia, the circumstances were peculiar, and something had to be done by the Bulgarians to enable them to escape from the embroglio which had arisen. The main purpose of the clauses of

the Treaty of Berlin, in 1878, in regard to Bulgaria,
were intended by the Great Powers as the means of
effecting the freedom of Bulgaria, under the suzerainty
of the Sultan, and yet they had been used by Russia
for the purpose of defeating this purpose. Therefore,
while Austria, Germany, and France agreed with
Russia in reference to the technical objections which
Russia raised against the strict legality of the Sobranje,
Austria, Italy, and Britain would not sanction any
hostile action by Russia against Bulgaria by means of
a Russian, or other foreign occupation of the Principality. In July 1887, the Grand Sobranje unanimously
elected Prince Ferdinand, who subsequently accepted
the nomination of the representatives of the people
of Bulgaria and Eastern Roumelia. Austria, Germany,
and Russia protested against his election; but have
left matters to take their course. Since his election,
Prince Ferdinand has, several times, been asked to
abdicate and retire from Bulgaria; but he refused to
comply, and says that so long as the Bulgarian people
stand by him, he will stand by them. He has now
been crowned Prince of Bulgaria, and is ready to make
his submission to the Sultan as his suzerain. Since
his elevation to the throne of Bulgaria, Prince
Ferdinand has shown wonderful pluck and resource,
prudence and discretion, in the difficult part he has had
to play; and the country has made considerable advance
towards peaceful consolidation and independence.
He has said that he will spend his life for a free and
independent Bulgaria. We shall soon see how far he can
stand by his brave words. In his efforts to defend,
maintain, and consolidate, the peace, prosperity,
and union of Bulgaria and Eastern Roumelia, all lovers

of freedom must wish him success.   Let the Bulgarians
be patient, and they will, I believe, succeed in baffling
their enemies and in securing their independence.

Future Bulgarian prospects.—The policy of absolutely excluding all foreign interference has worked
admirably well, and may, I hope and believe, be
worked with the same result for some time to come, or,
at all events, for the present and the immediate future.
How long Russia will allow Bulgaria to enjoy the
present happy condition of things in 1888, I do not
venture to predict; because France and Russia, Servia
and Bulgaria, may become at any moment, and might
have become any day for the last few years, grave
centres of European disturbances, which would inevitably end in a great European war.   While the peace of
Europe rests on such a precarious foundation as it
does at the present moment, we have to be thankful
that a great European war has not yet broken out.
The Bulgarian game of Russia was, and still is, to
regain the virtual predominating influence which
she had under the Treaty of Berlin, and which
she lost by the arrogant and blustering conduct
of her own Bulgarian Representatives.   That
game was, and still is, to get Bulgaria reduced to
a state of anarchy; then, to interfere in the Principality
by an armed force; and then, to declare that she cannot depart.   The Czar's interpretation of the Treaty
of Bulgaria is, that he was to be supreme in Bulgaria,
and, at the very least, as powerful in Bulgaria as
Austria was in Bosnia and Herzegovina.   Germany
has apparently favoured this view, and the events
which followed the Russo-Turkish war did the same
to all intents and purposes.   But Austria, Italy, and

Britain are against this view. In consequence of these diverse and opposing views, Prince Ferdinand has become *de facto* ruler of Bulgaria, and his position becomes stronger and stronger every day in the country of his adoption. Still, according to international law, he is not *de jure* ruler, and his position is, therefore, proportionately insecure. He has never, in fact, been recognised by any of the Great Powers as Prince of Bulgaria, and is not likely to be so until Russia voluntarily abandons her passive attitude, or a great European war breaks out, and solves the Bulgarian problem by the sword. Monsieur Stambouloff, the present prime minister of Bulgaria, like Prince Ferdinand, is in favour of the independence and extension of Bulgaria to the ancient dimensions of the Bulgarian Empire. But Monsieur Karaveloff, and a large number of the Bulgarian army with Pro-Russian or Pansclavonic aspirations, are in favour of the union of Bulgaria with or in subordination to Russia. Russia is determined, if possible, to get Bulgaria into her own hands in some way or other. Austria is determined that Russia shall not suceed in her Bulgarian aims. Further, the responsible statesmen of Austria, Germany, Italy, and Britain all declare that Bulgaria is not worth a great European war. Is Bulgaria, then, to be sacrificed to Russian ambition and continental necessities? No; by no means. The explanation of the whole matter is, that the Great Powers will endeavour to postpone hostilities as to Bulgaria, or any other pending dispute, as long as possible, and that they will settle the Bulgarian question, and some other questions and disputes between themselves, when they break out into a war begun by Russia, or France, or by Russia and France combined, in an effective manner, and will also establish the peace of Europe on something like a permanent basis, by imposing such terms of peace on the future offenders against the peace of Europe as are now established by existing Treaties, and as will cripple such offenders for any aggressive operations for a long time to come.   Primarily the Austro-Germanic-Italian alliance is meant to maintain the *status quo* in Europe, but it has also many far-reaching consequences in the event of a great European war.   Moreover, the policy of France is to regain her lost provinces of Alsace and Lorraine.   The policy of Russia is to be seated at Constantinople, and to become a great Mediterranean power.   As regards South-Eastern Europe, the permanent fact in the situation is that Russia is carrying out, and will, in future, try to carry out, the great traditional policy of Peter the Great, and make Russia the predominating and supreme power in the Eastern and Western Hemispheres.   That policy means the universal supremacy of Russia over all the nations of the world, and can never, and ought never, to be allowed to be realized.   France, for her own ends, is, at present, not unwilling to help Russia towards the partial realization of Russian policy.   Frenchmen would, perhaps, prefer an alliance with Russia and also with this country ; but an Anglo-French-Russian alliance at present is a wild, fantastic, and impossible dream. Mark what I am now going to say.   If Russia should make war on Austria, neither Italy nor Britain can long remain passive observers of the war.   As Italy is the close ally of Austria and Germany, and as we are and must be the allies of Italy in the defence of the *status quo* in the Mediterranean, we might be called on, at any moment, to strengthen and defend our fortresses and fleet in the Mediterranean, and, at once, be involved in a war between Austria and Russia, or between Germany and France.

Progress of Confederation in the Balkans.—All the Balkan States must have powerful allies to defend them. Therefore, while sometimes Russia, and sometimes Austria, predominates in their councils, the policy of all the Balkan States is one of neutrality or of national aggrandisement. This is also the policy of Roumania, which, under certain circumstances, would, as in 1878, be forced to assist Russia in the dismemberment and destruction of Turkey; but, under certain other conditions, *e.g.* by treaty obligations between Austria and Roumania, she might be induced strenuously to oppose Russian progress towards Constantinople. Roumania, and Servia and Bulgaria have all been national and patriotic and anti-Russian ever since the last Russo-Turkish war; because they all clearly saw that Russia aimed, not at their enfranchisement from Turkish slavery, but at their own subjugation to the Russian yoke, and at the advancement of aims which were destructive of their own national interests and aspirations. On the whole, Bulgaria, Servia, and Roumania, will, I think, look to the West for protection, and not to Russia. The Balkan States must, therefore, confederate together for their common protection and defence, or submit to be ruled by Austria or Russia. In the Balkans, Austria and Russia have the deepest interests at stake, and cherish the strongest jealousy against each other. There, the contest between them is for the leadership of the Balkan States; but the immediate object of Austria is to get down to Salonica,

and of Russia, to get possession of Constantinople.
The rivalry of these two great military powers does
not stop there. It involves their very existence as
great powers in Europe. The Balkan States, with
such powerful and warlike neighbours as Austria and
Russia surrounding them on every side, are too weak
to stand by themselves. They must gravitate towards
Austria, supported by Germany, or fall to Russia, or
confederate by themselves under a European
guarantee of neutrality. Another solution is, the
extension of the kingdom of Greece as far as, and so
as to include, all the Balkan States. This is the
Hellenic idea, and is frequently seen cropping up in
the shape of Hellenic excitement in Thrace, Macedonia,
and Thessaly. We live in an age of historical
revivals. As fondly as an ambitious and dispossessed
heir anxiously desires to get back to his paternal
acres, so do rising states anxiously desire to get back
to their conditions of former glory. For the present,
there is no firm or permanent solution possible. But,
in virtue of the Treaty of Berlin, Eastern Roumelia,
Bulgaria, and Herzegovina act as the outlying
bulwarks of Constantinople and Vienna against Pansclavonic aspirations and aggressions. In the meantime, the Balkan States themselves are making rapid
progress towards a confederation of some sort amongst
themselves. The policy of Austria in the Balkan
peninsula is based on the principle of excluding Russia
from asserting any forcible or military supremacy
over Bulgaria, and on the non-intervention of herself or
any other foreign power; on the development of the
independence and confederation of the Balkan States;
and on the maintenance of her present influence in the

Balkans, and of her supremacy on the Danube. This policy has received the sanction of Italy and Germany, and has also been approved of by England. It has also far-reaching consequences in regard to the Mediterranean, in which Austria, Italy, and Britain are deeply interested, and in which their interests have now been recognised by these three great military and naval powers as being practically identical. With the policy of Balkan independence, all the Balkan States are at one with the great central European powers. Under the guidance and protection of the Great Powers of Europe, this Balkan Confederation, I hope, will become an accomplished fact. It would most assuredly be the best solution for us, and the whole of Europe, and was the one most favoured by the great Lord Stratford de Radcliffe. But, on the other hand, although for different reasons, France and Russia do not agree with the Balkan policy of these great European powers. Russia makes no secret of her intention to avail herself of the first favourable opportunity of gaining a predominating influence in Bulgaria, and consequently, in the Balkan States generally, to enable her to carry out her traditional policy against Turkey, and plant her eagles on the church of St. Sophia. At sea, the French and Russian fleets can do nothing against Germany, or Austria, or Turkey, or Italy, or Spain, in opposition to the combined fleets of Britain and Italy. Hence the importance of the attitude of Britain and Italy in the conflict which I believe—I hope I may be wrong—is rapidly approaching, and which will pass over Europe like an overwhelming whirlwind in its suddenness and destructiveness.

Austrian and Russian rivalries for the succession of the Turkish Empire.—Austrian policy is clearly shown by her railway policy—as, for example, the railway between Metrovitza, the last stage on the Salonica line, and Salonica,—a railway, which would give to Austria' an opening to the Ægean for her trade, and thereby, in the course of time, for her political influence. By Turkish concessions, made in 1882, as to the Balkan railways, the railways to be built were to be constructed, by the month of October 1886, between Vienna and Constantinople and Salonica, through Pesth, Sophia, and Belgrade for traffic and passengers, and to be on the continental gauge, and not on the Russian. One of the railways now referred to runs from Vienna through Pesth, Belgrade, Sophia, and Salonica to Constantinople, and the other through Pesth, Belgrade, and Salonica. This railway policy is no new scheme. In 1872, a Convention was entered into between Austria and Turkey for an extension of railways, which were intended for the defence of Turkey. But that Convention was afterwards seen to be insufficient. Therefore, in order to defend and develop the territory covered by the Convention of 1872, and to satisfy local aspirations, that Convention has been modified by arrangements between Austria and Servia of a politico-commercial nature for defensive and offensive operations. Austria's policy then was disarmament; but it has been found to be impossible of realization. Railway communication between Vienna and Constantinople will soon be completed, and will have an important bearing and effect in any war by

Russia against Austria or Turkey. The old Turkish party is opposed to railways and Western civilization. All the same, the European powers, on grounds of high European policy, urge, promote, and enforce the construction of military and commercial railways in Turkey against all and every opposition. In the end of 1881, war nearly broke out between Austria and Russia in consequence of their rivalries in the Balkans. But Germany kept them from fighting. To get down to the Ægean, Austria requires the help of Servia, and she is not likely to get that on easy terms; for Servia has her own aspirations in regard to Macedonia, and yet Macedonia is necessary for Austria to enable her to get down to Salonica on the Aegean. The key to the situation in the Balkan peninsula since 1878 is that, by an arrangement between Austria and Germany, nothing can be done in the Balkans without Austria's consent. Nay more, the key of the European situation is, that the Eastern question must not be reopened for the present, May 1888, and that the Treaty of Berlin must be maintained. The policy of Austria is to extend the territories of Austria to Salonica, and to uphold her influence as supreme in the Balkans. The Eastern problem really is this : Whether Turkey, or Austria, or Russia is to hold Constantinople. Now, no matter what the Emperor of Austria, or his advisers, might be inclined to do by partitioning Turkey, the Hungarians will not allow Russia to obtain peaceful possession of Constantinople. In the composite Austro-Hungarian Empire, the Hungarians are very powerful in numbers and wealth ; and will therefore have a very great influence in deciding on the ultimate foreign policy of the Austro-Hungarian

Empire. But the Teutonic element in Austria-Hungary is the most powerful element in the Austro-Hungarian Empire. The Austrian Empire is largely Sclavonic, and is a state composed of very different and opposing elements, and is, indeed, a conglomeration of races and religions. Amongst the peoples of Austro-Hungary there is much friction and opposition. Towards the Emperor himself there is the greatest devotion by all of them, even by the Croates, who have given Austria the greatest recent trouble of all. In Austria, nearly one-half of the population are Sclaves; but the leaders and the governors are Hungarians and Germans. The most powerful element in Austria is Teutonic, and that element is naturally supported by Germany. Kossuth predicted the separation of Austria and Hungary, and urged Hungary to join Bosnia and Herzegovina, Servia and Russia. He was a Radical, and was opposed to the union of Austria and Hungary. He suffered exile in 1849 for his opposition to the House of Hapsburg. In January 1882, the Sclave population between the Black Sea and the Adriatic—in Dalmatia, which is roughly equivalent to Bosnia and Herzegovina— were in a very excited condition,—a condition which might have brought about a serious explosion at any moment. Bosnia and Herzegovina have been subjected to Austrian military service, and will, no doubt, be formally annexed by Austria on the earliest opportunity.

Austria as the heir of Turkey in Europe.—Turkey, is, I fear, doomed to destruction, in spite of Austrian, German, and British support. She is dying away by a nearly incurable disease. She cannot support herself;

and, for nearly two centuries, has become smaller every generation. Her officials are eating out her heart, and drinking up her best blood. She is dying of exhaustion and inanition. No power on earth can restore her for generations,—perhaps not for centuries, —probably never. It is bad enough to national unity and greatness to be governed by different laws, and to be placed under different judges according to nationality, as in Turkey; but to be so, and to find the peoples all devoted to their own selfish interests, is fatal to national existence. What power, then, is to succeed her? I say that Austria is the natural successor of Turkey in Europe. She stopped the progress of the Crescent in 1683, and fought boldly and well for the religion and civilization of Europe against the barbarism, militarism, and Mahomedanism of the Ottomans.

Russia's proposal for a partition of Turkey rejected by Austria in 1882.—The partition of Turkey has often been discussed, and under various conditions. A suggestion, for example, has been made for an alliance between Russia and France with the view of obtaining Constantinople for Russia, and Egypt for France. Before such a division could be carried out, Turkey must be defeated, and Britain and Austria must abandon their traditional policy in regard to Turkey. The Sultan has an army of 100,000 men in European Turkey; and in a month he can raise his army to 250,000, and in six weeks to 700,000 men. The Turkish forces are stationed in Constantinople, Adrianople, Macedonia, Epirus, Albania, Salonica, Scutari, and Erzeroum. Therefore, even as against Turkey alone, a hostile force has a difficult undertaking to accomplish before success crowned its efforts. No doubt, in European Turkey and Egypt, there are Christians as well as Mahomedans who have fought and shed each others' blood for ages; but the Christians and the Mahomedans have to be defeated before the Sultan's power in Europe is totally destroyed. All our own national interests are best secured by the Turkish Empire being maintained in its present dimensions; and the chief and dominating objects of Austria are equally strong for maintaining the *status quo* as to Turkey. But to carry out this policy effectively, and for any length of time, the corruption, and the treachery, and the impotence of Turkish officials must be extirpated, and greater liberty and freedom must be conceded to the rising nationalities of Turkey, and greater local government must be extended to them than hitherto. Reforms are also needed in Turkey to develop the great natural and material resources of the Turkish Empire. If, however, Turkey is to be destroyed, as it may well be in the next great European war, the question at once will arise, who is to be the Sultan's successor? This question, as I have already said, is the Eastern question. Russia says by her sovereign and by her foreign ministers that Russian policy is for peace; but still, all the same, she, in fact, prepares for war, and concentrates huge masses of troops on the Austrian and German frontiers. How long are these hollow pretences to continue? How long are we to wait for the war arrays, and the booming of artillery of hostile armies? About the end of 1882, a Russian Mission, under Count Lobanou, was sent from St. Petersburg to Vienna, to propose the partition of Turkey between Austria and Russia. Still more, indeed quite recently, rumours have been floating about the air as to the partition of the Ottoman Empire in the event of its bursting to pieces by its own weakness, corruption, and incapacity. I place no reliance on such rumours, which are merely guesses at probabilities by persons more or less acquainted with the secret causes at work. One of these rumours was that, in the partition of Turkey, Austria would extend her territory down to and be inclusive of Salonica; Germany would get Syria; Italy, Tripoli; and Russia, Constantinople; and, strange to say, France was to get nothing. This partition is ingenious; but is never likely to be put in force. If it ever took place, it would not, from its nature, last a generation. At the same time, let us be under no delusion. If we are not prepared to assist and defend our own interests, anything is possible as regards the partition of Turkey, or our supremacy in the Mediterranean, or our sovereignty in India. Whatever might be Austria's own inclinations in this matter, there were some men, in high and influential positions, not unfavourably disposed to the proposal of a partition, and yet they are most assuredly opposed to Count Andrassy's and Prince Bismarck's views. The influence of Prince Bismarck prevailed in 1882, and the proposed partition was rejected. The policy of Count Andrassy and Prince Bismarck was a close alliance between Austria and Germany, on the basis of the *status quo* in Europe, and one which would draw Italy and Servia towards them. But a joint alliance of Austria and Russia meant an aggressive policy against Turkey, and the partition of the Ottoman Empire between them. Prince Bismarck is opposed to this

aggressive policy; because Germany would be thereby
weakened in her policy of defence against France.
Still, there is a strong Anti-German feeling slumbering
in the breasts of the Austrian people. This arises
from a suspicion that Austrian policy is being too
much subordinated to German policy. But the
Austro-German alliance is strong by the hatred which
exists in Hungary against Russia, and by the wishes
of official and parliamentary Hungary and official
Austria.

4.—FRENCH AND GERMAN POLICY.

Long feud between France and Germany.—Between
France and Germany there has been a long and bitter
feud, which was intensified by the late war between
these two countries, that is to say, between Prussia and
her allies on the one hand, and France on the other.
For more than half a century, Prussia has been slowly
recovering from the injuries inflicted upon her by
France in the early part of this century, when the
King of Prussia was defeated by Napoleon I. Shortly
after that time, when the old Holy Alliance was dissolved by Napoleon I., the Netherlands were taken
from the German Empire, with Austria at its head,
and the Italian cities and the Rhine provinces were
torn from the German Empire, and South Germany
was broken into fragments. Prussia, however, as you
know, by taking the place of Austria in the Germanic
Empire, became, in our day, the head and leading power
of Germany; and the German national idea, under the
steadfast and courageous action of the late Emperor
William, was made a reality. In this great work, he

was ably supported by the military genius of Count Von Moltke, and the political sagacity of Prince Bismarck. The annexation to Prussia of Alsace and Lorraine at the conclusion of the late Franco-German war, after Alsace from 1681, and Lorraine from 1766, had been in the possession of France, has left a deadly feeling of hostility in the breasts of the French people against the present German Empire. The result is, that both parties are armed to the teeth, in the anticipation of an early and inevitable conflict between them.

Republican France.—Besides, France may, at any moment, be in the throes of a great national and internal revolution. The French people are heavily burdened with taxes, civil and military. They are dissatisfied with their present rulers. They seem to have no confidence in their present form of government, which may, ere long, be overthrown, and a monarchical, or despotic, form of government be adopted by them in its stead. If the French Republic should be overthrown, and Parliamentary Despotism, or Military Despotism, be established in France, the Chief of the State would be certain to be a soldier, or be ruled by the army. The result of that state of things would be, at least such is the belief in Germany, that an inevitable and speedy effort would be made by France to defeat Germany in war, and reconquer the lost provinces of Alsace and Lorraine, and break up the present German Empire. Some people may say that a war by France against Germany with such objects in view is insane; but their views of the matter will count for nothing with those who will have the decision in their hands. France is a great military power; but it is an unstable power. She even now boasts that she is the greatest military power in the

world, and she is making stupendous efforts to perfect
her offensive and defensive armaments at an enormous
cost. She is nearly at the end of all her politicians
of any eminence in public affairs. She may become
the victim of a charlatan and a humbug.

Boulangerism and French integrity.—The rise of the
coming saviour of France, in the person of General
Boulanger, is a surprise to most people ; and yet ought
not to be so in the present condition of political society
in France. Whatever may be General Boulanger's
views and ultimate aims, he is an opponent of the
present Parliamentary and Republican Government of
France, and he says that he is a true supporter of a
National Republican Government. What part is he
to play in the internal and external affairs of France ?
Is he to play the part of the Protector Cromwell, or of
General Monk ? Is he, in other words, to play the
part of Dictator, or that of the Restorer of the old
Monarchical family of France ? My expectation is
that he will try to play the part of Cromwell, and
that he will bring on another Franco-German war, and
be pitched from his temporary throne, and that he will
bring his country to disgrace and ruin. No matter what
General Boulanger says and wishes, Boulangerism means
the abrogation of constitutional government, anarchy,
and civil war, and probably foreign war as well. What,
I ask, does Boulangerism mean according to its authors
and supporters ? It means, they say, the integrity
and greatness of France. Integrity and greatness ?
When ? If before the late Franco-German war, that
means war with the German Empire and with its allies,
Austria-Hungary and Italy, so soon as General
Boulanger declares himself in favour of a *plebiscite*,

or appeals to the people to support him in destroying
the present form of French republican government. He
asks for a dissolution of the present National Assembly,
and also for a revision of the present constitution
of France, on the principles of the Revolution of
1789, *i.e.* no President and no Senate. The
Revolution of 1789 was the embodiment of pure
Jacobinism, and ended in the Military Empire of
Napoleon I. Its mottoes were, and are still, "No
religion, no morality, and no government." Are we to
have another repetition of ancient history in France?
Are we soon to have another great social and political
upheaval in France? Suppose he gets his revision of
the Constitution, and is elected President with dicta-
torial power, he would soon find that he must rest his
possession of power on the strength of the French army,
and on giving it employment in a war against Germany
or ourselves. The possibilities of the near future on
the Continent of Europe are discouraging and humili-
ating to all lovers of peace and civil progress in
Europe. The permanent factor of the Franco-German
situation is, that Germany will never give up Alsace
and Lorraine to France, unless at the point of the
sword, and after a crushing and irremediable defeat.
A war between France and Germany for Alsace and
Lorraine will be Titanic in its proportions, and stupendous in its results. Consequently, Germany has
entered into an offensive and defensive alliance with
Austria and Italy for the maintenance of the *status quo*
established by the Treaty of Frankfort in 1870, and
for the protection of Austria against Russia, and of
Italy against France. As yet, France has no reliable
ally in the whole world.

A forecast of future events.—We must never forget that France wishes to extend her influence in the Mediterranean—*e.g.* in North Africa, and in Morocco as well as in Tunis and Algeria, and that these wishes are adverse to the cherished aims of Italy and Spain. Moreover, the commercial and maritime policy of Italy and Spain are directly opposed to the commercial and maritime policy of France. The aims of France and Russia in the Mediterranean are alone sufficient to explain why Italy and Spain are rather in sympathy with German and Austrian policy than with French and Russian policy; for neither Italian nor Spanish interests and aims would be promoted by France, or Russia, converting the Mediterranean into a French, or a Russian, lake. Naturally enough, however, Spain wishes to be at peace, and on friendly terms, with all the Great Powers, and consequently is no party to the Austro-Germanic-Italian alliance. But she has aspirations of her own in regard to the future acquisition of Morocco. Spain holds that she, and not France, or any other European Power, can govern and civilize Morocco as she herself can. In this view, Italy and Britain will have something to say. Thus, here again the Mediterranean problem emerges amidst the conflicting interests and claims of Spain, Italy, France, and Britain. Then, again, Greece has a great part to play in any great future European war. If she can have patience, she will reap the fruits of the strong friendly feelings of Italy, Austria, Germany, and Britain. She must, however, have a regard for Bulgarian aspirations as well as her own; because Bulgaria and Greece set up diverse claims, and are supported by antagonistic interests. Greece must learn that she herself can accomplish nothing

in the way of realizing the Hellenic idea, or the Union of
all Greece and the Balkans in a compact and strong
confederation, and, perhaps, the restoration of the
ancient Byzantine Empire of Greece, nor even the
annexation of Epirus, Macedonia, and Crete, with the
view of obtaining Constantinople at some future time.
For all these purposes, active intrigues have been taking
place since 1878.   But with such allies as I have just
indicated, she can be raised, at no distant period, from a
minor power to a first or second class kingdom.   Still
further, Poland will also play a great part in the
approaching war—if war there must be—and she will
probably be restored to the rank of a united kingdom,
under the guidance and supremacy of Austria, or
Germany, and as a future barrier and bulwark against
Russian aggression and encroachment in Europe, and
for the defence of Austria and Germany, and also of
Europe and Western civilization.   Poland, you will
remember, was thrice partitioned, namely, (1) in 1772;
(2) in 1793; and (3) in 1796.   Unquestionably the
restoration of the Polish kingdom would have the
most important consequences to Russia, but it would
not be injurious to the peace of Europe. ˙ It will not,
however, take place unless at the end of a successful
war against Russia by Austria and Germany.   It will
never take place as a peaceful solution, based on the
advantages and interests of Europe.

Russian policy is also against the Turkish Empire.
—There are two policies in Russia.   One policy is
known as the Russian Traditional, Muscovite, or
Pansclavonic policy, and has always been directed
against the Turkish Empire, and is now directed
against the Austria-Hungarian Empire both as an end

and means,—that is to say, it is directed primarily against Austria-Hungary in order to compel the Austria-Hungarian people to allow Russia to take, occupy, and hold Constantinople ; and, secondarily, in order to draw all the Sclavonic races in Austria-Hungary to Russia herself. Again, you must never forget that the Pansclavonic or National aspirations of the Russian people are religious as well as political, and are meant to bring about the union of all the Sclavonic peoples into one Church—namely, the Eastern Church—and into one state or nationality under the Czar, who is the head of the Russian Empire and also of the Eastern Church. Whether primarily or secondarily, this policy of Russia would necessarily end in the destruction of the Austro-Hungarian Empire. Of the Russian national policy, the greatest official representatives are Count Schouvaloff and General Ignatieff. This Russian Policy is backed up and supported by the Russian army and people. It was the predominating factor in the last Russo-Turkish war, and was the cause of the so-called Bulgarian atrocities. The other policy is the Russian court, official, or St. Petersburg policy. Its greatest official representative is Monsieur Giers, who, after all, is but the hand of the Great Czar—who, although intensely national, is himself a great friend of peace. But the Czar himself can be a lover of peace no longer than may be consistent with the maintenance and increase of his power.

The Russian people may force the Czar's hand.— Whatever may be the views of the Czar himself as to war against Austria, or against Turkey, his hand may be forced by his people, as his father's hand was forced in 1878 ; and, then, the Czar, in self-defence, will, no doubt, prefer war against Austria, or Turkey, or Britain, or any other great power, rather than have civil war in his own country. Besides, Russia is pre-eminently a military despotism, and its most powerful classes are to be found in the army. In Russia, the rulers are the military classes; and there are no middle classes as in our own and other European countries. The military people in Russia hold the power and authority of the country in their hands. There are 80,000,000 of agriculturists in Russia; but they have no power in the Russian Government. In the event of a war by Russia against Turkey, Roumania and Austria will, I expect, oppose the passage of the Russians across the Danube. This plan was settled sometime ago, and will no doubt be eventually carried out; for Austria and Roumania are deeply interested in opposing Russia in any attempt to get on the south side of the Danube. For, if Russia were able to extend her territories to the south side of the Danube, all the Balkan States between the Alps and the Carparthians, down to the Bosphorus and the Dardanelles, and the Adriatic, would be subordinated to the Russian Empire, and Russia would become a great Mediterranean power. The Danube passes through Austria, Servia, and Roumania, and then enters the Black Sea. Stationed on the south side of the Danube, Russia could threaten Venice in the Italian, and Vienna in the Austrian kingdoms.

5.—RUSSIAN POLICY IN EUROPE AND ASIA.

Russian policy in Europe and Asia.—Russia has her eyes steadily fixed on the possession of Armenia,

which would help her towards the realization of her
dreams in a twofold direction, namely, (1) in the
direction of Constantinople, which is the great object
of her desire in Europe; and (2) in the direction of
India, which is the great object of her desire in Asia.
To gain command over Constantinople, she is pushing
forward her schemes to get strong fortifications into
her possession on the north of the Dardanelles, and
the Sea of Marmora, and also in the Balkans, and on
the banks of the Danube. She thus hopes to place
the Sultan of Turkey and his Empire under her feet.
A huge, barbaric power, and military nation, like
Russia, established in Constantinople, on the confines
of the Mediterranean, and acting like one man at the
will of the Czar, the Autocrat of Russia, would be a
grave danger to the peace and civilization of Europe.
Russia at Constantinople would also probably mean a
high protective tariff against our merchandise, and in
favour of her own, in all the present territories of the
Sultan, and also in the Steppes of Central Asia, to a
greater extent than ever. Moreover, Constantinople
in the hands of Russia means the Russian control of
Egypt and the Suez Canal, and the creation of Russia
as a Mediterranean power. Therefore, it would
involve the abandonment of our supremacy in the
Mediterranean, unless at an enormously increased
expense; and might also involve serious dangers to
our Indian Empire at no distant period.

Russian threats and their possible effects.—Russia
has, or can easily have, a plausible ground for war
against Turkey; for the Sultan is seldom able to pay
to the Czar the war indemnity agreed to be paid by
Turkey to Russia at the end of the last Russo-Turkish

war in 1878. We have already heard threats uttered by Russia against Turkey for the non-payment of this indemnity, and of seizures by Russia in Asia Minor for the protection of Russian interests, and also of Erzeroum, and perhaps of Armenia, in security for this indemnity. Russia is now, May 1888, and has for months, been collecting large masses of troops on her Austrian and German frontiers, and apparently expects soon to be able to force a solution of the great Eastern question in her own favour. Unless the other great powers are prepared to oppose her, she will be able so to do, and will unquestionably do it. But, all the same, Russia is a Colossus of clay, and not of brass and iron ; and is incapable of long, or successfully, contending against the great Western powers, who are very differently situated as to naval and military powers and financial resources from Turkey, or the Asiatic hordes who have been pounded into dust by her. She has long been engaged in her old game of stirring up disturbances in Asia Minor, Trans-Caucasia, and especially in Kurdistan, Armenia, and even Macedonia. According to her usual well-known methods, she is preparing the way in those regions for political disturbances, to be followed by Russian intervention and annexation as far as may be necessary, or prudent. Russia is clearly playing a waiting game. Indeed, she is believed not to be ready for war with Turkey, or Austria, till 1889. At present, she does not wish to enter into an alliance with Republican France. Nay more, if, by means of a European congress or conference, or by an agreement or an understanding with the great monarchical powers of Europe, the Czar could accomplish his ends as to Constantinople, he would gladly, and without delay, come to terms with Austria, Germany, Italy, and Britain. But his people, and especially the military classes, and the Pansclavists in Russia, are eager for war, and may not, and almost certainly will not, have patience to wait for a Franco-German war, which would possibly enable Russia to get all she wants, or, at least, as much as would satisfy her for a time.

The Triple Alliance and Britain are for the status quo *of Berlin Treaty.*—But, then, the policy of Austria, Germany, Italy, and Britain is the maintenance of the Treaty of Berlin. Russia is opposed to this Treaty, and will break through it on the earliest opportunity, and will try to get control over Bulgaria. Bulgarian independence is a matter of primary importance to Europe, and above all to Austria-Hungary, which is largely inhabited by Sclavs ; for, if Russia were on the south side of the Danube, Austria-Hungary would soon be undermined by Russia. If standing by herself, she would crumble to pieces in a very short space of time. Lord Beaconsfield was ready to go to war with Russia, if the Czar insisted on the maintenance of the Treaty of San Stephano. Why ? Because that Treaty utterly destroyed the Turkish Empire, and put Russia in its place. Consequently, Russia, under that Treaty, would speedily have become a Mediterranean power, and, perhaps, all powerful in Europe and Asia. The Treaty of Berlin was a compromise by all parties to prevent, or, at all events, to postpone, a great European war. To have been effective, it should have been followed up by an alliance between the great European powers. But this alliance was never entered into in consequence of reasons which I hope to explain, at full length, on some future occasion.

The Austro-German League of Peace.—The Austro-German league of peace, in all its phases, which are not a few, has peace and mutual defence as its chief and final end. But it is really an expensive and exhausting process of armed neutrality; and every power involved is increasing its naval and military armaments on a colossal scale, and at a huge cost, and there is no end in sight of this mad rivalry. This league began in 1879, and was originally intended to comprehend Britain. But its original scope was limited by the defeat of the Conservative Government and the retirement of Lord Beaconsfield from public life in 1880, and by the return to office of a Liberal Government under Mr Gladstone. Its terms were published to the world at a critical time, in February 1888, when war appeared to be inevitable between Austria and Russia. It is based on the common interests of Austria and Germany, and also of all those powers whose interests in the European *status quo* are identical with their own. It is primarily directed against any attack on Austria by Russia, or by France on Germany.

Austro-German Treaty.—The precise terms of the Austro-Germanic-Italian alliance have of course never been divulged; but the general terms of the existing Treaty are well known. The last treaty between Austria and Germany and Italy was made, in November 1887, for five years, and was for an offensive and defensive alliance between them. Its main purpose was to maintain the freedom and independence of Europe on the basis of existing treaties. Its general aim was to prevent a disturbance in the present balance of European power; prevent any attack upon the Austrian or German Empires, and prevent Russia's advance to Constantinople, or her absorption of the Balkan States. In such circumstances, it is plain that a breach of the present treaties immediately raises the question of the free navigation of the Mediterranean, and also of the general peace and stability of the Continent. This Triple Alliance is based on the supposition that it can prevent Russia from carrying out her policy in the Balkans, and can keep France at bay, and can, if necessary, defeat a Russian and French alliance. It also tends to promote the confederation of the Balkan States.

It is important to Britain and other powers.—It also has important consequences as regards the Balkan States, and Turkey, and Britain; and is of such a nature as to compel those powers to join Austria, Germany, and Italy as a necessary consequence, or to abandon the defence of their vital interests. For example, if Austria were to be defeated by Russia, and France were to be at war with Germany, there would be grave danger of the equilibrium in the Mediterranean being disturbed: for, if Russia defeated Austria she could easily advance on Constantinople; and then, Germany being engaged in a deadly struggle with France, Russia would be able, if we stood aside, to destroy the Turkish Empire. We will not, I believe, allow Constantinople, or the Balkans, to fall into the hands of Russia; and we will, I hope, support those central European powers, who have the same aims as ourselves in peace and in war. Neither Germany, nor Austria, nor Italy, nor we, will sanction further concessions to Russia in Turkey, or against the Sultan, or against the semi-independent Balkan States. Still, we must keep in mind that neither Britain, nor Turkey, is within the limits, the rights, and obligations of the Austro-Germanic-Italian alliance, and that neither Britain, nor Turkey, is in alliance with Russia or with France. If a disturbance of the equilibrium in the Mediterranean should be effected, an alliance between the great naval powers of Britain and Italy, and, perhaps, also of Spain, is inevitable. Than the resuscitation of Spain, nothing has been more important in the recent history of Europe. Spain is not, at present, a great naval power. But she can place 100,000 men on her frontiers in the event of war between Italy and France. Even since 1884, there has practically been an understanding between Germany and Spain for mutual aid in peace or war. Observe, and never forget, that, if Germany is the greatest military power in the world, we are the greatest naval power in the world. We should, therefore, take care that we can defend our territories, and interests, and allies, and be feared as foes, and courted as friends, in all that concerns the advancement of the prosperity and civilization of the world. Russia is strong in defence, but not in attack. Germany is strong in attack, and needs the assistance which Austria can afford to give. Germany is between two great military powers. One of them, France, asserts undying hatred against her, and the other, Russia, expresses undying hatred against her nearest and best ally. The fast approaching war will come upon us like a thief in the night, like a sudden clap of thunder in a clear sky. In a moment, the sky will be darkened, swords will flash in the face of enemies, and volleys of artillery will be heard; and thrones, and principalities, and powers will be shaken to their foundations.

The Eastern Question.—Till recently, Germany left her north-eastern frontier nearly unprotected. But now, the old forts of Thorn, Posen, and Dantzic, on that frontier, have been converted into fortified camps. Similarly, Austria is taking defensive measures in Galicia; and Italy is doing the same on her French frontier. Austria and Hungary alone are weaker than Russia. Still, Bohemia, Moravia, and Hungary are well defended by their frontier mountain ranges. Galicia, which is a part of the ancient Polish kingdom, and has lately got self government bestowed upon it, to the great happiness and contentment of all its people, stands outside that range. Italy, Austria, and Germany are all taking defensive measures on the basis of their being allies, and on their being opposed to France and Russia. If war should be made against Russia by Austria and Germany, the allied powers will probably invade Russian Poland. Hence Warsaw is being defended to the utmost by Russia. If, on the other hand, Russia should invade Bulgaria, or try to capture Constantinople by land or sea, Austria would declare war against Russia, and strike a counter-stroke at Russia in Russian Poland, where we may naturally expect the Poles will rise against Russia. For Austria and Germany, the Eastern question is this : Are they to allow Russia to surround them, and to predominate in South-eastern Europe ? For us, the question is this : Are we to allow our commerce of £200,000,000 a year in and through the Mediterranean to be dominated, interfered with, or diminished by Russia seated at Constantinople, and raised to the rank of a Mediterranean power. By our Imperial interests, the people of our empire have the deepest interest in this great question of International and Foreign policy. Shall the people defend their rights and interests? or shall they act like cowards in their defence, and to the lasting injury of themselves and their posterity for ever? Peace I prize as one of God's greatest blessings. But peace at any price I detest and abhor; and I feel confident that the great mass of the people of this country will not surrender their glorious birthrights, and will uphold and defend them against the whole world. Shall we, I ask, be less ready to defend our country's rights and interests than our forefathers? I say no—never!

Position of the Austro-Hungarian Empire.—Austria is the pivot of the Eastern question; and Russia can never obtain Constantinople unless through Vienna. She is fighting against Russia for her very life as a great European power. She, like Russia, is Sclavonic, and is ruled by a German dynasty. The Czechs are Pansclavonic in their national proclivities. The Hungarians are thoroughly opposed to Pansclavonism. Austro-Hungary is a composite State, a dual Empire, and not one nationality. The Emperor of Austria is at its head; but there are grave elements of disruption within its territory. It is composed of the two great kingdoms of Austria and Hungary, together with subordinate kingdoms or principalities of Bohemians and Czechs, possessed of a considerable degree of self government in the form of separate legislatures, or diets, and separate executive local governments. Thus, Austria-Hungary is a grave danger to herself and her neighbours; for her various peoples have never been firmly welded into a united Empire. Bosnia and Herzegovina were placed under the protection of Austria, and have now been virtually annexed by her since the Treaty of Berlin. Some people say that Russia demands these two provinces for herself. I do not think so. Russia would be content with Bulgaria and Eastern Roumelia; but she can and will, I hope, get neither of them. Austria is bent on having and holding the supremacy of the Balkan peninsula. Russia is the same. Nothing less than the sword can finally solve the dispute; and, strange to say, Italy and Germany, her late foes, are to back her up in this supremacy against Russia.

The fundamental principle of the alliance is protection of the allied powers against Russia and France.— The Austro-German alliance is fundamentally based on the necessity of Austria defending herself against the risk of being destroyed by Russia; and on the necessity of Austria being prepared, at all hazards, to support Germany against any attack by France, or by France and Russia combined. Prince Bismarck, Count Kalnocky, Signor Crispi, and Lord Salisbury are all in favour of the maintenance of the Treaty of Berlin, which was deliberately founded on the defence of Austria against Russian aggression. When Count Andrassy was lately asked if there was to be war, he said, and rightly said, "Ask the Czar." As between Austria and Russia, this last question contains the whole Eastern problem in a nutshell. We live in the midst of an armed peace, which, as Prince Bismarck lately said, may break down in ten days, ten months, or ten years. Will Europe be content to remain in this condition much longer? I very much doubt it. Still, this policy of armed peace is better than war,

and has been admirably worked out by the wonderful
foresight and political sagacity of Prince Bismarck,
who is one of the greatest statesmen of any age, and
is, by far, the greatest statesman of the present age.
Prince Bismarck does not believe, and no wise statesman ever did believe, in the doctrines of sentimental
Radicals, that is to say, in governing an empire by the
momentary views and passions of the multitude.
Prince Bismark overthrew Austria and France in arms,
and built up the German Empire in spite of the covert
and open hostility of the majority of his countrymen
in Prussia, and also of the popular representatives of
his country. He is now determined to support the
German Empire thus established. German and
Austrian interests are not, in many respects, at all the
same; but the Prince has fixed on a wise system of
defence of Germany and Austria. Supported by their
allies, before and behind, for the protection of their interests and integrity, Austria and Germany cannot fail to
be successful as long as it is maintained. Austrian
policy depends for its success on the independence of the
Balkan States; and German policy on the isolation of
France. Prince Bismarck long based his foreign policy,
as far as possible, on a Russian alliance; and will never
willingly give offence to Russia. But he will not allow
his general views in this matter to interfere, in the
least degree, with the most perfect and steady adherence to the Austro-German Treaty of alliance.
Here we have the key to the present European situation. The Prince's policy has always been essentially
friendly to Russia; but he will not endanger the
German Empire by sacrificing Austria to her rival and
enemy. This policy, which is essentially one of en-

lightened selfishness, may be called narrow and selfish.
But it is that upon which alone any lasting compact
between nations can be based. Notwithstanding all
the shifting scenes of Austrian policy, one great
principle is clearly deducible from them all, namely,
the duty of defending Bulgaria and Roumania against
Russian aggression and Russian invasion. This is the
policy which Germany must support as a plain and
evident duty. Therefore, Prince Ferdinand of Bulgaria,
if he acts with ordinary prudence, need have no immediate fear of being expelled by Russia from Bulgaria.
Austria will not allow Russia to conquer Bulgaria, or
Roumania, and thereby become the successful and
armed head champion of the Sclavonic race. She
knows, or at least fears, that the conquest of Bulgaria,
or Roumania, is the death-knell of her national and
imperial existence as a great power.

Future prospects of war and its consequences.—
Again, while German policy is friendly to the Czar,
and is keenly alive to French hopes of recovering
Alsace and Lorraine, Germany is determined never to
surrender these provinces to France. Germany did
not annex them for their riches, or for their commerce,
or from any lust of territory. She annexed them on
military and political grounds, for her own defence
and the completion of her national unity. That
Germany is to stand up for the permanent annexation
of these provinces is the key of the present situation
in Germany. To do so effectually she must have
Austria as her friend and ally. Germany, in self-
defence, cannot and will not abandon Austria, or allow
a new grouping of the great powers against herself.
Nor can, nor will, Austria abandon Germany, and incur

the risk of speedy dissolution at the hands of the
Russian people, eagerly desiring her destruction. The
continental map of Europe has been greatly changed
since 1860 and 1870, or within the small space of
thirty years; and now Germany is determined to
consolidate her Empire against all the world. War
between Austria and Russia is not imminent at
present; but disarmament is impossible by any one
of the great powers. There is, I fear, another Franco-
German war looming hideously in the not very distant
future. In such a war, Germany, if successful, will
probably not add any French territory to the German
Empire; but would, no doubt, willingly gratify any of
her allies with a slice of French territory. But, if
successful, Germany would probably annex the chief
French colonial possessions to herself, and would also
annex all the Dutch seaboard towns. Are we acting
wisely by standing aloof? or should we join the
Austro-German alliance? In the circumstances which
have now been developed, I say that our policy should
be self-defence, and preparation to defend our interests
at home and abroad. We now hold the issues of
peace and war in our hands. Let us keep our faces
steadily looking towards peace as long as we can.
The Austro-German alliance has already kept the
peace for ten years. We may help this alliance, now
strengthened by Italy, to keep it a little while longer.

Austria and Germany must stand or fall together.—
Alas! the peace of Europe hangs on a very slender
thread. It may be broken at any moment. The
policy of the kings of Prussia has been, for the last
three generations, to be on friendly terms with Russia,
and it has been eminently successful and profitable for

Prussia. Indeed, the Russian Czars think that the kings of Prussia have had the best of the bargain, and certainly think that they themselves have not got their proper share of the plunder. Till within the last few years, this traditional policy of the Prussian sovereigns towards Russia had been rigidly and scrupulously observed. For some years past, a tacit, if not express, understanding existed between the late Emperor William and the present Czar that Russia should not cause a great European war in the lifetime of the late aged monarch. This understanding was held by Prince Bismarck to be inadequate for the security of the German Empire, and accordingly the German Military Septenate Act was passed last year, 1887, by the German Parliament. The life of the Emperor Frederick hangs in the balances of life and death; and the character of his heir and successor is unknown. Let us hope that the peaceful temper of the Emperor Frederick of Germany will be long preserved, in the interests of peace and civilization; and that a fierce, cruel, and bloody war in Europe will be averted, if not for ever, at least for a long time. But do not let us forget that Germany's great enemies are France and Russia; and that they have, or suppose they have, good reasons for being enraged at her, and for seeking revenge by war. Thus, France is Germany's enemy because she was defeated by Germany in the war of 1871, and because she lost Alsace and Lorraine in the contest, and wishes to regain them for herself. Then, Russia is Germany's enemy because Germany is, on principle and by self-interest, opposed to Russian Pansclavism, which aims at reorganizing the world on a new socialistic basis, and at destroying the

Austro-Hungarian Empire, and also at establishing a
universal dominion and supremacy over all the peoples
and nations of the world.   Beyond all question, the
Russian Pansclavists, whose headquarters are at
Moscow, hate Germany for shielding Austria-Hungary
and Turkey from their blows and clutches, and also for
aiding Austria-Hungary to prevent Russia from being
supreme in Bulgaria.   We may rest assured that Germany will be faithful to her alliance with Austria-
Hungary.   Germany may possibly act as the honest
broker in the division of the Turkish Empire between
Austria and Russia; but if such a partition ever takes
place, she will do her utmost to strengthen, not weaken,
Austria-Hungary in so doing.   Austria and Germany
must stand or fall together against the separate or combined forces of Russia and France.   That they are so
determined is shown by many facts and circumstances
well known to you as well as to me, and upon which I
hope to speak more at large on a subsequent occasion.
Sir Charles Dilke holds that Germany cannot save the
Austrian Empire from dismemberment and destruction.
But he takes, I think, too gloomy a view of the Austria-
Hungarian position and resources.   He forgets that
it is the interest of Germany to defend Austria as
much as it is Austria's interest to defend herself:
for, if Austria was destroyed as a great power, there
would be the greatest danger of the German Empire
bursting into pieces by the effects of the combined forces
of Russia and France.   For the present, Russia stands
aloof from the Austro-German alliance, but the
alliance stands firm and strong as ever; and, to use a
strong yet expressive phrase, is cornered and hemmed
in by the Austro-German and Italian alliance.   Still,

we ourselves must be prepared for every contingency in South-eastern Europe ; because Russia has great advantages on her side by the wonderful tenacity of her rulers and her people in carrying out their national and traditional policy.

7.—THE AUSTRO-GERMAN AND ITALIAN ALLIANCE.

Italy joined the Austro-German Alliance.—Italy is a party, and an important party, to the Austro-German alliance ; and may be called upon, as a great naval power, to take an active part in any contest by the three allied powers against Russia and France.   The original offensive and defensive treaty between Austria and Germany and Italy was made in 1882.   It was renewed in 1887 for five years.   No doubt, Italy has been influenced in her foreign policy, in joining this alliance, by considerations which, in certain events, would affect her unity and nationality, and her relations with the Pope as the spiritual head of the Church of Rome, and the former temporal sovereign of Rome and its dependent states and cities.   The King of Italy will fulfil his existing obligations to the Pope ; but he will never agree to restore the temporal power of the Pope over Rome, his capital city.   In 1870, Italian unity was crowned by the acquisition of Rome ; and Italian aspirations for the restoration of her nationality were satisfied.   Italy will not listen to a separation of Rome from the Italian kingdom, or to a restoration of the Papal temporal supremacy over Rome.   For five years, all the statesmen of Italy have directed their attention to the Austro-German alliance for the peace of Europe and the maintenance of Italian unity in the Levant and in the Mediterranean. This is another prime factor in the European situation. What Italy has most probably in view in her recently formed alliance with Austria and Germany is to maintain and strengthen her influence in the Mediterranean and the Red Sea, and to get Tripoli, and to consolidate the Italians into a great and united people. A Franco-Italian alliance is, at present, out of the question. Still, the French and the Italians belong to kindred races and civilizations, and have more natural affinities between them than exist between the Italians on the one hand, and the Austrians and Germans on the other, and consequently the Italian people will not be easily moved to fight against France unless for some strong and powerful reasons.

Spain and Turkey.—Spain may also be drawn to the side of the Germanic powers in the event of a European war. Turkey herself, although not admitted within the charmed circle of intimate and close alliance, is also, unless the partition of Turkey is to be the German solution of the Turkish problem, an important factor in the League of Peace. Further, Turkey will never agree, nay more, will never be allowed to agree, to an alliance with Russia, or to a protectorate under Russia, or to a neutrality in the event of a war between Austria and Russia. Still further, unless Russia, France, and Britain should be in alliance against the Germanic League of Peace, no great power of prophecy is required to enable one to predict that the Germanic powers and their allies are sufficiently powerful to prevail against any combination which can be brought against them.

8.—BRITISH POLICY.

Britain will not go to war against Austria and Germany and their allies.—As regards our own interests in the Bosphorus, the Dardanelles, and in Egypt, our interests coincide with those of the parties to the Germanic League of Peace, and not with those of France and Russia. That Britain should be the ally of France and Russia against Austria and Germany is such an absurd supposition, considering all the facts and circumstances, and the interests involved, that it may be summarily dismissed from our minds without further discussion. Again, an alliance for a general future policy between us and France and Russia, or between us and either of them, is suicidal and absurd. Still, we must keep in mind that, in order to obtain a continuance of peace, the great powers may be inclined to sacrifice some of the weaker powers, and thus bring about an understanding on a peaceful basis, or, at the end of a great European war, by a new redistribution of power in North or South Africa, in European or Asiatic Turkey, or in Persia or Afghanstan in Central Asia. An Anglo-French alliance has no stability in it; for French interests are diverse from and antagonistic to our own. A recent Liberal Government• of this country sacrificed our just rights and interests to gain the goodwill of France, and all to no purpose. We ought always to remember how the Anglo-French alliance as to Egypt came to an end in July 1882, and was productive of nothing except procrastination and surrender, ill-will and heart-burning. Again, France and Russia cannot be our allies so long as their policy is aggressive and hostile to the Sultan of Turkey in Asia or in Europe. As regards ourselves, I have the most perfect confidence that, so long as we look after our own interests, and our statesmen are as patriotic as their predecessors, no combination of the great powers can be formed to put us in a corner, or deprive us of necessary allies, without the world being shaken to its centre. We are for peace, and so are the German powers, and we should never hesitate to take those steps which are necessary to carry the Policy of Peace into effectual execution. The Austro-German League of Peace has preserved the peace of Europe for nearly ten years. Many signs around us portend that its strength and efficacy will soon be put to the test. In certain contingencies, we hold the balance of European power in our hands, and can more effectively advance the interests of European peace by keeping our hands free than by tying them under treaties of any kind. Upon this point the leading statesmen of this country are agreed, and have agreed to act for the present.

Our Foreign Policy should be just.—Our foreign policy should be just, and based on the honour and integrity of our Empire. We should not be timid or aggressive, but courageous and self-reliant. The past history of our country, of the British Empire, is like a grand, noble epic poem in action. It is a grand display of noble deeds in the civilization of the world. It is not surpassed by the history of any other nation which has existed in the past, or in the most cultivated or heroic ages. As hitherto, so in future, we should defend ourselves, our allies, our colonies, and our possessions in every part of the world. We must not allow any power, military or naval, to injure our just rights.

The great European Drama progresses rapidly.— The great European drama, which will, I believe, involve all the great military and naval powers in Europe, and may cause a war between all the European powers, great and small, is rapidly developing, and may soon be commenced, with all its horrors, calamities, and disasters. It now proceeds in the intricacies of European diplomacy, in the occasional outbreaks among some of the minor combatants of the near future. When war does really break out, the results will be stupendous. Then the combatants will range themselves on the side of the Teutonic, or on the side of the Sclavonic race. The war will be Titanic in dimensions and results. Let us, therefore, calmly and deliberately decide on our policy in time of peace, and let us take care to be on the side of order, civilization, and peace. The real contest may yet, after all, be waged between the greatest military despotic power and the greatest maritime power in the world, or, in other words, between Britain and Russia. Britain is the most powerful Empire in the world by its wealth, industry, intelligence, and population. Our policy greatly affects every foreign power in the world. The ocean is the element on which we alone hold undisputed sovereignty. There we are supreme. But as wars are now sudden and decisive, we should always be prepared for all the reasonable contingencies of our Empire. On the other hand, Germany is the greatest and most powerful military nation in the world; is peaceful in its foreign policy; and is determined to keep the peace unbroken as far as it is concerned. Therefore, I say that, in the present circumstances of the great powers, the alliance, even the united action, of Britain and Germany is the best security which can be obtained for the continuance of peace, or the preservation of Western civilization in the event of a great European war in the near future. But, while Russia is steadily and yearly advancing towards Constantinople, Germany is as steadily pushing Austria forwards towards Constantinople. Our own duties and interests lie in the maintenance of the Treaty of Berlin, and of the liberties of Europe. The possession of Constantinople is a matter of vital interest to Austria, and consequently it is the same to Germany. It is also a matter of great interest, but not of vital interest, to us.

V.—CONCLUSION.

Our Foreign Policy should be only national.—I have directed your attention to an immense number of subjects, and have traversed the globe for the purpose of setting before you our real position, interests, and prospects. I hope I have done my work with fairness and impartiality. I certainly feel that my sole aim has been to guide your thoughts towards the happiness and greatness of our country, and the peace, happiness, prosperity, and freedom of the whole world. To the best of my ability, I have striven to base our foreign policy on the eternal principles of justice and truth, and to establish that policy on the firmest and best principles of good and just and prudent government. The true principles of national policy, as well as of individual action, are justice, sound policy, wisdom, and prudence, and I have done my best to apply these principles, and to exclude all other principles in this speech on our international policy, duties, and interests.   The European outlook is dark and gloomy, and points to a sudden war, which, whether swift and decisive, or slow and uncertain, will have grave and important consequences for the future of Europe. The masses of our own country are on their trial.   Will they show themselves fickle and unreliable in the hour of danger, or firm, steadfast, and just in the defence of our national honour and national and world-wide possessions ?   The age in which we live is momentous, and we must be prepared, at any moment, to defend our own rights, interests, and honour.   The war clouds daily increase in magnitude and blackness. A common policy between ourselves and Russia and France is wholly impossible as against Austria and Germany.   Besides, we have a great traditional policy to uphold, and we must prosecute that policy along with some of the great European powers, and these naturally are Italy, and Austria, and Germany.   Let us suppose, for a moment, that we became the ally of Russia or France.   If we were the ally of Russia, we would be obliged to give up Constantinople to Russia, and become the enemy of Austria, backed up by Italy and Germany and Turkey.   If we were the ally of France, we would be obliged to fight with Germany, backed up by Austria and Italy and Turkey.   Suppose, on the other hand, that Russia and France defeated Austria and Germany and Italy, we would have to fight Russia in Central Asia and India.   For Russian ambition is insatiable, and extends to a supremacy in Asia as well as in Europe.   How, then,

can we be the ally of Russia under any circumstances,
or for any length of time? To carry out our
Mediterranean policy, Austria and Italy are our
natural and inevitable allies, and we must act accordingly. Upon this point there is no room for dispute.
No wonder, therefore, that Mr Gladstone agrees
with Lord Salisbury's foreign policy. Britain is no
longer a sea-girt isle. She spreads herself all over the
world, and has possessions and rights and interests
in both hemispheres. The next great European war
will be gigantic in its proportions and results. Sooner
or later, and perhaps sooner than some people think,
war is inevitable in consequence of the present unstable
condition of Europe. Russia has not yet given orders
to her troops to march from Warsaw upon the long
extended Galician frontiers of Austria. France has
not yet given her orders to march to the Rhine. But
Russia and France are making huge military preparations for the approaching Titanic war. All Russia
needs is money. Can she raise the necessary loan for
war? The peoples of Europe are armed to the teeth
as they never were before, and Europe itself resounds
with the clang of arms in making ready for war.
As yet, they are not ready to go forth to battle.
They may be so at any moment. Let us, therefore,
see that we are in a position to act worthily of ourselves, our ancestors, and our country.

LECTURE

ON

JOHN GRAHAM OF CLAVERHOUSE,

VISCOUNT OF DUNDEE,

AND

HIS TIMES,

DELIVERED AT KEW ON 25TH JUNE 1889, AND

GREATLY ENLARGED,

BY

ALEXANDER ROBERTSON, M.A.,

BARRISTER-AT-LAW,

AUTHOR OF LECTURES ON THE GOVERNMENT, CONSTITUTION, AND LAWS OF SCOTLAND, 1875-78;
AND OUR HOME, COLONIAL, AND INDIAN AFFAIRS, 1879-80.

DUNDEE:

WINTER, DUNCAN & CO. 10 CASTLE STREET.

1889.

PREFACE.

THE following Lecture was intended to have been delivered in Dundee during the last Christmas recess, and thereafter at Kew, in Surrey, during last winter. For reasons of a personal and domestic nature, its delivery in Dundee and at Kew last winter had to be abandoned. But, having made arrangements to publish it in one volume in the course of this summer, along with my two Lectures on the Sciences of Law and Politics, and my two Lectures on Home and Foreign Affairs, I decided to deliver it, as far as possible, at Kew in the course of this summer. I, accordingly, omitted nearly the whole of the general historical features of the Lecture, and summarized several other parts, and delivered the Lecture thus abridged to a public audience at Kew on the 25th of June last. As printed, or written, before I delivered my abridged Lecture at Kew, I submit the full text of the Lecture to my friends and to the general public as a fair, honest, and impartial effort to give a true picture of the life and times of a most grossly and shamefully abused man. I hope we shall no more hear of the gallant Viscount as the " bloody Claverhouse," unless in the mouths of ignorant partizans and crazy bigots.

On the following page, the reader will find Wordsworth's stirring words, written in October 1803, in his Sonnet in the Pass of Killiecrankie as to the expected French invasion. Wordsworth's sentiments in this piece are admirable; but some of his facts are erroneous.

To Mr John MacLauchlan, Secretary, Albert Institute, Dundee, and Mr Robert Walker, Beaconsfield House, Kew Green, I take this public opportunity of expressing my sincere thanks for their many valuable suggestions to me while the following Lecture was passing through the press. I have to add that neither Mr MacLauchlan, nor Mr Walker, is responsible for any statement or opinion given in the following pages.

DANEBURY HOUSE,
KEW GREEN, KEW, SURREY, 24th July 1889.

IN THE PASS OF KILLIECRANKIE,

AN INVASION BEING EXPECTED, OCTOBER 1803.

"Six thousand veterans practised in war's game,
Tried men, at Killiecrankie were arrayed
Against an equal host that wore the plaid,
Shepherds and herdsmen.—Like a whirlwind came
The Highlanders, the slaughter spread like flame;
And Garry, thundering down his mountain road,
Was stopped, and could not breathe beneath the load
Of the dead bodies.—'Twas a day of shame
For them whom precept and the pedantry
Of cold mechanic battle do enslave.
O for a single hour of that Dundee,
Who on that day the word of onset gave!
Like conquest would the men of England see;
And her foes find a like inglorious grave."

—Wordsworth.

CONTENTS.

IV.—THE BATTLE OF BOTHWELL BRIDGE; THE CAMERONIANS; AND THE TEST ACT OF 1681.

V.—CLAVERHOUSE IS SENT BACK TO THE SOUTH-WEST OF SCOTLAND.

VI.—IMPORTANT EVENTS IN THE REIGN OF JAMES II.

VII.—GRAVE CHARGES AGAINST CLAVERHOUSE DISCUSSED; AND GENERAL CONDUCT TOWARDS THE COVENANTERS.

VIII.—THE REVOLUTION OF 1688.

LECTURE

ON

JOHN GRAHAM OF CLAVERHOUSE,

VISCOUNT OF DUNDEE,

AND

HIS TIMES

[INTENDED FOR DELIVERY IN THE CITY OF DUNDEE; AND ALSO AT KEW
IN THE COUNTY OF SURREY].

———

I.—EARLY LIFE.

INTRODUCTION.—John Graham of Claverhouse, first Viscount of Dundee, is indelibly associated with the cruel and bloody persecutions of the Scottish Presbyterians by the governments of Charles II. and James II., and also with the brilliant victory won by him in 1689 for the Stuart cause at the battle of Killiecrankie. By the Scottish Whigs and Presbyterians, he has been stigmatized as the "bloody Claverhouse;" and by the Scottish Tories and Episcopalians, he has been celebrated as a gallant hero and cavalier and "Bonnie Dundee." In this lecture, I propose to try to form a just and impartial estimate of his life, actions, and character, and to give a brief sketch of Scottish History connected with the times in which he lived; and to avoid all romance and exaggeration.

U

Birth and pedigree.—Claverhouse was born in 1643, and was descended from an ancient and noble family, which had the blood-royal of Scotland in their veins. He was the elder son of Sir William Graham of Claverhouse in the county of Forfar, and of Lady Jean Carnegie, a daughter of the first Earl of Northesk. He had one brother of whom I shall hereafter be obliged to speak, and two sisters of whom I shall have nothing further to say.

His education, appearance, and character.—On the 13th of February 1665, he and his brother matriculated as students at St. Leonard's College, St. Andrews. Till this date, nothing is known of his youth. What he did, or how he spent his time, at college, is equally unknown. Some authors have stated that he was then an earnest reader of the great actions recorded by the poets and historians of antiquity. Some have stated that he was a blockhead, and was possessed of no intellectual culture. But his university career is a blank. Claverhouse, says Scott in *Old Mortality*, was rather low of stature, and was slightly, though elegantly, formed. His gesture, language, and manners were those of one whose life has been spent amongst the noble and the gay. His features exhibited even feminine regularity. He had an oval face, a straight and well-formed nose, dark hazel eyes, a complexion just sufficiently tinged with brown to save it from the charge of effeminacy. He had a short upper lip, curved upwards like that of a Grecian statue, and slightly shaded by small mustachios of light brown, joined to a profusion of long love-locks of the same colour, which fell on each side of the face. His exterior appearance seemed to suggest that he was better formed for the court or the saloon than the field of battle ; and his manners seemed to indicate that he was more the votary of pleasure than of ambition. Under this exterior there was hidden a spirit unbounded in daring ; aspiring, yet cautious; prudent, yet magnanimous. In body and mind he was quick, untiring, and energetic ; and, in the pursuit of the business of his daily life, he was bold, courageous, and ambitious. Like most of his rank in life in his own day, he was a soldier of fortune both at home and abroad, and sought honour and glory and land as the reward of his military services.

His life till 1677.—Claverhouse appears to have gone to the Continent in or about the year 1668 to see the world, and seek his fortune as a soldier. In 1672, he is supposed to have taken service with the Duke of Monmouth, who, with a force of 6000 English and Scotch troops, had joined the French standard under Turenne. This force had been sent to France by Charles II., in conformity with a secret treaty between him and Louis XIV., and in return for large yearly subsidies to be paid by Louis to Charles for military aid to be given by Charles to enable him to crush the rising power of Holland, and to support the claims of the house of Bourbon to the Spanish throne. But, in 1674, he is known to have been in the service of William then Prince of Orange, and afterwards King of Great Britain and Ireland. There is a story that, when Claverhouse was in the military service of the Prince of Orange, and engaged in the long, bloody, and indecisive battle of Seneffe, near Mons, fought in 1674, between William and the Duke of Condé, he saved the Prince's life, and was made captain of William's own regiment of horse guards, commanded by the Count de Solmes, who subsequently, in 1690, led the English forces against James II. at the battle of the Boyne in Ireland. But how far this story is correct, and when, or why Claverhouse transferred his services from France to Holland, are utterly unknown, and rest almost entirely on conjectures. In 1677 or 1678, Claverhouse returned from the Continent to Scotland, and took service under Charles II. as a lieutenant of a regiment of cavalry, commanded by the Marquis of Montrose. Whatever or wherever his military services may previously have been, thenceforward till his death, in 1689, Claverhouse was a prominent figure, and played an important part, in the history of Scotland. In the year 1677, during a temporary lull of continental warfare, the Prince of Orange, the elected Stadtholder of the United Provinces of the Netherlands, was married to Lady Mary, niece of Charles II., and the elder daughter of James Duke of York, afterwards James II. Twelve years thereafter, in 1689, William and Mary became king and queen of this country. During these twelve years, great events were to happen in the annals of Scotland, and in the life of John Graham, the hero of the battle of Killiecrankie.

I must now ask your attention to a brief outline of some of the events which deeply concerned the history of Scotland during the period from 1679 to 1689; because, without some knowledge of these events, we cannot rightly understand the life of Claverhouse, or the times in which he lived.

2.—OUTLINE OF RELIGIOUS AND ·POLITICAL EVENTS IN SCOTLAND FROM 1677 TO 1689.

Presbyterianism established, dis-established, and re-established.—The Scottish Covenant of 1557 was followed by the overthrow of Popery in Scotland, and by the Reformation of the Church of Scotland under the leadership of John Knox, and by the establishment of the Scotch Presbyterian Church in 1560. The accession of James VI. to the throne of England brought about the establishment of an Episcopalian Church for Scotland in 1606. Then followed the opposition of the Scotch people to the Episcopal Church so established in Scotland, and to the illegal and despotic actions of Charles I. and Archbishop Laud. The Scottish Covenant of 1643 was followed by the great civil Revolution; by the English Commonwealth under Oliver Cromwell as Protector and the restoration of Presbyterianism in Scotland; and by the restoration of Charles II. and the re-establishment of Episcopacy.

Episcopacy re-established by King Charles II. in 1661. —At the restoration in 1660, the mass of the Scottish people, clergy and laymen, were weary of the religious and civil strife which had been waged since the time of John Knox. King Charles II. violently disliked Presbyterianism, and was himself a Roman Catholic at heart. Amidst the jarring discords of religious strife in Scotland, Episcopacy was again established in 1661 in Scotland; and James Sharp, who was then in London as the ambassador of the old Resolutionists, or Moderate Presbyterians, of Scotland, and as a great champion of the Scotch Presbyterian Church, returned to Scotland as Archbishop of St. Andrews and Primate of Scotland. A petition was then presented to the King by the Scottish Covenanters, denouncing religious toleration as a vast mischief, and as a specious pretence unjustifiably set up in the name of tender conscience. It prayed that schismatics, as well as papists and prelatists, should be stamped out of the land. But the Committee of the Estates answered their prayer by ordering the Covenanting leaders to be thrown into prison.

Important Acts passed from 1660 *to* 1663, *while Lord Middleton was Lord High Commissioner.*—On the restoration of King Charles II., a new Government was formed for Scotland in 1661. In it, Lord Middleton, a soldier of fortune, created an earl, was appointed Lord High Commissioner, governor of the castle of Edinburgh, and commander-in-chief of the military forces; the Earl of Glencairn, Lord Chancellor; the Earl of Lauderdale, Secretary of State; the Earl of Rothes, President of the Privy Council; and the Earl of Crawford, Lord High Treasurer.

Scotch Parliament of 1661.—A Scotch Parliament was held in 1661 under a Royal Commission from Charles II., and with Lord Middleton as Lord High Commissioner. At the opening of this Parliament the national honours, called the regalia, consisting of the royal crown, sceptre, and sword of Scotland, were produced, after they had been supposed to have been lost, or stolen, or destroyed, but were merely buried for safety in the parish church of Kinneff near Dunnottar Castle. The Scotch Parliament passed an Act rescinding all Acts passed since the year 1633.

This Rescissory Act declared the rescinded Acts to be invalid, and also to be repealed. What use there was of repealing statutes which were invalid is not easy to understand. But Gilbert Burnet, afterwards Bishop of Salisbury, says that most of the Representatives in this Parliament were men of affairs rather than men of accurate language, and that they were almost constantly drunk. If he is well informed, as most probably he is, accurate and measured language was not to be expected from them. Nay more, we need not be surprised that many of the Acts thus rescinded were also gradually restored by successive Parliaments. An Act was also passed in this Parliament concerning religion and church government, and declaring that His Majesty would settle these matters; and that, for the present, sessions, presbyteries, and synods should continue. Upon this Act, there was issued a royal proclamation, sweeping away the Presbyterian polity from the Statute Book, and establishing Prelacy and its discipline and government in its stead. There was also passed another Act, on the second of May 1661, for the restoration and re-establishment of the ancient government of the Church by archbishops and bishops. Thereupon bishops were appointed for the Scotch bishoprics, and the Covenant was burned by the hangman as a mark of contumely and disrespect. There was also passed an Act giving to the King an annual income of £120,000 for life. As this sum was in sterling money, and not Scotch, the amount was large in proportion to the wealth of the country at that time. Nothing was granted to him to help him to support a standing army; and the King had to get the funds for this object, from the King of France, by betraying the interests of his own country.

King's Privy Council created with great powers.—
Measures were then taken to strengthen the King's
Government over Scotland, and these followed the
precedents of the Parliamentary Government of twelve
years previously.   There was also created a Privy
Council with powers unknown to the old Secret
Council of Scotland.   This Privy Council virtually
took the place of the Estates during the intervals of the
sessions of Parliament.   It was thus an imitation of the
Committee of the Estates, not elected by the Estates
of Parliament, but virtually created by the Crown under
the royal prerogative.   It also acted as a court of first
instance for discovering how far persons charged before
it might be tried by the regular criminal tribunals,
and it also exercised many functions of a punitive
character under various Acts of Parliament.   After
the Union between England and Scotland, the Privy
Council of Scotland had practically the absolute control
of the chief internal executive functions of the Government, and exercised the prerogative functions of the
sovereign in Scotland.

*Measures taken to enforce Episcopal Church Govern-
ment.*—I must now deal with a succession of
measures taken to enforce the new order of Church
government, and to get people to abjure the old.   The
first Act was a statute, in 1662, making necessary a
declaration from all persons in offices of public trust to
the effect that the Covenant and the National League
were against the fundamental laws and liberties of Scotland.   This Statute extended not only to the Ministers
of the Crown, Judges, and other Officers of State,
but also to Members of Parliament, Magistrates, and
Councillors of Burghs, and persons having any other

public charge, office, and trust within the Kingdom.
There was also passed, secondly, a law against the clergy
who had not been presented by the patrons of churches
since 1639, unless they were formally presented by
the patrons, and unless they accepted Episcopal collation; and also declaring that, where Presbyterian clergy
had only Presbyterian ordination, they must accept
Episcopal collation. The clergymen who complied
with this Act were unpopular with their flocks.
Those who would not comply with it were driven from
their manses and churches, and deprived of their
stipends. Whereupon the expelled ministers began
to hold church and other assemblies of their own. Then
Parliament denounced these assemblies as unlawful
meetings and conventicles, and nurseries of sedition.
As this Statute against recusants did not contain any
penalties for non-compliance with its terms, the Privy
Council, as representing the Estates between sessions,
issued proclamations regulating the enforcement of the
Act. Hence, the Privy Council made laws to gave force
to a statute, which, in its terms, was inoperative. These
proclamations laid the country desolate, and increased
the hatred of the people towards the bishops. Three
hundred and fifty ministers were driven from their
churches and their benefices, and the bulk of their con-
gregations followed them. Then an Act was passed to
compel the people to attend their parish churches on
the Sabbath, and imposing penalties on absentees
according to their rank. But this Act was found to
be impracticable, even although husbands were subsequently made liable for fines imposed on their wives.
Women, it has been wisely observed, have always been
more enthusiastic for religion and for ideal truth than

men. Thereafter the Privy Council passed an Act of Council, called the Mile Act, commanding recusant ministers to reside within their parishes, and imposing the punishment of sedition on the disobedient.

Court of High Commission restored.—The religious warfare had so much increased that it was necessary to relieve the Privy Council, the Court of Justiciary, and the inferior Courts, by the establishment of a special court for ecclesiastical causes. In 1664, the Court of High Commission, abhorred and dreaded in England and Scotland, was restored in Scotland to deal with ecclesiastical offences. This Court was empowered to summon and call before it all Popish traffickers, all contemners of the discipline of the Church, all keepers of conventicles, all obtruders into parishes, all who did not attend the parish church or keep the sacraments, and all who traduced Acts of Parliament or of the Council in relation to Church affairs. In two years it had sunk into utter contempt, and was allowed to expire.

Parliament of 1662.—The Parliament of 1662 sat about eight days; that is to say, it devoted one day to the election of the Lords of the Articles; and then adjourned. The Lords of the Articles then went over, drew up, and prepared such Acts as were to be passed in that session. They having done this, Parliament had its second and last meeting, when all the Acts were read, debated, voted, and passed. The Lord High Commissioner then went up to Court in London along with the Lord Clerk Register, who had, in the meantime, put the Acts into the ultimate statutory form which they were to assume. All the Acts of the Scotch Parliament either were touched by the sceptre in the hands of the King; or, where the King had appointed a Commissioner to act for him, in the hands of the Commissioner.

Military forces appointed to enforce the Acts for conformity to Church.—To give effect to the new ecclesiastical order of things, military forces were sent to aid the civil authorities in the most disturbed districts in the South-west of Scotland, the head-centre of the Remonstrants, who then formed the extreme Presbyterian party in Scotland. Thither Sir James Turner, a rough and unscrupulous soldier, was sent in 1665, to command the troops. The result was to create license, oppression, and insult, and to make the soldiers a curse to all the people over whom they had any control. The soldiers were quartered on the non-conforming citizens to enforce the levying of fines and impositions. The excessive and extortionate cess or quartering money, and the exaction of illegal cess, and the imposition of illegal fines against the innocent as well as the guilty, drove the people to rise in rebellion. Turner was defeated at Dalry, in Galloway, in November 1666, by a body of Covenanters, who were soon afterwards, on the thirteenth of November 1666, defeated by General Dalziel at Rullion Green, in the neighbourhood of Edinburgh. Very soon thereafter, in 1667, the policy of the Scotch Government was changed from one of harshness to one of leniency, and the soldiers who had been stationed in the Western counties of Scotland were ordered to retire from them.

The First Indulgence, 1669.—The first indulgence was issued from Whitehall in June 1669, on the sign-manual, countersigned by Lord Lauderdale as Secretary

for Scotland, and addressed to the Scottish Privy
Council. It purported to wish the restoration of the
well-behaved ministers expelled under the Act of the
Privy Council of 1662, but under the condition that
their parish churches were vacant. It gave them the
glebe and manse, but not the stipend, which the
Privy Council was directed to collect, and thereupon
allow a maintenance to the ministers under licenses of
indulgence. It also declared that whoever should
preach, expound the Scriptures, or pray at any of the
meetings in the fields, or who should convoke the
people to those meetings, should be punished with
death and with confiscation of goods. While many of
the expelled ministers took advantage of this indulgence the recusants had new and severe measures of
the law brought against them. Lords Rothes and
Lauderdale were rewarded with dukedoms for their
services in connection with this indulgence. Lord
Lauderdale was a strange character. In his youth, he
had been a zealous Presbyterian; but, trimming his
sails to catch the breath of royal favour, he had
become a zealous Episcopalian. In 1641, he was a
Whig; and twenty years later he remorselessly persecuted the Whigs. His great ruling passion was his
own personal aggrandisement, and he was neither
better nor worse than the self-seeking Scottish
politicians and courtiers of that age.

The Western sectaries.—A small party, the Remonstrants, in the West of Scotland became the centre
of a great religious body, which was separated from the
Prelatic party and from the Presbyterians who availed
themselves of the first indulgence. This party looked
upon that indulgence as a snare, and would not have

anything to do with it, or with those who had. But the Government determined to force them into compliance with the law. Hence, in 1676, appeared a new legal Writ, under the title of Letters of Intercommuning, prohibiting intercommuning, or holding intercourse, with persons who had broken the laws as to conventicles, and holding the intercommuners guilty as principal offenders. By this writ, an act of Christian charity— clothing the naked, feeding the hungry, or hiding the pursued person—was an intercommuning. Heavy penalties were imposed on intercommuners, and tempting rewards were offered to informers, by the Privy Council, which authorised and issued the new writ, and which, on many occasions, overstepped the constitutional rights and privileges of the ancient Secret Council of Scotland. For, undoubtedly, to impose penalties on a new class of offenders was a legislative, and not an executive act, under the old Constitutional Government of Scotland.

Severities against them.—In 1678, the Government availed themselves of an Irish force collected to enforce the law against intercommuning, and to keep order in Ayr and Renfrew shires, where disaffection to the Government was most prevalent. The using of this force, associated with a barbarous and savage Highland force, accustomed to rapine and plunder, was a grave scandal to the Government ; for neither the Irish, nor the Highlanders, observed the laws of civilized warfare, but maimed, and killed, and plundered their opponents, and even their allies, in the most undistinguishing and disgraceful manner. The orders of the Privy Council were, that the troops in the disturbed and proclaimed districts should have free quarters, and have power to disarm those districts, and to be free from all civil and criminal actions or indictments for what was done, or the Privy Council or their Committee should order, in the King's service, by killing, wounding, apprehending, or imprisoning all who might oppose the King's authority, or by seizing such as they had reason to suspect, "the same being always done by the Privy Council, their committee, or by the superior officer." In the West, all had to endure this pestilent scourge of plunderers, unless they had the special protection of the Privy Council, by the granting of bonds for the good behaviour of themselves and their tenants. This force of thieves and cut-throats, and mostly Highlanders, amounted to from 6000 to 8000. Some of the Ayrshire gentry remonstrated against this savage horde being employed amongst them, and proposed to go to London to remonstrate with the King; but the Privy Council issued an order forbidding them to cross the border. The Western counties had to suffer this barbarous host amongst them for a season, until, in a few months after their services commenced, the barbarians returned to their own homes laden with all manner of spoil. Even Lauderdale became ashamed of the necessary tools of his policy in the West of Scotland. On the complaints of the Duke of Hamilton and others in London to the King, the Highlanders were ordered to return to their homes. In Fifeshire, where the people were passionately devoted to conventicles, the landed gentry entered into bonds, and were relieved of the presence of the Highland host, whose headquarters were at Stirling. In the West, forfeitures and fines became lucrative to large numbers of common informers and greedy lawyers; and, although primarily belonging to the Crown, were often gifted away, and never benefited the royal exchequer at all. The recusants were unfortunately and shamefully left by the Government to the tender mercies of personal greed and personal spite; and were exposed and pursued by the Episcopal clergy of all grades with venomous rancour and hatred.

Position of the Church in the reign of Charles II.— In the West of Scotland, there were numerous fierce fanatics, and also, in some degree, in Fifeshire; but, generally speaking, the people in Scotland were outwardly content to conform to the law then existing as to religion and religious worship. Still, the politicians and prelates succeeded, by violence, harsh cruelty, and injustice, in alienating from the Established Episcopalian Church and from the Government of Scotland, not only the lower classes, but all those of the upper whom strong party feeling, or want of court interest, did not attach to their standard. During the reign of Charles II., the Church was the pivot upon which the Government of Scotland turned. Archbishop Sharp, a Presbyterian apostate, sitting at the Privy Council, eagerly examined and sentenced the recusants, and often acted as president at the Council Board. He had also succeeded in getting the election of the Lords of the Articles under the control of the bishops, and thereby practically in placing the Scotch Parliament under the control of the hierarchy; for, under his auspices, the bishops chose eight temporal peers, and the eight temporal peers chose eight bishops, and the sixteen thus chosen chose eight lesser barons and eight burgesses.

Character and opinions of the Covenanters.—The
recusant Covenanters were very serious and earnest
people in religion and politics, and were incapable of sepa-
rating religion from politics. They became the Whigs
of politics at a subsequent period, and put conscience
above all things in this world. They fought for civil
and religious freedom after their own fashion, and were
as confident of being in the right as their opponents,
who then held the supreme power of the Government
in their hands. Loyalty and Whiggery thus became
opposed to each other; and yet, in the nature of
things, there is no contradiction between them any
more than between Toryism and popular or representative government. Extreme loyalty becomes
absolutism; and extreme Whiggery, anarchy. If the
principles either of loyalty or of Whiggery are carried
to their logical results, both Loyalists and Whigs
would naturally and necessarily become persecutors.
Those who were, about this time, called Whigs in Scotland were a remnant of the Presbyterians, who had been
Covenanters in 1643. Against these Covenanters, struggling for civil and religious freedom after their own
narrow and bigoted fashion, Charles II. and James II.,
and their instruments in Scotland, *e.g.* Claverhouse, were
harsh and cruel, and so were the Parliaments which supported them. But, we must remember that, if these
recusant Covenanters had gained the upper hand and
the supremacy in Scotland, there would, so far as they
were concerned, have been no such thing as real civil
and religious freedom as long as they could prevent
it. The recusants were enthusiastic and zealous in
the pursuit of religious truth, but their enthusiasm
was sullied by fanatical zeal, and soured by the spirit

of self-righteousness. The recusant Covenanters were extreme Puritanical Presbyterians. They were fiery in their temper, language, and conduct. They were narrow-minded, arrogant, and gloomy. They condemned all elegant studies and innocent exercises, and were envenomed with the rancour of political hatred, and firmly held that all men must be of their religious and political party, or they must be wrong, and damned in this world and the next. Such principles and such conduct are false in politics and unchristian in religion, and were never those of the great body of the Scottish Presbyterians. In these days, every one feels shame at the tyrannical and oppressive government of Charles II. and James II., and at the misrule, license, and brutality of their soldiers; at the executions of the recusants on the scaffold; at the exactions and free quarters imposed on them by military law; and at the Parliament by its placing the lives and fortunes of a free people under the heel of military despots. But our higher civilization, and our more enlightened views of civil and religious liberty than formerly existed in Scotland, have been the fruits of centuries, and are the results of the sacrifices of good, noble, heroic, and patriotic men of former generations, and of Monarchists as well as of Republicans. I honour the recusant Covenanters for their steadfastness to their principles. I pity them for the cruelties and injustice which they suffered at the hands of their opponents and enemies. But I condemn their principles as narrow, bigoted, and false. Liberty is a precious gift of God to man; and must be preserved free, unsullied, immortal, and universal, as God's best gift to the human race.

The Whig Remonstrants of 1660.—On the twenty-
third of August 1660, a party of the old Whig Remonstrants of Scotland drew up and signed a supplication
to King Charles II., praying for the preservation of
the Reformed Church of Scotland in doctrine, worship,
discipline, and government ; and for the reformation
of the Churches in the kingdoms of England and
Ireland ; and for the carrying on of the work of uni-
formity in the religion of the three kingdoms ; and for
the extirpation of Popery and Prelacy ; and also praying
that all places of power and trust in the three kingdoms
should be held by such as have taken the Covenant.
This supplication was never presented.   Those who
signed it were, as I have said, committed to Edinburgh
Castle as conventiclers, that is to say, as persons meeting
in assemblies unauthorised by the law.   They were a
remnant of the Remonstrants of the West of Scotland,
and disliked the Stuarts, and had been furious at Cromwell for not allowing them to assail nearly the whole
of the human race for not accepting their religious
beliefs.   They did not represent the general feeling
of the Scots at the Restoration, at which time
the religious feeling was either Episcopalian, but
especially and above all Presbyterian, and tolerant.
They raved about Presbyterianism being extended to
the whole three kingdoms of England, Scotland, and
Ireland ; and were ignored by all parties in the state,
and afterwards suffered very severely at the hands of
the Government.   From the very first, Charles II.
was strongly inclined towards Episcopalianism rather
than Presbyterianism, and with the despotic doctrines
then popular with Episcopalians, such as, non-resistance ;
the king can do no wrong ; and absolute obedience.   At

the time of the Restoration, there were three great ecclesiastical parties in Scotland, namely, the Episcopalians, supported by England and the court party; the extreme Presbyterians in the West; and the moderate Presbyterians spread all over the country. Those last mentioned unquestionably formed the majority of the Scotch people at that time and since.

The Whigs and the Tories.—Whiggery really sprung from the East of Scotland; but grew most potently in the South-west. At Mauchline, in Ayrshire, a large body of men met under the auspices of the Earl of Eglinton, a zealous Covenanting nobleman. They formed themselves into a military party, and marched to Edinburgh, but did not effect anything of any importance. These people were the "Whigamores" of 1648. They were subsequently led by the Earl of Argyle, and were defeated by Sir George Monro in an attack which they made upon Stirling Castle in 1648. Subsequently, Argyle opened up negotiations with Oliver Cromwell, and, by the Protector's assistance and support, Argyle's party became supreme in Scotland. The name of Tory as a political designation came into use in Scotland in connection with the proposal made, in 1680, to exclude James II., then Duke of York, from the Scottish throne on the ground that he was a Roman Catholic. It was applied to all royalists who upheld the hereditary and absolute right of the royal family to the crowns of England, Scotland, and Ireland as of divine right. But, although the great body of the Scotch Presbyterians objected to the interference of the sovereign in their ecclesiastical matters, and hated Popery with a bitter hatred, they strongly protested against the execution of Charles I. Indeed, as soon as they knew that they had

protested in vain, they at once proceeded to acknowledge
Charles II. as the legitimate heir and successor to the
Scottish crown. With this class, the hereditary right
of their kings to the crown was a fundamental principle
of their political creed; but the divine right of kings to
rule as absolute monarchs was absolutely rejected by
them as false and blasphemous. The Revolutions in
the middle and at the end of the seventeenth century
have finally substituted the supremacy of Parliament
for the royal supremacy in our government.

The Regular Army in Scotland very small.—When
we have been always accustomed to see around us
large bodies of armed men as soldiers, prepared for
military service at home or abroad ; and when we see
police constables in large numbers spread all over the
country, and that the soldiers are ready to be called out
for the protection of the Empire in any part of the world,
and the constables for the protection of our lives and
property at home; we cannot easily realize the state of
the country at a time when there were no regular troops
and no regular policemen, and when the country was
dependent on bodies of local militia to guard our shores
and defend the lives and property of our ancestors against
foreign invasion, and when the citizens themselves had
to protect their lives and property at home against
neighbours or bands of marauders and thieves from a
neighbouring district or clan. Still, the condition of
Scotland really was such that, in the sixteenth and
seventeenth centuries, it was nearly dependent on
these imperfect and unreliable means for protection
and defence. In the reign of James VI. there were
no regular troops in Scotland, and the defence of the
kingdom was entrusted to the national militia, which

was essentially a compulsory force for defensive purposes. Even in the reigns of his son and his two grandsons, the regular and disciplined troops of Scotland were very few, and were almost exclusively used as a body-guard for the sovereign. Under the name of personal retainers, the great and princely feudal lords of Scotland had large bodies of men for their own protection. Royal volunteer cavalry bands, however, were occasionally raised in Scotland for special service.

Character of the Scottish volunteer soldiers.—Here I have to observe that many young men of good families enlisted as volunteers into the ranks of the cavalry thus raised, and also into the ranks of the Royal Scottish life-guards, of whom we now hear almost for the first time. These two facts augmented the pride and self-confidence of those troops, which were often engaged in acting as the agents of the Government in levying fines, and in exacting free quarters, and in otherwise oppressing the Presbyterian non-conformists in Scotland. Their birth, their habits, and their duties made them licentious and oppressive in their characters; and their superior officers being frequently rash, head-strong, incompetent, or indifferent, the common soldiers and the subaltern officers were often allowed to do very much what they liked. In fact, as a rule, they were all, officers and men, so much accustomed to such duties as I have mentioned, that they conceived themselves at liberty to commit all manner of irregularities with impunity, as if they were exempted from all law and all authority. Most of those volunteers, men and officers, had usually betaken themselves to a military life from poverty, the stress of circumstances, their

own misconduct, or disinclination to the simple yet
honest life of agricultural labourers or small farmers.

Archbishop Sharp murdered at Magus Muir.—
On the third of May 1679, James Sharp, Archbishop
of St. Andrews and Primate of Scotland, had been
dragged from his carriage at Magus Muir, near St.
Andrews, and cruelly murdered. His death struck
terror into the breasts of the more active members of
the Government and of their subordinate agents. In
particular, it instilled a fierce desire into the mind of
Claverhouse to punish and slay the assassins of the
Primate, who had been an early friend and patron of
Claverhouse at St. Andrews. The chief actors engaged
in the Primate's death were Hackston of Rathillet,
Russell of Kettle, and John Balfour, often designated
as of Burley, but really of Kinloch in Fifeshire. They
were assisted by nine or ten peasant-farmer recusants.
All of them had been on the look-out for Carmichael,
sometimes designated as deputy-sheriff of Fifeshire,
and at other times as a commissioner of the Primate
or of the Privy Council. He had been energetic
in enforcing the penal laws passed against the non-conformists. In the execution of his duties, he was aided
by a military force. These recusant Covenanters in Fifeshire had had some of their goods seized by his orders for
non-appearance before tribunals, at which, they said,
their conscience forbade them to appear. Carmichael
was warned of his danger, and escaped out of their
hands. When they had learned that Carmichael had
escaped, they saw the Primate's coach approaching
them. They then cried out to each other, in the fury
of their excited imagination and misguided zeal, that
the Lord had delivered the Primate into their hands.

Hackston refused to head the attack of this body of bloodthirsty murderers.   Balfour then said to them, " Gentlemen, follow me."   He, with nine or ten men, dragged the Primate out of his carriage, and, with their swords and daggers, put him to death in the presence of his daughter, who vainly tried to ward off death from her aged father by exposing her own life to extreme danger.   This bloody deed is without justification in law, or morals, or expediency.   In the eyes of the extreme Covenanting Presbyterians of those days the Primate's death was a just and righteous judgment; and in those of the Episcopalians and of the moderate Presbyterians, it was a brutal murder.

Character of the Archbishop's murderers.—These cruel and bloodthirsty assassins of the Primate were types of the incapacity and folly of those times. They themselves thought and said that they were doing God's work in murdering the Archbishop, and that they were working for the glory of God in so doing. They had the dangerous gifts of coarse and uncouth eloquence, which was plentifully garnished with Scripture texts, and admirably adapted to excite and influence poor, ignorant, and unsophisticated peasants. They were not the men who were the real and genuine sufferers of the Covenant for the sake of conscience. The real sufferers in those times of national disturbance and revolution were patient and humble men, distinguished for the simplicity, sincerity, and piety of their lives and morals.   For a time, the assassins of the Archbishop all escaped the just punishment of their wicked and murderous actions, and at once fled from Fifeshire to the sympathetic West country, where great events were

in progress towards an armed insurrection and civil war.
They joined those rising in the West of Scotland.
But, ultimately, they were almost all slain in civil war,
or suffered death at the hands of the public executioner.
In the end of the seventeenth century, religious toleration was neither practised nor understood by any party,
religious or political, in Scotland.

III.—CLAVERHOUSE'S LIFE AND CONDUCT IN THE

SOUTH-WEST OF SCOTLAND.

*Claverhouse appointed a commander of a troop of
cavalry.*—Although Claverhouse was appointed a lieutenant of a volunteer troop of cavalry in 1677 or 1678, he
had seen no actual service in Scotland, and apparently
did not understand the obstinate character of his
countrymen when stirred up by religious or political
enthusiasm. The policy of persecuting the Covenanters being resolved upon, and resumed by the
Government with renewed vigour, in 1678 three
new troops of cavalry were ordered to be raised for
special services in the West of Scotland. Of one
troop, the Earl of Home had the command; of
another, the Earl of Airlie; and of the third, and, by
the King's desire, Claverhouse. Each troop seems to
have consisted of about fifty men. The discharge of
his military duties took Claverhouse to Dumfries-shire.

His duties in South and West of Scotland.—At this
time, the great civil officer of the county of Dumfries
was Sir Robert Grierson of Lagg, the sheriff or steward-

deputy.   He was a coarse and brutal man even for
those times, and was the cause of much of the odium
which has fallen on John Graham.   Claverhouse's new
duties were dangerous, undignified, and not to his
taste, and really consisted in hunting after recusant and
non-conforming Presbyterians ; and, at first, in sending
or taking them to the deputy-sheriff for punishment.
He was badly supplied with money to pay his men, or to
pay for provisions or forage.   His men therefore often
lived at free quarters on the inhabitants unknown to
their commander, or unpunishable by him, and they were
undoubtedly guilty of numerous acts of cruelty and
oppression.   In March 1679, Claverhouse, under a royal
and special warrant from Whitehall, was appointed
deputy-sheriff of Dumfries-shire ; and Andrew Bruce
of Earlshall, one of his lieutenants, was appointed
deputy-sheriff along with him.   On the 21st of April
1679, Claverhouse suspected that the conventiclers in
his neighbourhood were openly and ostentatiously
preparing to hold a great conventicle on an early day,
and in violation of the law.   Generally speaking,
although the conventiclers were goaded by oppression
and cruelty towards actual rebellion, yet the great
majority of them were opposed to it.

The Conventiclers rise in rebellion at Rutherglen.—
On the 29th of May 1679, and nearly four weeks after
the Primate's murder, was the anniversary of the King's
birthday, which had been publicly appointed as a
day of national rejoicing.   The conventiclers objected
to all holidays on principle ; and, on this occasion, had
determined to make a counter-demonstration on their
own account, and fixed on Glasgow as their place of
meeting for this purpose.   They abandoned Glasgow

for Rutherglen, very near to Glasgow. There, with Robert Hamilton, the brother of Sir William Hamilton the laird of Preston, as their military leader, and Thomas Douglas, one of their fire-breathing ministers, as their spiritual guide, and Balfour of Burley, or rather of Kinloch, and Russell of Kettle, and seventy or eighty of the common people, they duly arrived, and extinguished the bonfire which was blazing in honour of the King, and lighted a bonfire for themselves, and solemnly burned all the Acts of Parliament and Royal Proclamations passed or issued since Charles's restoration. A protest against all interference by the English Government as to the Presbyterian Church was read, and nailed to the market-cross, and then the Covenanters withdrew. This protest was called the Declaration and Testimony of some of the true Presbyterian party. During these lawless proceedings, Claverhouse was at Falkirk. As soon as he heard of them, he rode off to inflict punishment on the contemners of the King's government. He met Lord Ross in Glasgow on Saturday the thirty-first of May, and then proceeded to Rutherglen to make further inquiries in regard to the rioters. He apprehended several of the Rutherglen ringleaders. Hearing of a projected meeting by the conventiclers on the following day, Sunday, at Loudon Hill, a steep and rocky eminence which marks the junction of the counties of Ayr, Lanark, and Renfrew, he set off to Loudon Hill in search of them. On his arrival there, early on the first of June 1679, he saw, with his own eyes, that the conventiclers were collected in great numbers in the neighbourhood of that hill, and not far from the hamlet of Drumclog, now consisting of a single house.

Description of Drumclog battle-ground and hostile forces.—The region in the neighbourhood of Loudon Hill seems to stretch farther than the eye can reach, without much grandeur or dignity, yet it is striking by its huge proportions as compared with what is adapted to cultivation and fitted for the use of man. Much of it was then totally useless for cultivation, but large portions of it have since been, and are now being, brought under cultivation. There is a steep and winding path from the level moor into the hills on the north. At the top of this path is the brow of the hill. From this point the ground slopes downwards on one side in a southerly direction for about a quarter of a mile, and then the slope terminated in a marshy level, which was traversed in its whole length by what seemed a natural gully or deep artificial drain, broken by trenches filled with water, whence peats and turf had been dug, and where, at intervals, some alder bushes were to be seen. Beyond the ditch or gully the conventiclers were drawn up. Their infantry stood in three lines. The first was provided with firearms; the second, with pikes; and the third, or rear line, with scythes on straight poles, hay forks, and other rustic tools, converted into instruments of war. On each flank, and a little backward from the bog, was a small body of cavalry, indifferently armed, and worse mounted, but full of zeal for the cause they had espoused, and composed of small landed proprietors or well-to-do farmers. On the side of the hill, above the conventiclers, were their women and children. The ground was well taken up by the insurgents, and the defence was well planned by men of some military skill, that is to say, by Hackston of

Rathillet, Patton of Meadowhead, and Cleland, who afterwards died at the defence of Dunkeld. The total numbers of the insurgents were about one thousand men, of whom one hundred rode on horseback, and of these not one-half were tolerably well armed. Some of their officers had seen military service abroad as soldiers of fortune in foreign service. The royal forces numbered about two hundred and fifty dragoons.

Claverhouse commenced the battle.—No opposition by the insurgents to the progress of the royal forces was attempted in the narrow path or defile to which I have referred. But, as soon as the royal forces were seen by their opponents, the religious meeting was broken up, and the armed conventiclers took up a defensive position on the farm of Drumclog. The land so occupied now grows meadow grass; but it is surrounded even now by deep bogs. As soon as the royal horsemen arrived at the summit of the hill, at the end of the defile, the trumpets and kettle-drums of the royal forces sounded a bold and warlike flourish. In reply, the conventiclers defiantly raised their voices to God in psalms. No time was lost by Claverhouse in attacking the conventiclers. Shortly before the battle of Drumclog he had told his men that, on the first opportunity, he and they must attack the conventiclers at all hazards.

The character of the insurgents at Drumclog.— At Drumclog, the assembly was mostly composed of extreme Presbyterians, who were subsequently known in Scottish history as Cameronians, and were high-flying and crack-brained fanatics. It also contained a few moderate Presbyterians, who were men of peace, and would have been satisfied with a free toleration of their religious doctrines and observances.

Balfour, Hackston, and the murderers of Archbishop Sharp, in self-defence, naturally wished to force their co-religionists into civil war and rebellion. The conventicle and expelled ministers practically agreed with the murderers of the Primate, but for very different reasons. These wished to fight, as they sincerely thought, for the honour and glory of God, and His true religion, and against the King and his courtiers and their broken oaths in promising to support the Solemn League and Covenant. Feuds hotly raged amongst the insurgents as to whether Charles II. ought to be acknowledged as king, and whether they ought to be content with the free exercise of their own religion, and whether they should insist on the re-establishment of Presbyterianism as of supreme and universal authority. The country gentlemen and most of the clergy who joined the insurgents were moderates; but the country people were zealots and extremists. Robert Hamilton, the leader of the insurgents, was a man of good family, and scrupulously refused to assume his rank and title as his brother's successor. He would never take the family estate or title; because he could not take the oath of obedience to an uncovenanted monarch. The conventiclers as a body, like the Jews of old, thought themselves to be a chosen people of God in the midst of the people among whom they dwelt. They did not spare their enemies who fell into their hands; and they thought that they were God's servants, called upon to do justice to their enemies as His enemies. They were Anti-Popish, Anti-Prelatic, Anti-Erastian, Anti-Sectarian, and thought that they were the true remnant of the Church of Scotland. They looked on the English Prayer-Book and the Scottish Prayer-

Book as remnants of the Roman Catholic Mass, and also on Prelacy as little better than Popery.

The battle of Drumclog.—At the battle of Drumclog, Claverhouse rode on a sorrel-coloured horse, supposed by his enemies to have been given to him by the Devil himself. A party of royal dragoons, or mounted infantry, proceeded down the hill to the brink of the ditch at the bottom, and opened a brisk fire on the conventiclers. This skirmishing party tried to cross the ditch, and failed to do so, and lost several men in the attempt. Hamilton ordered his men to advance; and Cleland, at the head of a numerous body of men on foot, advanced against the royal dragoons. Claverhouse then called in his skirmishers, and the engagement became general. Scythes and pitchforks were used by the insurgents against the floundering horses; and Claverhouse had his own horse wounded by a pitchfork. The royal troopers fell back; and Balfour pursued them with his horse. In charging the royal cavalry, the conventiclers scattered them, and killed thirty-six of them, and lost only three of their own number on the field. The fight ended in a general rout of the royal forces. In writing to Lord Linlithgow, Claverhouse stated: "I saved one of the standards, and made the best retreat the confusion of our people would suffer." He further acknowledged that he lost eight or ten cavalry and many more dragoons. On the other side, the Covenanters said that their own loss did not exceed five or six men. The victorious conventiclers pursued Claverhouse's men, who fled over the hill and across the moorland to Strathavon, about six or seven miles distant, and then fled to Glasgow, a distance of

about twenty miles, and never drew rein till the sur-
vivors were all safe in Glasgow.   Claverhouse himself
calmly and resolutely retreated with great ability, and
brought up the rear-guard.   Many of his soldiers,
who would have been slain by the men of the conventicle force, were saved by the humanity of the
women who were with the conventiclers, whose policy
was to slay their enemies and spare them not.   They
rejected all cries for mercy from their opponents, and
acted towards them with fiendish cruelty.   Stranger
still, they acted after this fashion in the name of God
and heaven's decrees !

*State of affairs amongst the insurgents after the
battle.*—In the camp of the conventiclers at Drumclog
the seeds of disunion were thickly sown amongst
them.   The moderate Presbyterians were in favour of
peace, constitutional government, equal laws, and the
substitution of reason and mildness for persecution
and intolerance.   The extreme Presbyterians were for
war to the knife.   The moderate and rational Presbyterians in the Drumclog camp, and out of it, gravely
doubted whether their efforts and struggles for civil
and religious liberty would be crowned by God with
success, because of the blood-guiltiness of Balfour and
his colleagues in the cruel and wicked murder of
Archbishop Sharp.   Most assuredly, a good cause is
never advanced by cruelty, vindictiveness, and
oppression.   Victorious at Drumclog, the all-important
question for the victors was this : What were they to
do next ?   On this vital question diverse and contradictory opinions were entertained in the camp of the
insurgents.   Some of the leaders were for dispersing,
and some were for marching on Hamilton, Glasgow,

Edinburgh, and London. Some were for converting
Charles II. to their religious and political views, and
some were for setting up and establishing a Free
Republic in Scotland. Some were for a Free Parliament
of the Scottish Nation. The most sensible of them
were for a Free Parliament and a Free Assembly of the
Kirk. As usual in almost every insurrectionary movement, the efforts of the moderate or rational party
were defeated by the fanaticism and violence of the
extreme parties in the two opposite camps.

*The Conventiclers march on Glasgow and are
defeated.*—On the night of the battle of Drumclog, the
captains of the insurgent army stayed at the house of
Lord Loudon; and, in his lordship's absence, were hospit-
ably entertained by Lady Loudon his wife, who, like
many of her sex in Scotland at the time, was a violent
and uncompromising Whig and Covenanter, and stood
up boldly, and in spite of all consequences, for what she
thought the true religion of God. Next day, the
conventiclers marched to Glasgow, where Hamilton
divided his forces into two bodies or divisions, to
enable him to attack the city from different points.
But, by the time of their arrival, the royal forces had
erected strong breast-works within the city. With
Claverhouse and Lord Ross at their head, they defeated
one division of the conventiclers, and chased it out of
the city, and saw the other division flying to join the
division which had been defeated. The two divisions
being joined, they halted at Lord Loudon's house.
But hearing Claverhouse's trumpets sounding the alarm
to horse, they fell back on Hamilton Palace, and were
left undisturbed near Bothwell Bridge, which is close to
the Palace.

Claverhouse ordered to Stirling, and afterwards to Western counties.—Claverhouse was ordered by the Privy Council to join Lord Linlithgow, the commander-in-chief of the Scottish forces. Thus, his independent command ceased for a short time. But when, a few days afterwards, a large army was concentrated at and despatched from Edinburgh against the insurgents, encamped near Bothwell Bridge, he was made captain of a troop of the Royal Scottish life-guards. After the battle of Bothwell Bridge, he obtained a new commission, and was sent back to his old work in the disturbed Western counties. In the interval between the battle of Drumclog and the resumption of his old duties under his new commission, events of the greatest importance were taking place in Scotland. To these I now wish to draw your attention, in order that you may have a proper understanding of the events which properly belong to Claverhouse's biography.

IV.—THE BATTLE OF BOTHWELL BRIDGE; THE CAMERONIANS;

AND THE TEST ACT OF 1681.

The Scottish Government alarmed, and the Covenanters elated.—Immediately after the battle of Drumclog, the Privy Council of Scotland, totally unprepared to cope with a serious insurrection, ordered a concentration of the military forces of the kingdom to take place at Edinburgh; called out the militia, except in the disaffected counties; and denounced the insurgents as traitors, whom they summoned to surrender at discretion. The Covenanters were also

Y

busy. They were frantic with exultation; for they had lately been more successful than they had ever anticipated. Men in large numbers, varying from 5,000 to 10,000, flocked from all parts of the South-west of Scotland to the standard of the Covenant. The conventicle meeting of the first of June had assumed gigantic proportions, and had ended in open rebellion against the established Government of the country. The position was serious and critical. The majority of their ministers spent their time in preaching against the Pope and Prelacy, and their military leaders quarrelled amongst themselves. The moderate Cove-nanters, called Erastians by the extremists, with John Welsh and David Hume at their head, asked no more for themselves or their party than they were willing to give to other people. They had no serious quarrel with the King's government and the bishops of the Established Church, and merely wished to worship God after their own fashion. The extreme, or high-flying, Covenanters were led by Robert Hamilton, Donald Cargill, and Thomas Douglas, Hackston and Balfour. Cargill and Douglas were ministers, and both were violent and disloyal in speech and action. This extreme party talked much of liberty, freedom, and God. But their political and religious ideas were confused, unreason-able, and extravagant. The extreme Covenanters were unanimously against the King's indulgence to tender consciences in matters of religion. They, and they alone, as they thought, knew what was the true religion, and were prepared to force other people in Scotland to worship as they thought fit to dictate.

Monmouth sent to Scotland as commander-in-chief.
—The state of Scotland at this time was, therefore,

very alarming; and the King and his English
Council doubted the ability of the Privy Council of
Scotland to put down the insurrection which had
arisen, and to restore peace in Scotland. Accordingly,
the Duke of Monmouth, with a commission as commander-in-chief, and with full powers to negotiate
and settle terms of peace with the insurgents, was
despatched from London by the King and the
English Government. These powers were put in
force on the day before the battle of Bothwell Bridge
through the medium of Lord Melville. But the
Covenanters would not agree to lay down their arms,
and the negotiations consequently came to an end.
Other negotiations, to which I shall presently refer,
were equally fruitless. Monmouth was the King's
eldest illegitimate and favourite son. He was even
said to put forth pretensions to be legitimate, a son born
in lawful wedlock. He had not a shadow of foundation
for this pretension. He had served in the Low
Countries under the French General Turenne, and also
under William Prince of Orange. He was popular,
polished, and a Protestant. Though a libertine, he
was a favourite of the Puritans. He was ardent and
intrepid in the field of battle, and effeminate and
irresolute everywhere else. He had great personal
courage, and personal graces of mind and body.
Indeed, the Duke was celebrated for his manly beauty
and his personal graces and high accomplishments.
But, when he ought to have been prompt and decisive
in action, he was vacillating and uncertain. Monmouth
left London on the fifteenth of June, and arrived in
Edinburgh on the eighteenth of June 1679. He at
once took the field against the insurgents.

The Cameronian and Moderate Presbyterians in the insurgent camp.—In the insurgent camp, there were several fierce and fanatical leaders, who had great influence over the multitude, and who regarded every proposal which was not based on the solemn League and Covenant as null and void, impious and unchristian. These leaders were strong Calvinists, who believed in predestination in all things spiritual and temporal, and consequently in the happening of human events as God allows them, and independently of any freewill on man's part. The extreme Covenanters afterwards became Cameronians. These men were severe in aspect, morose in temper, and haughty of heart. They believed that the pale of salvation was open for them exclusively, and that all other Christians, however slight were the shades of difference of doctrine from their own, were, in fact, little better than outcasts or reprobates. The moderate Presbyterians were very different from these extremists. Their object was the re-establishment of peace on fair and honourable terms, by securing their own religion and their own liberty. They disclaimed any desire to tyrannise over the conscience, or liberty, of other people.

Description of the Royalist camp.—The Duke of Monmouth took up his camp on Bothwell Muir, an open common, two miles distant from the Clyde, on the other side of which was the camp of the insurgents. On the twenty-second of June, he reached Bothwell. His advance-guard held the little town of Bothwell, about a quarter of a mile from the river; but his main force remained encamped on the moor. Monmouth was the general in command of the royal army, and Dalziel was his lieutenant. The Marquis of Montrose commanded the cavalry, and Lord Linlithgow the foot. The royal forces were of considerable magnitude. Monmouth was said to have had 15,000 men under his command; but his total force did not exceed half that number. Still, he had under him three or four English regiments, and the flower of Charles's army. There were also the Scottish life-guards, with Claverhouse at the head of a troop of them, burning with a strong desire to avenge their late defeat at Drumclog. There were also other Scottish regiments there assembled. There was also a large body of cavalry, composed partly of gentlemen volunteers, and partly of the tenants of the crown, who were bound to perform military service for their fiefs. There were also several large bodies of Highlanders, under their respective chiefs, with strange language, religion, and manners, and with keen eyes to the forfeitures and fines and plunder likely to arise to themselves from the defeat of the insurgents. These Highlanders formed a formidable part of the royal army. A complete train of field artillery accompanied the royal forces. By a miracle alone could the ill-equipped, ill-disciplined, and tumultuary army of the insurgents escape utter destruction.

Monmouth and Dalziel described.—At daybreak on the twenty-second of June, and on a knoll near to and on the north of Bothwell Bridge, there was a conference between Monmouth and a deputation from the insurgent camp. This knoll commanded an extensive view of the distant country, and of the insurgent camp. The Duke I have already described. His lieutenant, Thomas Dalziel, was a very different man from his Grace. Dalziel's dress was composed of

chamois leather, curiously slashed, and covered with
antique lace. He wore a breast-plate, over which
spread a hoary beard which had never been
cut since the execution of Charles I. His high
and wrinkled forehead, his fierce grey eyes, and
marked features, evinced strength unbroken by
age; and also evinced stern resolution, unsoftened
by humanity. He was more feared and hated by the
Whigs than even Claverhouse himself. He was also
as much feared for his cruelty and indifference to
humanity and human sufferings as he was respected
for his undeniably steady loyalty and undaunted
valour. For my present purpose, I have already
sufficiently described Claverhouse.

*Terms offered by Monmouth to the insurgent deputa-
tion.*—The members of the deputation from the
insurgent camp were Welsh, Hume, and Ferguson
Caithoch. The Duke received them courteously, and
patiently heard them read the Hamilton Declaration,
which they submitted to him as a detailed statement of
their grievances and demands. The grievances were
indisputable; and the demands were moderate. The
demands of the Moderates were a free exercise of
religion, a free Parliament, and a free General
Assembly of the Church. The Duke said, in answer,
that he could not treat with armed rebels; and that,
if they would surrender and lay down their arms, he
would do all he could to get pardon for them for the
past, and also toleration for them for the future. He
allowed them an hour to decide on their course of
action. He could not have acted in any other way; for
insurgents must win, or must suffer the punishment of
rebellion. The deputation returned to the insurgent

camp, and there they found tumult and disorder added to want of discipline, and their own lives endangered by the fury of Hamilton against them. The terms of peace offered by the Duke were neither rejected nor accepted by the insurgents. What really happened was, that the time, allowed to accept or reject them, was permitted to elapse, and the fight was begun without further parley.

Insurgent preparations for defence.—A guard was placed by the insurgents at the long and narrow bridge of Bothwell, over which the royal army must necessarily advance to the attack. But this guard was divided and disheartened, and entertained the idea that it was engaged on a desperate and impossible task, and meditated a withdrawal to the main body. Such a withdrawal would have brought speedy, irremediable, and utter ruin to them and their friends. Beyond the bridge was a wide and open plain, and consequently unfit for the protection of undisciplined troops against the attack of a regular army. On the insurgents' side of the river were two or three occupied houses, and some thickets of alder and hazel. At the points where the bridge was, the Clyde is narrow, swift, and deep. The bridge itself was then twelve feet wide, and was guarded by a strong gate-house in the centre. It was then more defensible than it is now; for the bridge has since been widened, and the level of the approaches raised to the height of the centre, instead of having a steep incline from the centre to the ground on each side of the river. Hackston of Rathillet, with a few men, had taken possession of the gate-house. Balfour of Kinloch, with a few more men, had planted themselves among the alder bushes. The passage by the bridge was blocked, and the gates of the guard-house were closed. Videttes were posted by the insurgents to watch the march of the royal army. At first the insurgents, who were holding a day of humiliation for the sins of the country, refused to obey the commands of their officers, and reeled to and fro, hither and thither, in the greatest alarm and trepidation, and were agitated like waves of the sea. They were a confused, unorganised mass; a helpless, stupid rabble. The timid and the prudent withdrew from the field of battle, and gave up their cause as lost. The rest were proposing to elect new officers in the very sight of the royal army. Although they were from 4,000 to 6,000 men in arms, the insurgent army was in danger of falling to pieces without a single blow. Nothing is more true than that mobs, as well as mob-leaders, are easily excited and as easily depressed. As no answer was returned to the Duke by the insurgents to his proposal, he gave the order to his troops to advance.

The royal forces advance to the attack.—Supported by squadrons of cavalry, the glittering masses of English foot-guards directed their march towards the bridge. The artillery were quietly engaged in. planting their guns against the bridge, and the Highlanders were eagerly engaged in searching for a ford to cross over the river. Too late, the insurgents sent off reinforcements to support the guard on the bridge, and their officers set to work to get their men into their ranks. They tried to raise a psalm, and so far succeeded, amidst fear and consternation. The royal army shouted; the Highlanders yelled; the cannon began to roar on one side, and the muskets began to be fired on both sides ; and Bothwell Bridge and the adjacent banks were enveloped in wreaths of smoke.

The insurgents defeated on the bridge, and the royalists victorious.—With great spirit the royalists commenced to attack the bridge. The two regiments of foot-guards were formed into close column, and quickly rushed toward the river. One corps, deploying along the right bank, commenced a galling fire on the defenders of the gate-house ; and, at the same time, the other corps pressed on to occupy the bridge itself. The insurgents sustained the attack with great constancy and courage. While a part of their number returned the fire across the river, the rest maintained a discharge of musketry upon the royalists at the end of the bridge itself, and upon every avenue by which the royal soldiers endeavoured to approach it. The royalists suffered severely ; but still they gained ground. Then the insurgents near the bridge were reinforced from their main body, and began a heavy fire, and the royal soldiers returned it. The firing was vehement on both sides, and the issue of the action seemed doubtful. Monmouth, riding a white charger, had remained on the top of the knoll, which I have already described. Thence he urged, entreated, and animated the exertions of his soldiers. By his orders, the cannon ceased to fire on the main body of the insurgents, and was directed against the defenders of the bridge. Still the issue seemed doubtful. He then threw himself from his horse, and led the foot-guards, and was followed by Dalziel with the Lennox Highlanders. The ammunition of the defenders of the bridge began to fail. Messages for aid

were sent to the main body of the insurgents, but
no aid ever arrived in answer to these messages.
Hackston and his men fought an hour in defending
the guard-house of the bridge, and completely
exhausted their store of powder. Hamilton ordered
Hackston to retire, and he was obeyed. The portal
gates were then broken down; the obstacles removed
and thrown into the river; and the insurgents, after
fighting bravely, had to retire and defend themselves
in the houses and copsewood on their side of the river.
The royalists poured over the bridge and formed for
attack in the open, and to all intents and purposes they had won the day; and the battle of
Bothwell Bridge, if battle it can be called, was
practically at an end.

*Claverhouse and Dalziel pursue, slay, and seize the
rebels in large numbers.*—Claverhouse had been im-
patiently waiting for the defeat of the Covenanters.
When the bridge was carried by the royalists, he
crossed over it, and formed his cavalry in line on
the moor. He then fell on the insurgents, and hewed
them down right and left. The insurgent ranks were
broken to atoms, utterly routed, and fled in all
directions from the field of battle. The cries of
" Kill! kill! "—" No quarter! " resounded from the
royal army, and were carried out to the letter.
Dalziel was busy on the field of battle with his Highlanders, armed with their broadswords, which flashed
in the sunlight as they were brandished against the
Covenanters flying in all directions for life and safety.
Dalziel's carnage was fearful; but his hand was
stopped by Monmouth's orders. Dalziel would have
quenched the rebellion by the utter destruction of the

rebels; and, I believe, Claverhouse would gladly have done the same.   But Monmouth was not of their way of thinking in this affair.   He was merciful and mild; they were merciless and cruel.   The dead and wounded were numerous on both sides.   Balfour of Kinloch was wounded in the sword arm and disabled. Hamilton, the military commander of the rebels, fled, and, as Wodrow states, left the world to doubt whether he acted most like a traitor, a coward, or a fool.   Of the insurgents, 1200 surrendered, and were taken prisoners to Edinburgh, and suffered great cruelties by being huddled together for several months in the churchyard of Greyfriars Church.   Most of them were discharged on their own bonds for their good behaviour.   Two hundred of the most resolute and obstinate of them were shipped off to the plantations, and were wrecked and drowned in the Orkneys.   Four or five hundred of the Covenanters, states Wodrow, were slain in the fields.   Not many of these were slain on the bridge.

Duke of York's administration.—In 1680, the Duke of York was sent to Scotland by his brother, King Charles II., and placed by him at the head of the administration of that kingdom.   At or about the same time, the Exclusion Bill was under discussion in England, and was vehemently promoted by the English Roundheads, who opened up negotiations with the oppressed Scotch Presbyterians, who then endured an oppression and cruelty far greater than the Non-conformists had ever known in England.   The Duke of York was hard and stern by nature, and was unpopular by reason of his religion.   He was sent to Scotland about the time that the savage and barbarous

Lauderdale was sinking into his grave. The Duke of
York's administration in Scotland was worse, harsher,
crueller, and more unparallelled by odious laws and
punishments than the Duke of Lauderdale's administration. The Scottish Privy Council had power to
put state prisoners to the rack. Although the
members of the Privy Council often could not stand
the infliction of the rack on prisoners, yet the Duke
of York took pleasure in the cruellest of such punishments. After the Parliament of 1680 was ended, the
Duke of York returned to London. He went back to
Scotland in 1681 to preside over the deliberations of the
Scotch Parliament of that year. During his vice-
royalty in Scotland, he was personally affable and
courteous, and gained the good opinion of all sorts of
people in Scotland. In consequence of the Test Act,
the Dukes of Monmouth and Hamilton resigned their
offices in the Scottish Government; and the Duke of
York, refusing to take the oath, resigned his office of
Lord High Commissioner of Scotland; and the Earl
of Argyle ultimately lost his life by taking the oath
under such restrictions as appeared to him just and
reasonable, but which was held to be unjustifiable and
treasonable.

*Succession and Test Acts passed in the reign of
Charles* II.—During this Parliament of 1681, two
important Acts demand our special attention, namely,
(1) as to the succession to the crown, and (2) as to the
tests for official employments. By the first Act, it was
asserted that the kings of Scotland derived their royal
power from God Almighty alone, and succeeded
lineally thereto according to the known degrees of
blood, which could not be interrupted, suspended, or

divested by any act or statute whatsoever; and that any attempt to alter the succession to the Imperial crown of Scotland was rebellion. It was also thereby further declared that the right to the crown devolved on the next heir, and that no difference of religion, and no assent of Parliament, could alter or divest the right of succession and the lineal descent of the crown to the nearest and lawful heirs. The second Act was entituled, An Act anent Religion, and the test to be taken from every person holding office in the Government or in corporations; and extended downwards to schoolmasters and clerks on the civil side, and to the rank and file of the army on the military side. The oath to be taken under this Act expressed belief in the Presbyterian religion as contained in the Confession of Faith of the first Scottish Parliament of James VI., and adherence thereto for life, and for the education of children. It also recognised the king as supreme governor in all causes, ecclesiastical as well as civil. The Test Act was aimed at the Papists and the Covenanters, and, as a rule, would be refused by all of them; for the Papist would see that the Test Act was aimed at the Pope, and the Covenanter, that it was against his own principles as too Erastian. By this Act, power was given to the king's officers and soldiers to put the oath to all persons; and also to search, examine, and apprehend all persons suspected of disloyalty to the king and the laws. Under it, men taken with arms in their hands were to be shot; and rebels without arms in their hands were to be tried by the Privy Council, or by a civil or military officer entrusted with authority from the Crown or the Privy Council, or at common law. This harsh and fantastic

Act of Parliament aroused the deadly hatred of the Covenanters against the Government. It had even to be explained by a Declaration of the Privy Council before it was accepted by several of the King's most sincere friends.

Observations on Test Act and Argyle's execution.— The Act of Settlement contained a declaration that the Act was to be permanent, and unalterable by subsequent Parliaments. Such a declaration was clearly *ultra vires*, and not binding on subsequent Parliaments. This Act was, in fact, repealed by Parliament in 1689 and rejected thenceforward by Parliament. No supreme Parliament can bind another supreme Parliament. At some future date this principle may yet have an important application in regard to the Union between England and Scotland in 1707, and, *e.g.* to the operation of the Union Treaty in regard to the Established Church of Scotland. With some few exceptions, the Test Act was taken by nearly all to whom it was offered. These exceptions were the Cameronians and the Earl of Argyle. The Earl was the son of the Marquis executed in 1661, and who was himself inprisoned in Edinburgh Castle, whence he was released in 1663, when Middleton fell from power, and when the Earldom of Argyle, but not the Marquisate, was restored to the Campbells. The Earl's power was great amongst the Presbyterians, and his estates and hereditary offices were tempting possessions to the rapacious courtiers and nobles of Scotland at that time. Argyle refused to take the oath of the Test Act unless with a special interpretation, " so far as consistent with itself and the Protestant religion." He fell into a trap of his enemies. He was indicted for treason " by leasing-making" before the Earl of Queensberry as justice-general, with four other judges on the bench, and with fifteen noblemen as jurymen, on the thirteenth of December 1681. He was found guilty on the twenty-fourth of December, and was condemned to be executed, and his estates were forfeited. His extensive heritable jurisdictions were divided amongst the King's courtiers or their friends. His estates were, after the Revolution of 1688, restored to his son Lord Lorne. He himself escaped from Edinburgh Castle and reached Holland, where he planned a descent on Scotland, and was defeated in 1685. He was executed in Edinburgh on this judgment for leasing-making in 1681, and not for invasion in 1685.

The Cameronians and their opinions.—For the purpose of clearness and brevity, I shall now, and once for all, dispose of the tenets of the Cameronians, whose great leaders were Donald Cargill and Richard Cameron, who entered Sanquhar in Dumfries, on the twenty-second of June 1680, at the head of about twenty men, and published the Sanquhar Declaration, which clearly shows that the Cameronians had political as well as religious objects in view. The Sanquhar Declaration was read and nailed to the market-cross of Sanquhar by Cameron, and it became the great leading testimony of all who were subsequently designated Cameronians. This Declaration announced that the Lord's discontent with His people was in not disowning Charles Stuart for his perjury and usurpation in Church matters, and for his tyranny in civil matters. The declarants claimed to represent the True Presbyterian Kirk and Covenanted Nation of Scotland; and disowned Charles Stuart as having

any right or title to the crown, which, they alleged, he
had forfeited years before by his perjury and breach of
the Covenant between God and His Kirk, and by his
usurpation of the crown and of the royal prerogatives,
and of his many breaches in matters ecclesiastic, and
of his tyranny and breach of the *leges regnandi* in
matters civil. They declared that they placed themselves under the standard of the Lord Jesus Christ.
They further declared war against him as an usurper,
and against all the men of his practices as enemies
of the Lord Jesus Christ and His cause and Covenant.
They also denounced the Duke of York as a professed
Papist, and as a man repugnant to their principles and
to their vows to the Most High God. Subsequently,
the Scotch ministers of state, and Charles II., and
his brother the Duke of York were excommunicated
by Cargill, and were thereby, as they thought and
alleged, cast out of the true Church; and, under the
powers and authority claimed by him as a minister
of the true Church on earth, were delivered up to
Satan. Such language would sound strange in our
ears even if uttered against the meanest subject of
the realm, and still more so if it were now uttered
against the Queen, or any of her ministers. A league for
mutual defence was also formed amongst the
supporters of the Sanquhar Declaration. The
members of this league, numbering from 70 to 300
horse and foot, took up a position at Aird's
Moss, in Ayrshire; and, on twenty-second of June
1680, had a scrimmage with Claverhouse's regiment,
then commanded by Bruce of Earlshall, by whom
they were defeated. Richard Cameron was killed
at this battle. But he had the honour of giving

his name to a religious sect which exists and flourishes under the ecclesiastical title of the Reformed Presbyterian Church of Scotland, and also to a regiment which, in the British army, has been distinguished for bravery and heroism in all parts of the world. Cargill and Hackston of Rathillet were made prisoners at the contest at Aird's Moss, and were taken to Edinburgh, where they were tried and executed. The fight at Aird's Moss was the last pitched battle of the serious insurrection in the previous year in the South-west of Scotland.

Severities against the Covenanters after the Test Act.—The murder of Archbishop Sharp, the battles of Drumclog and Bothwell Bridge, the Sanquhar Declaration, and the armed combinations spread all over the South-west of Scotland, having all taken place within a few months, the Government resolved on a course of strong repressive measures to stamp out the dangerous political and religious opinions of the Covenanters, and also to enforce conformity to the then existing Church government, and to compel attendance at church on Sunday. With the last-mentioned object, lists were regularly made up, and the names on the lists were called out, and the absentees were marked, and the obstinate absentees were severely punished by fines and imprisonment. The Government, in fact, resolved to wage a fierce war against the Cameronians, sometimes also called society men, hill men, mountain men, and wild westland Whigs. The Cameronians then issued an Apologetical Declaration of their views and intentions. This Declaration denounced killing for differences of opinion, and stated that they would punish those who were their enemies, *e.g.* such

as bloody militiamen, malicious troopers, soldiers, and
dragoons, and their aiders and abettors. The Privy
Council of Scotland asked the opinion of the Court of
Session as to the lawfulness of this Declaration against
the King's officers; and then issued a Proclamation declaring that the Lords of His Majesty's Privy Council
ordained that any person who owned, or would not
disown upon oath, the said Declaration, which was
alleged to be treasonable, whether such person had
arms or not, should be immediately put to death in
the presence of two witnesses and of the person or
or persons commissioned by the Council to that effect.
This royal Proclamation was an order for military
executions, and without trial before the ordinary courts
of law. Commissions in conformity with this Proclamation were accordingly issued by the Privy
Council. Another form of commission was also issued
by the Privy Council. This gives the form of an oath
of abjuration against the Cameronian Declaration.
It was issued in the form of a commission, applicable
to a limited district in the South-west parts of Scotland, and the commissioners were authorised to indict
those who refused to take this oath of abjuration, and
also to call fifteen men as a jury, and allowed the jury
to judge the persons indicted, and authorised the immediate execution of the sentence of death on such as refuse to disown it, or to answer the questions put to them
before the jury. Both forms were liable to gross abuse.
Persecution had hardened the society men, and turned
them against all civil government, and especially
against monarchical government. The persecuted sects
of Scotland brooded over the severities inflicted on
them, and mistook their own feelings as the oracles of

God, and therefore looked upon their own enemies as the enemies of heaven.

The Covenanters firmly bore the cruelties inflicted on them.—After the Union of the crowns of England and Scotland, the Privy Council of Scotland had, in practice, great judicial powers, as well as the general superintendence of the executive department, vested in it. The Privy Council of Scotland assembled in the ancient Gothic room adjoining the Parliament House in Edinburgh. When a prisoner was examined before the Privy Council, he was interviewed *vivâ voce*, and he was liable to be tortured by the thumb-screw and the steel boot to extort confession from him. The Privy Council had the power of condemning and punishing prisoners to fine, imprisonment, and banishment. The thumb-screw and the boot caused exquisite pain, and a doctor was present at the examination of prisoners brought before the Privy Council to see and determine how far the prisoners could bear the tortures inflicted upon them. I pass over the details of the horrible cruelties inflicted by the Government on the persecuted Covenanters about this period; because they in no way help us to understand what manner of man Claverhouse was. But I cannot pass over the great and indomitable courage and obstinacy which the Covenanters displayed on the battle-field, and in the presence of the tribunals before which they were tried. They defied the civil power, and courted martyrdom as the greatest and most glorious reward which could be conferred upon them in this world. In all their troubles and adversities, they looked forward through this vale of tears from mortality to immortality, from a brief life on earth to life everlasting in heaven, and there to be

with God's saints for evermore.   Through all the days
of the persecution, the Covenanters displayed mar-
vellous firmness and constancy to their religious
opinions and political doctrines.

*Monmouth returns to England, and persecution of
Covenanters continues.*—After the battle of Bothwell
Bridge, Monmouth hastened back to London, and
prevailed on the King to try the effect of gentle
measures for the brutal folly and cruelty of Lauderdale's Government.   But the recall of the Duke of
York, the King's brother, from Holland in 1680, about
the same time as Monmouth arrived at Court, put an
end to these humane counsels.   Monmouth himself
was soon afterwards in exile, and nothing was done
to carry out his policy of conciliation towards the
Covenanters.   Lauderdale's power, however, had already passed its meridian ; but, for the present, the old
policy of religious persecution was continued as before.

V.—CLAVERHOUSE IS SENT BACK TO THE SOUTH-WEST
OF SCOTLAND.

Claverhouse returns to the West counties.—After
the battle of Bothwell Bridge in 1679, Claverhouse
was sent back to his old employment in the South-
west of Scotland ; and, by order of the Privy Council
was, as I have already said, entrusted with the control
of the disaffected counties.   He, in fact, was entrusted,
by his commission, with the rights and privileges of
what was practically martial law, which, in all cases
where it exists, supersedes the ordinary law of the land.
Although great exaggeration has taken place as regards

the persons injured under the commissions issued by the Privy Council, there is no doubt whatever that great harshness and cruelty were perpetrated in carrying out the abjuration oath. Claverhouse himself confessed to acts of barbarity enough to make the blood of the present generation run cold: as, for example, in the case of John Brown of Priestfield, even although Brown's case fell within the terms of the commission by the Privy Council to Claverhouse. Still, with the sufferings of the Covenanters in the South-west of Scotland there was not much general sympathy in the other parts of the country.

Claverhouse suspended from all his public offices.— Claverhouse, under his new commission from the Privy Council, levied fines, seized arms, horses, and other movable property belonging to the insurgents, rebels, and non-jurors. In consequence of unjust charges being brought against him by the Scottish treasurer, the Marquis of Queensberry, in connection with not properly and regularly accounting to the Treasury for the fines and property seized by him under his commission, he was somewhat harshly and peremptorily suspended from all his public offices in the West of Scotland. Hence, Bruce of Earlshall acted in the West in his place for sometime. At the court in London, and in the Privy Council in Edinburgh, and also in the West of Scotland, Claverhouse had many enemies. Having gone to London to see the King in regard to those charges, he, as appears from the orders of the Privy Council of the third and twentieth of February 1681, satisfied the King of his innocence.

He is restored, and raised to colonel, &c.—In 1681, and in the second year of the Duke of York's administra-

tion of Scotland, and the year of the Test and
Succession Acts, Claverhouse was reinstated in his
commission. In the following year, the Duke returned
to England, and there was, says Wodrow, a respite of
severities in the South-west. Claverhouse's new commission made him sheriff of Wigtonshire, and deputy-
sheriff of Dumfries-shire, and steward of Kirkcudbright
and Annandale. By this commission, he was authorised
to hold criminal courts in Wigtonshire, and try
delinquents by jury. His letters to the lord treasurer
of Scotland, in the early part of the year 1682, show
his policy and his proceedings then. Claverhouse did
not like the harassing and imperfect schemes patronized
by his superiors for the pacification of the disturbed
counties in Scotland. He wished and proposed to
raise a permanent garrison for this excellent purpose ;
but his scheme was not adopted. He never was a
favourite with the old Scottish aristocratic courtiers,
who did not like to have projects laid before them by
a *novus homo*. Besides, they had their own selfish aims
to advance as well as to forward the interests of their
King and country. In Scotland, in the time of Claverhouse, two hundred years ago, in order to rise in the political world, one must have no personal opinions, but must
profess to be humble and obedient, and be all things
to all men, and especially to the men in power, or who
seek to be in power. If Claverhouse had not acquired
the favour of the King and of the Duke of York, he
would have been ruined by the network of intrigue which
surrounded him on every side. Amongst other enemies,
Claverhouse had the misfortune to incur the enmity
of Sir James Dalrymple of Stair. Sir James's family
had been settled in Galloway for many generations.

Sir James himself had been professor of philosophy in
Glasgow for a time.   He was one of the greatest lawyers
Scotland ever produced.   He was a staunch Presbyterian.   As he would not take the oath under the
Test Act, he, in 1681, was dismissed from his office
of president of the Court of Session in Edinburgh.
Moreover, Claverhouse was no favourite with the
Duke of Lauderdale ; because he advocated gentler,
and yet more effective, measures against the Covenanters than suited Lauderdale.   *Vide* Claverhouse's letter
to Queensberry on the fifth of March 1682.   Sir James's
son, Sir John Dalrymple, afterwards Lord Advocate
of Scotland, and the instigator and prime mover of the
wicked and detestable massacre of Glencoe, brought a
charge of extortion and malversation in the Privy
Council against Claverhouse.   On the other hand,
Claverhouse brought counter charges against his
accuser Sir John Dalrymple.   The Council decided
against Sir John, and found him guilty of employing
rebels, and winking at treasonable practices, of stirring
up the people against the King's troops, and of grossly
misrepresenting Claverhouse to the Privy Council.
Sir John was also fined £500 and costs, and was ordered
to be imprisoned in Edinburgh Castle till the fine and
costs were paid.   Claverhouse himself was acquitted.
Further, by a commission, dated the twenty-fifth of
December 1682, he was promoted by the King to a
colonelcy of a royal regiment of cavalry.   In the
following March, he was sent to England with
despatches from the Council to the King, and also to
the Duke of York, who was then, at all events, nomi-
nally Lord High Commissioner for Scottish affairs.
Claverhouse returned to Scotland in May 1683.   He

was sworn in as a member of the Privy Council of Scotland in 1684 and 1685. In 1688, he was a major-general.

He becomes owner of Dudhope, and Constable of Dundee.—Up till 1684, Claverhouse had not any means of increasing his modest private fortune, or enlarging his patrimonial lands and estates, which were almost all scattered about in the parishes of Dundee, Monifieth, Tealing, Glamis, and Kirriemuir, in the county of Forfar. His civil and military appointments, and his long and devoted services to the Government, gave him, as he thought, some claims on his official colleagues for a share of the confiscated estates which were divisable amongst the court officials of the day. In general, the Scottish politicians of the seventeenth century were an army of hungry and ravenous vultures seeking for prey and plunder out of the public treasury, and not very particular as to the rights of parties who stood in their way to the gratification of their avarice, or of their aggrandisement. Thus, after the Duke of Lauderdale died in 1682, his successor, Charles Maitland of Hatton, and then Earl of Lauderdale, was officially attacked in connection with his office as master of the Mint. At the instigation of Sir George Gordon of Haddo, who had been made president of the Court of Session, lord chancellor of Scotland, and Earl of Aberdeen, a commission was appointed to inquire into the condition of the coinage of Scotland. By this commission, Maitland of Hatton was declared to have misappropriated £70,000 of the public money. To satisfy this claim, he had to strip himself of a great part of his property, and particularly of the estate of Dudhope, and of the office of hereditary constable of

Dundee, both conferred in 1673 upon him and his heirs by the King, soon after the death, without leaving issue, of John Scrimgeour, third Viscount of Dudhope, and created Earl of Dundee and Lord Scrimgeour and Inverkeithing in 1661. This estate of Dudhope, *etiam constabularium castri de Dunde,* had been in the family of the Scrimgeours from the year 1296, when they had been conferred on the Scrimgeours by Sir William Wallace. Claverhouse now pressed his claim to the estate of Dudhope and the office of constable of Dundee. His colleagues tried to play him false as to the estate of Dudhope and the constableship of Dundee. But the arrangement was ultimately carried out in 1684.

An outrageous claim as Constable and Provost of Dundee repudiated.—In 1688, King James nominated Claverhouse provost of Dundee, and as such, and also as constable, Claverhouse claimed to have the custody of the Charters of the town, and to have jurisdiction over its magistrates. The elected provost of Dundee rightly repudiated Claverhouse's demand, which could not be legally maintained, inasmuch as the town of Dundee was then and had long been a Royal Burgh. In the following year, Claverhouse having violently attempted to enforce his claim, Provost Fletcher courageously summoned his townsmen to his aid, and forced the new hereditary constable to fly from the town for his life. Claverhouse returned soon afterwards with a body of followers to enforce his alleged rights over the town. But Mrs Maxwell of Tealing saw him and his followers crossing the Sidlaws, which are a line of mountain-spurs from the Grampians, and lie between the valley of Strathmore and the ground sloping down to

the river Tay.   As she suspected that they were marching towards the town with no friendly intentions, she,
therefore, promptly forwarded information to the
provost of Dundee of what she had seen.   In consequence of this information, Provost Fletcher and his
fellow-townsmen   were   prepared   for   Claverhouse's
arrival, and gave him such a warm reception as compelled
him to abandon all future attacks on the town to enforce
his supposed rights.   Baulked in their revenge, Claverhouse and his men set fire to the Rotten Row, or
Hilltown, which was then a row of houses outside the
walls of the town of Dundee, and which now forms a
part of the town or rather city of Dundee, which has
extended itself so marvellously in every direction, and
has been lately so much increased in population,
wealth, public institutions, and general importance.

*Claverhouse exerts himself on behalf of some
prisoners in Dundee.*—When Claverhouse was staying
with his wife at Dudhope, in August or September
1684, he found a number of prisoners in the tolbooth
of Dundee under sentence of death.   Their gravest
offence was theft.   Therefore, he exerted himself on
their behalf, and had milder sentences imposed upon
them ;   and   obtained   permission   from   the   Privy
Council to deal with the same class of offenders
in future.   *Vide* Privy Council Register, 10th
September 1684.

*Claverhouse was married to Lady Jean Cochrane,
who bore him a son.*—Claverhouse was married to Lady
Jean Cochrane, the granddaughter of the Earl of
Dundonald, and daughter of William Lord Cochrane
and his wife Catherine, the daughter of the Presbyterian
Earl of Cassillis.   Lady Jean   was   the   youngest

JOHN GRAHAM OF CLAVERHOUSE.

daughter of seven children; and had the reputation of
being very beautiful. Her mother was of Whiggish and
Presbyterian proclivities. Claverhouse himself was a
Tory and an Episcopalian, and a Privy Councillor of a
Tory and Episcopalian Government in Scotland.
Through his wife he might, therefore, be suspected of
being tainted with Whiggish and Presbyterian tendencies. Therefore, on the 19th of June 1684, he
wrote to Queensberry as follows : But, ere long, I will,
in despite of them, let the world see that it is not in
the power of love, nor of any other folly, to alter my
loyalty. He also wrote to his lordship on the very
same day : " The young lady was right principled, and
he would answer for her ; " and again : " Had she not
been right principled, she would never, in despite of
her mother and her relations, have made choice of a
persecutor." The contract of marriage was signed at
Paisley on the 10th of June 1684, and the marriage
was celebrated on the following day. The lady's
jointure was fixed at 5,000 merks Scots, which would
be equal to about £250 of English money, and was
secured on property in Forfarshire and Perthshire.
The lady's dowry was 40,000 merks Scots, or £2,000
sterling, which, in her day, was a considerable fortune
for a younger child. Lady Jean exercised no influence
over Claverhouse in one way or another. She re-
appears in history in the stormy period which preceded
the battle of Killiecrankie ; but, although he seems to
have had a fond regard for her, and she for him, he and
she were never much in each other's society after their
marriage. Indeed, on the very day of his marriage,
he received news that the Whigs of Glasgow were
astir, and were bent on mischief, and he at once

hurried away on his public and military duties from
his newly married bride. In the following August,
while enjoying the society of his wife, he grew weary
of a quiet country life in a few days. *Vide* his letter
to Queensberry on the 25th of August 1684. Active employment was a necessity of his existence. By Lady Jean
he had a son, who was born in 1689, and died in infancy.
After Claverhouse's victory and death at Killiecrankie,
Lady Jean was married to William Livingstone, Lord
Kilsyth. A popular rumour long prevailed that
Claverhouse's death was caused by the hand of an
assassin, whose action was instigated by Lady Jean's
second husband. For this popular story there is no
proof whatever. These few observations must suffice
for what I have to say as to Claverhouse's brief
married life. I must now resume my remarks as to his
public career, and as to the events which led to the
battle of Killiecrankie.

VI.—IMPORTANT EVENTS IN THE REIGN OF JAMES II.

The accession of James II.—Charles II. died on the
sixth of February 1685, and as a member of the Roman
Catholic Church. His brother, the Duke of York, succeeded him to the throne as James II. At the restoration of Charles II. in 1660, the people went mad with
rejoicing. But, at the accession of James II., one
party—the Covenanters—in Scotland looked forward
to a continuance of oppression, and another party—
the Episcopalians—feared a possible retribution. The
members of the Roman Catholic Church re-appeared
from their hiding-places. All over the country fears
and apprehensions of civil war abounded, and were

partially converted into a reality in Scotland in May 1685 by Argyle's invasion. But all fears of invasion or of civil war were ended by the collapse of Argyle's descent upon the West coast of Scotland, and by the utter defeat of Monmouth at Sedgemoor in 1685. King James II. was by nature stern, imperious, obstinate, unforgiving, and deceitful. James was zealous for his religion and wholly under the control of the Jesuits. At his brother's death he had promised to maintain the Established government in Church and State; but he speedily began to undermine the foundations of both. To carry out this policy against his own country, he, like his brother, had to depend on Louis XIV., who was then the most powerful monarch of Europe. James II. followed his brother Charles II. in his foreign policy. But the marriage of his daughter Mary to William Prince of Orange largely helped to defeat her father's policy. The Princess Mary was a staunch and un-flinching Protestant of the Broad Church stamp. Lord Chancellor Hyde, father-in-law of James II., during a great portion of his son-in-law's reign, performed the chief duties of the English administration. He was an Episcopalian, and hated the Puritans in England and the Presbyterians in Scotland.

The Home and Foreign Policy of James II.—All the efforts made in the latter part of the reign of Charles II. to preserve the executive functions of the state to the King had failed, and the Parliament of England had obtained possession of all the chief pre-rogative functions of the Government in England and in Ireland. The Parliament of Scotland had similarly, and yet not so completely as in England, obtained possession of them in Scotland; and the Parliaments

of England and Scotland were daily becoming the
predominant powers in the state.   Unless during the
military usurpation of Oliver Cromwell, they have
remained   so   ever   since.   I must   also   remind
you that all the efforts made to exclude James
from   the   throne,   on   the   ground   that   he   was
a Roman Catholic, had entirely failed.   In 1680,
the Exclusion Bill was passed by the English
House of Commons, and was rejected by the English
House of Lords.   In the following year, the English
House of Commons would accept nothing, and would
pass nothing, except the Exclusion Bill ; and the
English House of Lords would not consent to pass it.
Soon after the accession of James II., a violent Whig
re-action sprung up in England and Scotland, and
strong evidences were soon given that the royal
prerogatives were to be put to the issue.   The contest
ended, as you all know, in the defeat of absolute
monarchy and the victory of Representative or Parliamentary Government in the British Empire.   I must
also remind you that, as James could get no pecuniary
assistance from his Parliaments, he became the
vassal and hireling of Louis XIV. of France, as his
brother had been before him.   From the Restoration
in 1660 to the Revolution of 1688, the foreign policy
of our kings, though not of the people, was
dependency on France, and not alliance with Holland
and Sweden against France.   By a secret treaty
made in 1670, Charles II. had agreed to support
Louis' ambitious schemes on the Continent, and
Louis had agreed to support him against rebellion.
Louis XIV. had reduced the king of this country to
the disgraceful position of pensioner and vassal of the

throne of France. Louis' great scheme was to unite the Dutch provinces and Alsace and Lorraine to France by conquest, and to annex Spain to France under a claim to be made by his wife. The Revolution of 1688-89, and the elevation of William Prince of Orange to the English throne, defeated Louis' gigantic schemes of annexation, and James's despotic and religious aims against his country. James's whole reign was a mass of confusion and indecision, in which the king struggled for his religion, and abandoned his duty as a patriotic sovereign. His foreign policy was opposed to the national interests and wishes; but he could not, or would not, abandon his foreign policy, and its disgraceful and mercenary dependence for a national foreign policy against Catholic France, and on behalf of Protestant Holland, combined with a moderate policy in church and state at home. He stuck to his religion, and lost his kingdom in the end.

The King and the Parliament as to the Roman Catholics and Indulgences.—James II., a Roman Catholic king by public profession, struggled for toleration to his own Church; but he found that, in order to obtain his end, he would require to extend toleration to all the Presbyterians and the Quakers. What he really wished was to restore the Roman Catholic religion in England, Scotland, and Ireland. In April 1685, the Scottish Estates met and re-enacted the Test Act, and added a severe clause against conventicles. This new clause was to the effect that all such as should thereafter preach at a fanatical house or field conventicle, as also such as should be present as hearers at field conventicles, should be punished by death and the confiscation of their goods. The King then appealed to the Estates of Scotland for toleration to his own Church. He said that the members of it were loyal and peaceable, and that they should have the protection of the laws and government of their country, and that they should not be suffered to lie under obligations which their religion could not admit. A Bill was accordingly prepared by the King's ministers in Scotland to the effect that Roman Catholics should be under the protection of the laws, and have power to exercise their religion in private, but should not have power to exercise it in public. It was accepted by the Lords of the Articles, and also by a few of the nobles. But it was rejected by the lesser barons, and it was stubbornly opposed by the burgesses in Parliament. It was clear that Scotland would never pass this Bill. The King resolved to carry out his aims in some way or another. He could not bear to be thwarted. Accordingly, in September 1686, the Privy Council of Scotland received a royal command to embody the Bill in an Act of their own, and to proclaim it as thus sanctioned by the King in Council. Objections in the Scottish Privy Council were raised against this command as insufficient legal authority for the suspension of penal statutes passed by the Parliament. The Scottish lord chancellor, the Earl of Perth, said that the royal command was sufficient warrant. The King's instructions were accordingly complied with. Three imperfect indulgences, under stringent conditions, were issued in favour of the Presbyterians and others. At last, in May 1688, a fourth indulgence was issued, and was a full and complete indulgence to the moderate Presbyterians. In all these indulgences, the King spoke " by his own sovereign authority, prerogative royal, and absolute power, which all our subjects are to observe without reserve." Such expressions had hitherto been unknown in the royal proclamations of Scotland, and they then aroused two spectres—the fear of Popery, and the dread of absolute power—which eventually drove the Stuarts from the throne of England, Scotland, and Ireland. Since the Union of the crowns of England and Scotland, the royal prerogative had been growing, and was even declared, not without some foundation, to be as great in Scotland as in despotic France. Foreign political and religious events are often strangely intertwined. As the massacre of St. Bartholomew ruined Queen Mary, so the revocation of the Edict of Nantes in 1684 by Louis XIV. drove the French refugees into England and Scotland, and was not without its effect on Scotland and England at the time of the Revolution of 1688-9.

Severities against the Conventiclers—The law for punishing conventiclers was not allowed to lie idle. Royal proclamations were issued to punish, destroy, and root them out of the land. The conventiclers said that the prosecutions against them by King James were more cruel than ever. Many ships, full of men, honest and conscientious sufferers for their faith, and driven to madness by the cruelties inflicted on them, were sent to Jamaica, New Jersey, and Barbadoes, and often never reached their destination, and never without losing large numbers of their human freights on the passage by the heart-rending cruelties and indignities inflicted on them. During the killing time, as it is called, comprehending the latter part of the reign of Charles II. and the early part of James

II., the iron entered into the souls of the conventiclers, and made them fierce and cruel. To many of the exiled Scottish conventiclers the Puritan settlers of New England offered an asylum of future peace and prosperity. The King's first proclamation of indulgence was to the Roman Catholics; and not to the Presbyterians or Independents. The cause of this priority was, that the Roman Catholics were the King's own co-religionists, and that they and the Quakers held the principle of passive obedience as regards sovereigns and princes; and that neither the Presbyterians nor the Independents held that doctrine, but held that they could lawfully fight against tyrants. In England, the House of Commons asked King James to enforce the penal laws against the Nonconformists, while he himself wished to repeal the Test Act. The Conventicle Act was, in my opinion, cruel in its terms, and was atrociously enforced. To punish men for speculative or religious opinions may fill the prisons, and make martyrs, but it will never advance the truth, or make people one whit better. People should be punished for their actions, and for writings or speeches when they incite to such actions as are criminal according to the established laws.

State of religious parties in the reign of James II.—Between the last indulgence of James II., in 1688, and the accession to power of the new government of William and Mary, the Presbyterians were in the majority in the South-west of Scotland, and were there quietly resolving themselves into Presbyteries and Synods. Meanwhile, the indulged Presbyterians would not help the King in his direst extremity; for he had joined the Roman Catholics with themselves in his

indulgence of religious toleration, and he had filled the
chief offices of state in Scotland with Papists, or by
persons favourably inclined towards Popery.   Yet,
although a conspicuous opening for promotion in the
public service was before the eyes of all men in Scotland,
few availed themselves of it.   Amongst the converts to
the old religion and the religious faith of the King,
was the Earl of Perth, lord chancellor, and his brother
Lord Melfort, who was afterwards Secretary for Scotland
to James II.   Claverhouse remained an Episcopalian.

*Pacification of Scotland, and new outbreak and
harshness.*—After the death of Cameron and Cargill
in 1680, the pacification of Scotland made great progress for three or four years.   The Test Oath was
generally taken, and the civil and religious turmoil
of the preceding years appeared to be at an end.
Unexpectedly, however, in June 1684, a meeting was
held by armed Covenanters on Blacklock Moor, on the
borders of Lanarkshire and Stirlingshire.   Dalziel set
out in search of this armed body of men; but could get no
trace of them.   Claverhouse hurriedly rode away from
his bridal party on the same errand, and met with no
better success than Dalziel.   But Colonel Buchan,
Claverhouse's lieutenant, found the party at Lesmahago,
where there was a party of 200 Covenanters, who
fired on his men and wounded one of them.   In the
following July, as a body of Claverhouse's troops were
escorting sixteen prisoners to Dumfries, an attempt at
rescuing the prisoners was made.   Some of the prisoners were killed; some of them broke their necks at
Enterkin Hill in attempting to escape; and only two
of them were taken to Edinburgh.   Then the Government resumed energetic measures against the Cove-

nanters, and dreading a general outbreak, increased the
forces in the garrisons of Scotland.

Claverhouse's promotion and troubles.—In 1688,
Claverhouse was raised by James II. to the
rank of a brigadier of horse and foot in Scotland;
and James Douglas, the brother of the Marquis of
Queensferry, obtained the same military rank, with a
right of precedency by priority of the date of his
commission. But early in the spring of 1685,
Claverhouse was summoned, as I have already stated,
by Queensberry, the then Lord High Treasurer, to
discharge his obligations under his bond for the
fines due under his commission in Galloway. He
asked for more time, and said that his brother, the
deputy-sheriff of Galloway, was collecting the fines.
The Treasurer offered to give him five or six days.
Claverhouse said that this period was the same as no
delay. "Then," said Queensberry, "you shall have
none," and Claverhouse was accordingly obliged to
pay the money. In the following autumn, Claverhouse was summoned to London to be heard on the
complaint he had made to the King against Queensberry. Claverhouse pleaded his own cause with the
King, and the Treasurer was ordered to refund the
money he had compelled Claverhouse to pay. He,
accompanied by Lord Balcarres, returned to Edinburgh
on the 24th of December 1685. In the year 1688, he
was promoted to the rank of major-general, and in
March of the same year he was unjustly nominated
Provost of Dundee by the King. On the 12th of
November 1688, at a time when the King's affairs
were in a most critical state, and almost in a desperate
condition, he was, in London, created Viscount of

Dundee by King James II., with a right of succession
to the heirs of his body, and, whom failing, to his
other heirs, and was succeeded in the title by his son
and afterwards by his brother.   If the title had not
suffered attaint and forfeiture by Act of Parliament,
it would have fallen to the family of Graham of
Duntroon, near Dundee.

VII.—GRAVE CHARGES AGAINST CLAVERHOUSE DISCUSSED;

AND GENERAL CONDUCT TOWARDS THE COVENANTERS.

*As to the grave charges of cruelty against Claver-
house.*—Before I lead you onwards to the years 1688-89,
I wish briefly to discuss the charges of wanton and
illegal cruelty alleged to have been perpetrated by
Claverhouse, and upon which his popular reputation
is almost entirely based.   These charges cover a period
of six years from 1679 to 1686.   They are six in number,
and in every case Claverhouse has been unjustly
maligned, or his conduct is defensible on the ground
that he merely executed the laws of his country.
How far a man is morally justified in executing
inhuman laws and inhuman sentences has often been
discussed by moralists and jurists.   Upon that problem I do not now propose to enter.   For the present,
I have to deal with abuses of trust, which involve
legal culpability.   But I may here say that divine
and moral duties must be kept within the sphere of
moral obligations, and decided according to our
consciences; and that, independently of individual conscientious convictions, national and constitutional laws

must be enforced and obeyed by all in the state as an essential condition of national existence. Claverhouse, in his dealings with the Covenanters in the West of Scotland, was a voluntary and willing agent in executing the laws against the conventiclers, and against those who refused to take the Test Act passed by the Scottish Parliament. These laws were not only religious but also civil in their nature, and were enforced against those who were then supposed to be enemies of, and offenders against the State. To compel people to go to the Church at that time, but not now, established by the National Assembly of Scotland, was considered as obligatory on adults and children, as the duty of children to attend elementary schools in the present age is now considered obligatory. This duty of church attendance would have been as sternly enforced, as a civil duty, by the Covenanters if they had had the power, as it was by the Episcopalians of that period. During the Commonwealth, Presbyterianism, 200 years ago, in Scotland, was as dogmatic and persecuting as Episcopalianism there in the end of the 17th century. Freedom of conscience was believed in neither by Presbyterians, Episcopalians, nor Roman Catholics of that age. With these observations, I shall now take up the gravest charges made against Claverhouse, and briefly give you the conclusions at which I have arrived in regard to each of them.

(1) *Wigtown Martyrs.*—Claverhouse has been charged with being concerned in the drowning of Margaret Maclauchlan and Margaret Wilson, the Wigtown Martyrs, on the 11th of May 1685. He had nothing whatever to do with this matter. These two women were tried by commissioners of justiciary

and a jury, and sentenced to death on the 18th of April 1685. They were remanded on the 30th of April, but were drowned as heretics on the 11th of May. The actual offences charged against these two poor women were, that they refused to abjure the Covenant, and refused to attend the Established Episcopalian Church of Scotland. Claverhouse was neither at the trial, nor at the execution of the sentence. The commissioners and judges at their trial were Grierson of Lagg, a great persecutor of the Covenanters, and David Graham, a sheriff-depute of Dumfries-shire, appointed in 1683, and brother of Claverhouse.

(2) *Execution of John Brown.*—Claverhouse has been charged with shooting John Brown in the presence of his wife and child, on the 1st of May 1686. In a letter which he wrote to Queensberry on the 3rd of May 1686, he gives an account of this man's death. He refers to John Brown the elder, and John Brown the younger. He stated that the elder John Brown refused to take the oath, and would not swear that he would not rise up against the King, and further said that he knew no King. Moreover, Claverhouse states that he found bullets and match and treasonable papers in Brown's house. He states deliberately that he caused him to be shot. I, therefore, reject the popular story that his soldiers refused to obey his orders on this occasion. I hold Claverhouse's official account of this execution to be more reliable than the statements of Wodrow or any of his follow-ers. I am not aware of any cotemporary proof of the shocking incidents connected with John Brown's death, and accepted on the evidence of Wodrow, who was not a contemporary, and of Wodrow's followers and co-

religionists. That Brown was put to death by the
orders of Claverhouse, acting under a legal commission
of the established Government of the day, has never
been denied, and cannot be denied. But that
hundreds of Covenanters were fined and imprisoned
by Claverhouse, is no reason for designating him as a
blood-thirsty man. He then proceeds to state that
he had apprehended John Brown the younger at Bothwell; that this man had been guilty of rescuing prisoners
from the King's soldiers at Newmills; and that he had
handed him over to the lieutenant-general to be tried.
This John Brown the younger was a proscribed rebel.
The Act under which Claverhouse acted in ordering
John Brown the elder to be shot, contained these
words: " Any person who owns, or will not disown,
the late Treasonable Declaration, on oath, shall be
immediately put to death; this being always done
in the presence of two witnesses, and the person or
persons having commission to that effect." *Vide*, An
Act of the Privy Council of Charles II. in 1685. The
treasonable declaration referred to in this Act was the
Declaration published by Renwick in October 1684,
to the effect that the Declarants would put their
enemies—the King's servants—to death, " as enemies
to God, and the covenanted work of the reformation,"
just as their enemies had put their friends to death.
Such a declaration, as I have already said, was untenable and treasonable under any theory of civilized
government. The Declaration is given at full length
in Wodrow, IV. 148-9. In taking away the life of
John Brown the elder, Claverhouse acted upon the
authority of the laws of the land, and of the King's
Commission, sanctioned by Parliament, and, therefore,

the act cannot reasonably be said to be either wanton or illegal. If it was a judicial murder, the blame must fall on the Scottish Council who passed the Act of 1685. Claverhouse put Brown the elder to death as a rebel and traitor.

(3) *Death of Gillies and Bryce.*—Claverhouse has been charged with being concerned with the death of Gillies and John Bryce, who were hanged at Mauchline on the 6th of May 1685. Gillies and Bryce were tried before General Drummond and fifteen soldiers on the 5th of May 1685, and were hanged on the following day. Claverhouse had nothing to do with their death.

(4) *Hislop's execution.*—Claverhouse has also been charged with being concerned in the death of Andrew Hislop, who was the son of a poor widow, and was put to death in 1685, as guilty of refusing to take the oath of Abjuration. At the instigation of Johnston of Westerhall, an apostate Presbyterian, Claverhouse asked Hislop to take the oath, and on Hislop refusing so to do, Claverhouse had Hislop shot. Claverhouse here again acted within the terms of his commission, and he appears to have tried to save the unfortunate young man from the sentence of death. But he was overpersuaded by the apostate Johnston. Claverhouse had about this time incurred the anger of his masters the Privy Councillors in Edinburgh, and appears to have been afraid to incur the danger of further disgrace at headquarters. Acting from such motives, I think that Claverhouse was very blameworthy in this case.

(5) *Death of Graham of Galloway.*—Another charge against Claverhouse is that he caused the death of Graham of Galloway in 1682. As military executions

were not sanctioned by law in that year, this charge,
if true, would have been one of murder against
Claverhouse. But the charge is without any foundation, and was neither more nor less than the exaggeration of a charge in the indictment in 1682 against
Claverhouse by Sir John Dalrymple for oppression
by excessive fines and the illegal quartering of troops,
and of malversation in office, and so forth. This
specific charge was made by Defoe, who made another
charge of ruthlessly putting to death Matthew
Mackellwrath in Clanroneld in Carrick. This latter
charge is also absolutely false.

(6) *Death of four men at Auchencloy.*—Another
charge against Claverhouse is that he put four men
at Auchencloy, on Deeside, to death on the 18th of
December 1684. This charge must, I think, be
dismissed by every person who considers the circumstances under which these men were put to death,
and the legal authority which Claverhouse exercised
at the time. On the 11th of December 1684, and
almost immediately after the publication of Renwick's
Declaration, a body of men murdered Peter Peirson,
the minister of Carsphairn, at his own door. Peirson
had made himself obnoxious to the Covenanters; but
his conduct was no justification for his murder by a
rabble. One of this murderous gang was one of the
four men put to death by Claverhouse on the 18th of
December 1684. On the very same day, a body of
Covenanters, 100 strong, burst into Kirkcudbright,
killed the sentry, challenged the soldiers to fight, broke
open the gaol, and went off with as many of the
residents as would go with them. Now, the body of
men, of whom four were put to death, was a part of

the body of men who broke into Kirkcudbright; and, therefore, Claverhouse not unreasonably concluded that they were men engaged in an armed insurrection against the laws of the land, and as such, falling within the military jurisdiction which he exercised in that neighbourhood, which was in a state of anarchy and civil war at the time. All ought to deplore such excesses, and the military powers which sprung out of them for their suppression; but we must also remember the character of those times, the weakness of the executive civil powers, and the authority of the Parliament and also of the regular Government of the country as ample justification for Claverhouse's own conduct.

Opinion as to Claverhouse's general conduct towards the Covenanters.—I shall now briefly state what I believe to be the true position of Claverhouse in regard to what I look upon as the lamentable folly, cruelty, and oppression perpetrated upon the Scottish Covenanters in the reigns of Charles II. and James II. Claverhouse was a soldier of fortune, and usually executed the orders of the National Government with as much moderation as his duty to the Government would permit. That he was a savage and cruel man who executed his military and judicial duties with harshness is a statement totally unsupported by proof, and is utterly untrue. He was not a capricious and vindictive oppressor of a God-fearing and inoffensive peasantry; but a soldier waging civil war against a turbulent and fanatical body of men carrying arms, and using them. Tried by the law of the country at the time, he was executing just, and, in many cases, well-deserved punishment. A cruel Government, if you will, and as I myself think, drove large bodies of men to fight for their lives, their liberties, their wives, their children, and their property. But, then, Claverhouse was merely the instrument of a cruel Government, backed up and supported by an ignorant, or a servile, Parliament. He himself had no vulgar thirst for blood. As shown by his letter of the 9th of June 1683, he was often sorry for the victims of his severity, and would gladly have preferred to have punished the ringleaders of the poor peasants, who were driven into rebellion by more cunning heads, and more wicked hearts than their own. He was not cruel by nature, or reckless of any man's life. Indeed, judged by the manners of his age, he stands high amongst the military men of his time, and was as gentle, merciful, and humane as any of them. Taking him all in all in regard to his actions against the Covenanters, his conduct would bear a favourable comparison with any of the military men who have been engaged in quelling the tumults, insurrections, and rebellions of ancient or modern times. To call him bloody Claverhouse is a great injustice. Claverhouse was a strong and sincere Episcopalian and Monarchist, and was opposed to a general religious toleration. Those who think that he was a self-seeking soldier and statesman, whose rule of conduct was the King's wishes, have read neither his published letters nor the opinions of his contemporaries who were intimate with him and knew him well. In support of my opinions, which are so much at variance with the popular opinion which has been derived from Wodrow and Covenanting writers, I have to refer to published letters of Claverhouse ; the Memoirs of the

Earl of Balcarres; and the Memoirs of Cameron of Lochiel.

VIII.—THE REVOLUTION OF 1688.

Great national crisis approaching.—The affairs in England, Scotland, and Ireland were rapidly hastening towards a great and an inevitable crisis. For fully three years, between May 1685 and October 1688, there is little worth referring to in the life of Claverhouse's own personal history. Between these dates, however, or rather between the accession of King James II. on the 6th of February 1685, and the 18th of December 1688, when William Prince of Orange landed at Torquay in Devonshire, the royal diadem of the Stuart dynasty was gambled away by a short-sighted and bigoted King, whose fortunes, in the end, rested almost solely in Scotland on the courage, devotion, and ability of Claverhouse.

The Scotch Army of James II. marches into England. —Two months previous to Claverhouse being made a Viscount, King James II. announced to the Privy Council in Edinburgh that there was imminent danger of an invasion of England by William Prince of Orange, and that the regular troops in Scotland, numbering between 3,000 and 4,000, should, by levies in the Highlands, be increased to 12,000, and be distributed on the English border. Preparations were accordingly made to carry out the King's instructions. Edinburgh and Stirling were munitioned for war; the militia were called out, and volunteers were enrolled in every town all over the country. A subsequent

despatch from the King ordered the regular troops to
march at once for England, and to join the army under
Lord Feversham.   Resistance by the Privy Council
against the King's express commands was useless, and
the Scottish army immediately set out for England in
the beginning of October 1688.   The full strength of
the Scottish contingent numbered 3,763 men, of
whom 2,922 were infantry under the command of
Douglas, and 341 were cavalry under Claverhouse.
The cavalry marched to London by York, and reached
London early in November; and the infantry reached
Salisbury, where the Royal Army was encamped, on
the 10th of November 1688.   In the camp at
Salisbury, everything was in confusion.   Disaffection
was rapidly spreading; and the King, anxious and
deserted, broke up his camp.   Without a stroke for
his crown, he returned to London, and soon afterwards
left Whitehall for the Continent.

The interview between King James II. *and Balcarres
and Dundee in London.*—Of all his courtiers and
officers, Balcarres and Dundee were the most faithful to
King James II. at the moment of the greatest crisis in
his fortunes.   On the 17th of December 1688,
James had an interesting and important interview
with Balcarres and Dundee at Whitehall.   While the
King walked with his two faithful friends and
adherents, they assured his Majesty that they would
never forsake him.   He told them that he was to
leave England for France; and that, after he had
arrived there, he would send a commission to Balcarres
to manage the civil affairs of Scotland; and that he
would send a commission to Dundee to take the command of the royal military forces in that country.

For a short time, Dundee stayed in London, but his regiment was disbanded by James's orders. The Duke of Hamilton and the victorious Presbyterian party urged William Prince of Orange to exempt certain members of the Scottish Privy Council from the general amnesty. William peremptorily and wisely said "No." Balcarres and Dundee were asked to take the oath to William. They refused; and when Balcarres avowed his commission from King James, William said to him, " Take care." William assured Dundee that, if he would remain quiet, he would not be molested. Dundee's answer was, " that if he could, he would." Early in February 1689, Balcarres and Dundee left London for Edinburgh, to attend the Convention which was there to be held in March 1689.

State of the Whigs and Tories in the spring of 1689. —There was no fear of civil war in England, but there was a danger of it in Scotland. In the northern kingdom of Scotland, the great nobles and other high dignitaries professed loyalty to William; and yet there was no security that the Whigs of one day might not be Jacobites on the next. In March 1689, at the opening of the Scottish Convention, the Bishop of Edinburgh officiated as chaplain, and prayed that God would help to restore King James to his inheritance and throne. In the Convention, the Duke of Hamilton led the Whigs, who were now the Royalists, or the new Court party; and the Duke of Athole was at the head of the Jacobites, or the Opposition party. Hamilton was supreme in the Western Lowlands of Scotland. Athole, who had coquetted with the Whigs, was the most powerful nobleman in the Highlands. The Duke of Gordon held Edinburgh Castle for King James II., and

refused to surrender it.   After about two months'
delay, the Duke surrendered the Castle of Edinburgh
to William's Government in June 1689.   If the
political morality amongst the Scotch nobles was
lax, as undoubtedly it was, the aristocratical
sentiment amongst them was powerful.   Further,
while most of the leading public men in Scotland were
then the most disreputable time-servers the world
ever saw, the great body of the common people
were inflexible and pertinacious in the support
of their principles.   With the majority of the
Scotch nobles of this period, conscience had
lost all meaning, and yet amongst the great
mass of the people it was the most sacred possession
in the world.   At the end of James's reign, the bulk
of the common people were Whigs and Presbyterians,
and the minority were Tories and Episcopalians.   In
the Western shires the Covenanters sacked the
houses of the Episcopal clergy, attacked the Glasgow
Cathedral, stormed Holyrood Palace at Edinburgh,
and gutted James's Roman Catholic Chapel at Holyrood.   In this state of affairs in Scotland, William, in
the early part of 1689, summoned a Convention of the
Scotch Estates, to be held on the 14th of March 1689.

The Whigs victorious in the Convention of Estates.—
In the elections for the Convention, the Test Act of
1681, unjustly depriving all the Presbyterians of the
Parliamentary franchise, was overruled and set aside
by the Prince of Orange at the request of a deputation
of Scotch nobles and others, held in London in January
1689.   In the Scotch Convention, the Whigs carried
everything before them.   Hamilton was chosen president
by a majority of fifteen votes against Athole, and a large

number of Jacobites then went over to the Orange,
Whig, or Court party. If the representatives of the
Counties and Burghs had been elected under the
franchises then legally existing, the Jacobites would
have been in a majority in the Scotch Convention.
Even although the franchises and elections had been
manipulated in favour of the Presbyterians, the victorious party, in their first trial of strength, would have
been defeated by a change of eight votes to the Jacobites.
How, sometimes, do great events in the history of
the world, as well as of individuals, appear to depend
on the what appears to us petty and insignificant !

The Jacobites given up to despair.—A letter, written
by James II. to the Scotch Convention, signed and
countersigned by Lord Melfort as Secretary of State,
was read to the Convention on the 14th of March
1689. This letter breathed nothing but obstinacy,
cruelty, and insolence. Adversity had taught the King
nothing ; and James's cause was irremediably ruined.
The arrival of the Duke of Queensberry from London soon
afterwards raised a faint hope amongst the Jacobites
for the restoration of James II. ; but this hope soon
died away without effecting anything whatever for
the bigoted King. The hopes of the Jacobite party
were completely quenched. After the Lords of the
Articles had been appointed, and had reported to the
Convention their resolutions on the measures to be
adopted for securing the liberty and religion of Scotland, the parliamentary Jacobite party dwindled
rapidly to insignificance ; *e.g.* Athole, Mar, and
Annandale had joined William's party.

*Resolutions of Convention of Scotland and Scotch
Crown accepted by William and Mary.*—Since the

Union of the Crowns, the Government of Scotland had been carried on upon the supposition that the King was absent, and by means of letters communicated by the King to the Scottish Privy Council, or to the Scottish Parliament, in Edinburgh. Moreover, James had never been in Scotland since he became King; and therefore could hardly be said to have abdicated the throne. The Committee of the Convention, therefore, proposed that their resolution should be in conformity to the facts of the case, and should declare that, by his misconduct, King James II. had forfeited the Scottish Crown, and also his right to the allegiance of his Scottish subjects. When the question was put on the Committee's resolution, Athole, Queensberry, and some of their friends withdrew from the Parliament House, and the resolution was passed, with only five votes against it. After the resolution had been passed, Athole and Queensberry returned, and said that they had scruples about the throne being vacant; but, since it had been declared to be vacant, they thought that William and Mary should fill it. Then the necessary resolutions were passed by the Convention, and William and Mary were proclaimed at the Cross of the High Street of Edinburgh as King and Queen of Scotland. The Convention then approved of the claim of right, and the list of grievances to be remedied by law, both of which had been drawn up by the Lords of the Articles. Then Episcopacy was declared illegal and outrageous to common-sense, and the power exercised by the bishops to be pernicious, unscriptural, and unchristian. Although the Parliament abolished Episcopacy in Scotland in 1689, no other system of Church

Government was set up in its stead till the following year. No man could, at this time, understand what was the then existing established Church Government in Scotland. Nothing further required to be done by the Convention of the Scotch Estates, for the time being, than to appoint commissioners to go to London and to offer the Crown of Scotland to William and Mary. Accordingly, Athole, as representing the peers, Sir James Montgomery, as representing the commissioners of the counties, and Sir John Dalrymple, as representing the commissioners of the towns, were appointed the parliamentary commissioners to perform this high and important duty. The Convention then adjourned for four weeks. Before the adjournment, the States empowered Hamilton to take measures to protect the public peace. On the 1st of May 1689, in the Banqueting Hall of Whitehall, the coronation oath for Scotland was taken by William and Mary, with their hands held up to heaven, after the Scotch mode of taking an oath. Clause by clause, the oath was repeated by their Majesties. When William came to the clause promising to root out all heretics and all enemies of the Church of God, that is to say, in other words, according to the Scotch Presbyterian opinion of that period, all Christians who were not Presbyterians, he paused and said that he would not be a persecutor. Being told that he was not obliged to be one, the oath was taken in the terms settled in Edinburgh.

Government for Scotland appointed.—At the Revolution, Scotland was a poor country as to material wealth, and yet was rich in clever and self-seeking politicians. Where very many were claimants for office,

many had to be disappointed.   The Duke of Hamilton
was appointed Lord High Commissioner ; the Earl of
Crawford was appointed President of the Parliament ;
and Lord Melville was appointed to the office of
Secretary of State for Scotland.   The Secretary of
Scotland, though not the highest in rank, was then
the most influential officer of the Scotch Government, and he usually settled down at the English
Court, and became the regular organ for communications between the King and the Scotch Government
in Edinburgh.   At a later period, and until recently,
the Lord Advocate of Scotland performed the duties
of the Scotch Secretary of State.   As a right-hand
man in London as to Scotch affairs, William had
Carstairs, the royal chaplain for Scotland, and a
Presbyterian clergyman.   Carstairs was a good scholar,
an able man of business, a supple and consummate
politician, and was possessed of great self-command,
judgment, and secrecy.   Montgomery, Annandale,
Ross, Hume, and Fletcher were driven into opposition
to the new Government by being passed over in the
distribution of offices.   They very soon formed themselves into a club in opposition to the Government.
The great body of the Jacobites saw this division of
their enemies with delight, and hoped to profit by it, and
to bring about the restoration of the banished King
James II.   In March 1689, Hamilton rode in state up
the High Street of Edinburgh to open the Session of
the Convention at Edinburgh ; and Crawford took the
Test Oath as President.   But scarcely had the Convention been converted into a Parliament in June than
the fight of faction began, and the ascendency of
the club was seen to be supreme in Parliament.

This club was composed of Republicans, Whigs, Tories, zealous Presbyterians, and bigoted Prelatists, and acted as one man in Parliament, and made Government impossible in Scotland. Thus we see that parliamentary obstruction is at least two hundred years old. The old patricians hated the new plebeian officials, such as the Dalrymples. The Parliament also claimed the right to veto the King's nomination of the judges. It stopped the supplies for the King's Government, and declared none would be granted till the Bills upon which they had set their hearts had been passed, and had been touched by the sceptre. Hamilton refused to be thus coerced.

The Jacobites decided to hold a counter Convention, and failed.—On the 16th of March 1689, the Jacobites decided to hold a counter Convention at Stirling, where the Earl of Mar held the Castle, and promised to be faithful to James II. and his adherents. Athole promised to have a Highland force in readiness to support this party. As soon as the Convention assembled, John Graham, now Viscount of Dundee, became alarmed for his personal safety in Edinburgh; and complained to Hamilton that his life was in danger. He was told, not very truthfully, that his fears were unbecoming a brave man, and was advised to apply to the Convention for protection. He accordingly applied to the Convention; but that body refused to interfere on his behalf. Then, Athole wished further delay before he started from Edinburgh. But Dundee would not stay any longer in the capital; and Balcarres told Dundee that he would ruin all their plans by his haste. Dundee was headstrong, impetuous, and obstinate. A few days afterwards,

Balcarres was seized, and subsequently imprisoned in the Castle of Edinburgh. Thus the plans for a Jacobite restoration were ended in Scotland for a time.

Dundee leaves Edinburgh and rides to Dudhope.— Dundee joined his troopers, who numbered between forty and fifty men, and left Edinburgh on the 18th of March. Before he left Edinburgh, Dundee clambered up the western side of the rock on which the Castle of Edinburgh stands, and had an interview with Gordon, stationed at the western postern gate of the Castle, immediately above the place where Claverhouse stood. What passed between them is unknown. But tradition gives out that, in answer to a question by the Duke of Gordon, Dundee replied, " I go where the spirit of Montrose shall lead me." To this incident, Scott refers in his ballad of *Bonny Dundee.* Of this spirited ballad, I propose to read the three following verses :—

To the Lords of Convention 'twas Claver'se spoke,
" Ere the King's crown shall fall there are crowns to be broke ;
So let each Cavalier who loves honour and me,
Come follow the bonnet of Bonny Dundee.

"Come fill up my cup, come fill up my can,
Come saddle your horses, and call up your men ;
Come open the West Port, and let me gang free,
And it's room for the bonnets of Bonny Dundee !"

The Gordon demands of him which way he goes—
" Where'er shall direct me the shade of Montrose !
Your Grace in short space shall hear tidings of me,
Or that low lies the bonnet of Bonny Dundee."
Come fill up my cup, &c.

He waved his proud hand, and tho trumpets were blown,
The kettle-drums clash'd, and the horsemen rode on,
Till on Ravelston's cliffs and on Clermiston's lee,
Died away the wild war-notes of Bonny Dundee.

Come fill up my cup, come fill up my can,
Come saddle tho horses, and call up the men,
Come open your gates, and let me gae free,
For it's up with the bonnets of Bonny Dundee!

On through Stirling and Dunblane, Dundee galloped to Dudhope, where his wife was soon to be the mother of Dundee's only child. He was accompanied by George Livingstone, Lord Linlithgow's son, who proceeded to Lord Strathmore's house at Glamis, while Dundee himself remained in quietness for a week at Dudhope.

The Government orders the country to be placed in a state of defence.—The city of Edinburgh was in a state of uproar, confusion, and alarm until it was known that Dundee had ridden northwards, and then the tumult within the city began to cease. But the Parliament ordered the kingdom to be placed in a state of defence, and all Protestants, from sixteen to sixty, to assemble on the first summons. Fortunately for the new Government, three Scotch regiments, which had been in Holland, arrived at this time from the Thames, and were on board an English man-of-war in the Firth of Forth. They numbered about 1,100 men, and were commanded by Andrew Mackay, a Highlander of good family, and who had long served as a soldier of fortune on the Continent. On the 25th of March, he was appointed commander of all the forces of the Scotch Convention. I shall have again to speak of Mackay as the opponent of Claverhouse in the Highlands and at the battle of Killiecrankie.

Dundee is denounced a rebel, and fled to Glen Ogilvy.—On the 26th of March, Dundee was summoned by Hamilton's messengers to lay down his arms, and return to his duty in the Convention of Estates, or to be proclaimed a traitor and an outlaw. He replied to Queensberry, the President of the Estates, on the following day, recapitulating the designs in Edinburgh against his life, refers to his wife's condition, and refuses to obey Hamilton's summons. His letter was read to the Estates on the 30th of March; and on the same day, John Graham, Viscount of Dundee, was proclaimed a traitor, with all the usual ceremonies; that is to say, he was thrice called within the House, and thrice without the House of Parliament, and thrice at the Market Cross of Edinburgh with sound of trumpet, to make his appearance to answer the charges made against him. James II. was in Ireland at the time of these proceedings, and thinking that the time for action in Scotland had arrived, sent a commission to Dundee, appointing him his lieutenant-governor and commander-in-chief in Scotland. Letters were also sent by Lord Melfort to Balcarres and Dundee. But the letters of Melfort fell into the hands of Hamilton and were read in the Convention; and, being like their author, wild, foolish, and violent, caused a tremendous uproar in the Estates of Parliament. Of course, the newly-fledged Whigs were the loudest as to the dangers to which their love of religion and country had exposed them, and were the most urgent for prompt and energetic measures against their political

and religious opponents.   To escape arrest, Dundee
fled to the Highlands, where the only remaining hope
of the Jacobite party in Scotland then was.   There the
elements of disturbance were always at hand.   There
the inhabitants passionately loved war and fighting
for their own sake as well as for the advantages which
they conferred on the victors.

Character of the Highlanders.—The Highlanders,
then, were dangerous as friends as well as fierce as foes.
They had hereditary feuds of long standing amongst
themselves ; and they considered themselves strongly
bound by the ties of blood relationship.   Although the
feudal system had long been established in the Highlands
of Scotland, the old patriarchal system of a previous age
had never been superseded.   Although the chief of a
Highland clan might pay homage to a great lord, such
as Argyle or Athole, yet, amongst the clan, the chief
alone was king, and his word was law.   The Highlanders disliked military service for a lengthened
period ; and they knew nothing of military science,
and were not amenable to ordinary military discipline.
They won their battles by a rush, and retired to
their own homes with their booty ; or lost the battle
and then fled to their homes as fast as their feet would
carry them.   At the time of the Revolution of 1688-9,
the Celtic part of Scotland was scarcely known to England, or even to Lowland Scotland ; and what was known
of it was loathed, hated, and despised.   There, law and
police, trade and industry, were in a very backward
condition.   There, numerous chiefs held petty courts,
and were guarded by their clansmen.   There, as petty
kings, they dispensed rude justice to their clansmen,
waged fierce war against their enemies, and concluded

treaties of peace and of war in total disregard of the
King of Scotland or the King of England. They
wreaked terrible vengeance on their hereditary foes
for quarrels which had long before taken place. They
looked upon robbery as innocent and honourable.
They disliked industry. Their men hunted, and fished,
and fought; and their women laboured in the fields
at home. Their food and clothing were coarse; and
their dwellings squalid and dirty. They were courageous, and attached to their tribes and patriarchs and
families. They were faithful to allies and hospitable
to guests. Proud of their birth, they despised labour
and delighted in warlike exploits. In war the Highland
Celts were intrepid, strong, fleet, and patient under cold,
hunger, and fatigue. Usually, the chief of the clan
was colonel; the major was the chief's uncle or
his near relation; the captains were the tacks-
men or tenant farmers; and the company was
composed of the peasants. Amongst the Highlanders there was no fear of desertion, and no need
of Mutiny Acts; and they always followed their
pipers boldly and resolutely against their foes. Still,
they could not accommodate themselves to large
and sustained general movements, or be made subject to
strangers as their commanders. Their mode of warfare was a rush from an eminence, and a hand-to-hand
encounter; and their leaders must be their chiefs, or
their well-known and recognised substitutes. Their
wars were conducted as personal encounters, after the
fashion of Achilles, Ajax, and Ulysses amongst the
Greeks, as celebrated in the Iliad. These were
celebrated by their bards after the same fashion as
Homer may have sung the glories and the war exploits

performed by the Grecian warriors before the walls of Troy. Dundee proposed to introduce regular military discipline in the camp at Lochaber ; but, at the suggestion of Cameron of Lochiel, abandoned the idea as useless and inopportune. Blood relationships were overwhelmingly powerful amongst the Highlanders of two centuries ago. The Highlanders, the men as well as the women, were graceful, dignified, self-respecting, and sensitive. They were fond of poetry and oratory, which exercised great influence on their public deliberations and private meetings and assemblies. They were acute, tender, and vigorous. At the Revolution, and up till 1745, the English looked upon them, just as upon the Celts of Ireland, as savages and slaves, cut-throats and thieves, enemies and Papists. After the Rebellion of 1745, and the abolition of feudalism in the Highlands of Scotland, the Highlands were subjugated to law and civilization, and have now entirely changed their customs. Before this new state of things was reached, a political and social revolution took place in the North of Scotland, and the powers of the chiefs had to be broken, and the predatory habits of the people had to be abandoned, through the energetic, yet merciful, reign of law and firm government. In no other way can savages in Scotland, or Ireland, or South Africa, or India, or anywhere in the wide world, be brought under the *régime* of law and order, industry and civilization. Jacobitism in the Highlands of Scotland was not devotion to the Stuart cause so much as rebellion against the civilization and law of the Lowlands.

Dundee's early adventures in the Highlands.— Dundee was driven into rebellion by the Government. He escapes from Dudhope Castle and then from Glen

Ogilvy, and crossed the Grampians in April 1689. He then went to Inverness, where he had a disagreeable experience of the mischief arising from the hereditary feuds of the Highlands. On the 1st of May 1689, Dundee arrived at the camp of Macdonald of Keppoch, who was then besieging the town of Inverness on his own account, although erroneously said to have been sent to conduct Dundee to Lochaber. Dundee arranged the dispute between Keppoch and the town of Inverness; promised to meet Keppoch at Lochaber on the 18th of May ; and then marched through Badenoch and Athole ; swooped down on Perth in the early part of May; and carried off a large quantity of powder, provisions, money, and horses, of all which he stood much in need. He was off before the startled citizens of the Fair City knew the real situation of affairs, and the weakness of their enemy. He recrossed the Tay ; refreshed himself at Scone at the expense of Lord Stormont ; and appeared before the town of Dundee, where the gates were shut against him by Mackay's lieutenant. He then saw Lady Dundee for the last time in his life. He afterwards proceeded to Lochaber, whence had been sent the fiery cross calling the Jacobite clans to assemble for war. When Dundee arrived at Lochaber, Lochiel, the chief of the Cameron clan, was there with 600 broadswords ready against William and Argyle, and for James and Dundee. There also were soon assembled Macdonald of Sleet with 700 men from Skye, and Maclean of Mull with 500 men, and other Highland chieftains and their clansmen, and all enemies of the great Argyles, now once more restored to honour and power. Lochiel had many personal reasons for standing up for

the royal house of Stuart.   He had fought under Montrose for Charles I., and under Middleton for Charles II.
He had been knighted by James II.   He was brave,
generous, and loyal.   Then, the former chiefs of the clan
of Macdonald had once been the lords of the Hebrides
and of all the mountain districts of Argyleshire and
Inverness-shire, and had been largely stripped of their
possessions by the hated Campbells.   Moreover, Lochiel
and his Highland allies and neighbours had been formerly
subjected to a tribute in men and money, as feudal
vassals to the Marquis of Argyle, and had been, or hoped
to be, released from it.   Therefore all of them welcomed
the chance of completely and permanently gaining their
freedom from the odious and hateful bondage of the
Argyles.   Affairs had been completely changed in their
favour by the attainder of Argyle in 1685, and now
Lochiel and his Highland compatriots foresaw the return
of Argyle's supremacy over them and their estates.

The rebel muster at Lochaber.—On the 18th of May,
Dundee found every Cameron assembled, and the chiefs
of the Macdonalds, of the Macleans from Mull, of young
Stewart of Appin from Loch Finnhe, of the Mac-
Naughtons from Loch Fyne, of Grant of Foyers, and
of Grant of Urquhart, with their respective followers
in large numbers.   From the Lowlands there were
Sir Alexander James of Coxtone, Sir Archibald Kennedy
of Cullean, Hallyburton of Pitcur, Murray of Aber-
cairney, and other landed gentlemen with their followers and retainers.   The total muster at Lochaber
amounted to not less than 1,300 men, and, according
to some authorities, 2,000 men, together with fifty
troopers.   With such a force, Dundee naturally hesitated
to put the Stuart cause to the peril of a contest with the

new government. His instructions from James were to keep quiet till he received regular forces from Ireland; and he had, as yet, received no reinforcements or assistance from Ireland. As there had been no great rising in the Lowlands of Scotland, he well knew that, as he was then situated, he was unable to carry on a successful war in the South. Although Dundee was ardent and sanguine in temperament, he, at first, had no great confidence in the military abilities of his allies. He, therefore, proposed, as I have already said, to put them through a course of regular military discipline. Lochiel, however, knew his men much better than Dundee, and persuaded him to abandon such an idea, and assured him that there was no time to learn a new and modern method of warfare.

Condition of affairs at Lochaber.—Dundee asked James, and urged and entreated Lord Melfort, to send the long-promised succours from Ireland. In his last letter to Melfort on the 27th of June 1689, he speaks of Tarbat as a great villain for trying to seduce Lochiel and other Highland chiefs from their fidelity to James, and states that many of James's supporters had fallen away. He also stated that Panmure, Strathmore, Northesk, and Kinnaird had remained true to his king and master. He was then still hopeful of regaining old supporters, and obtaining new ones. The ardour, he wrote, of many of the supporters of the new government was greatly abated in many cases, and not a few secretly wished for the restoration of the exiled king. But the truth was, that the people to the north of the Tay were indifferent to the course of political events in the country. Some were opposed to the violent changes lately made on the hereditary succession to the throne; and some were opposed to another change of government; and some thought that, in the divided state of opinion in Scotland, and with the almost unanimous opinion of England in favour of the new government, opposition against it was hopeless. He received no effective answer to this letter. His entreaties for military aid from Ireland were practically made all in vain. But his tact, good temper, courtesy, and liberality won the hearts of all his allies. He spent his own money on the adventure, and in obtaining supplies was ably supported by his wife, and also by his brother-in-law the laird of Auldbar, and he shared in the hardships of his meanest follower. The power and influence which Dundee had over these lawless men shewed that he had genius and capacity of a high order in managing men. By degrees, Dundee had the most perfect confidence in the courage and fidelity of his followers; and they felt a similar confidence in him. Confidence begets confidence; and distrust begets distrust. At Culloden, an old chief, in his rage and passion, when he saw how matters were there mismanaged, cried out, " Oh ! for an hour of Dundee."

Mackay returns to Edinburgh, and Dundee disbands his forces.—I do not propose to trouble you with the marches and counter-marches of Dundee and Mackay in the Highlands in a game of hide-and-seek, in which Mackay was no match for Dundee. During the whole time nothing occurred of any importance, unless a skirmish between Barclay's dragoons and the Macleans at Colmnkill, where, if there had not been treachery in some of Mackay's forces, the Macleans would have been annihilated to the number of 200 men, and according to Mackay, of 600 men. In June, Mackay placed garrisons in the fortified places of Inverness-shire and Perthshire, and sent the rest of his men into winter quarters, and returned to Edinburgh. About the same time, Dundee disbanded his forces, and dismissed them on the understanding that they would return to Lochaber when required. As we shall find, scarcely a month elapsed before the fiery cross was raised to call the Jacobites to arms.

Position and circumstances of Dundee.—From the middle of June to the end of July, Dundee was not idle. He plied the arms of diplomacy with vigour. His last letter to Melfort gives a graphic account of his proceedings, his position, and prospects. It is dated the 27th of June 1689, and was written at Moy, in Lochaber. He says he was acting on the defensive; that he had neither commission, nor money, nor ammunition; that Gordon had surrendered the Castle of Edinburgh on the 13th of June; that Mackenzie and Athole had gone to England; that the Earls were cautious; that the Bishops "are the church invisible," and that the poor ministers generally stood right. He proceeds to state that Queensberry and his brother had gone over to William; that Tarbat was a great villain, and had endeavoured to seduce Lochiel from James's cause by means of money. He then proceeds to point out that blank commissions must be sent to Scotland; and also a commission of justiciary, with powers to judge all persons except landed men; and that, first of all, and above all, he wanted 5,000 or 6,000 men. From a postscript to this letter, and added, of course, before it was despatched, he appears to have received a letter from Melfort, who complained of the dislike which was entertained against him in Scotland, but who gave no promise of help to King James's commander in

Scotland. Dundee adds, in his postcript, that he had not twenty lbs. of gunpowder at his disposal. Such, then, was the plight of his lordship exactly a month before the battle of Killiecrankie.

Mackay proposes to garrison the Highlands.—From Inverness Mackay, in June, advised the Duke of Hamilton and the Scotch Parliament to place a strong force in the castle of Inverlochy, and other places in the North, and stated that the Highlanders would never be subdued until they did so. He also stated what he had done in the Highlands, and that he would be in Edinburgh very soon. General Mackay clearly saw that something must be done by the new Government to establish a permanent force in the Highlands of Scotland, and in the very heart of the discontented clans, and able to overawe the Macdonalds, the Camerons, and the Macleans. He accordingly determined to erect, as soon as possible, a chain of fortresses, to be commenced near the sea, on the West coast of Scotland, and stretching from the Atlantic to the German Ocean, and in the very centre of the discontented clans. When, about the beginning of July, Mackay actually arrived in Edinburgh, he found quarrels and intrigues rampant within and without the Parliament House; and all the political parties manœuvring for place and power, and totally indifferent to their foes beyond the mountains in the North. He also found that nothing had been done to carry out his policy for the pacification of the Highlands. He also soon found out that Dundee had been able to take possession of Athole, Badenoch, and other parts of the Southern Highlands, but that Elgin and Inverness stood out against his lordship. Moreover, Lord Murray, the son of the Marquis of

Athole, urged and besought Mackay to come to his
aid in Athole. Although the expedition to Inverlochy
was practically abandoned, Mackay decided at once
to start to the aid of Lord Murray, and fixed on Perth
as his rendezvous.

*The Athole tenantry refuse to join the Whig Lord
Murray.*—Lord Murray, who had taken up the
revolution at an early stage, and had faithfully and
resolutely stuck by it, went to Blair Athole early
in July 1689, and there found Stewart of Ballechin,
his father's factor and confidential agent, in possession
of Blair Castle, and refusing to give it up to his lordship.
Lord Murray was married to a daughter of the Duke of
Hamilton. Stewart of Ballechin was a Jacobite and a
Roman Catholic. At this time, he had the virtual command of the Athole tenantry, who refused to obey Lord
Murray. Instead of obeying their lord's son and heir,
they drank to King James's health in the rivulet of
Banovy, and, unless to the number of 200 or 300
men, they deserted him as soon as they knew
that he was acting in the interest of the new
Government. The Athole tenantry were then largely
devoted to the Jacobite cause. One word from the
Marquis would have added 2,000 strong and good
men to the cause of King James. But the Marquis
himself was false, fickle, and pusillanimous. He was
a Jacobite and a Williamite by turns, and nothing
long, and was regarded with contempt and disgust by
the great two parties in the country. He gave promises of support to the new Government in Edinburgh,
and then slunk off to England, and was evidently waiting to see how the contest in Scotland was to go. If it
went against William, he would throw in his fortunes

with James, and preserve his family honours and estates; and if it went against James, he would throw in his fortunes with William, and preserve these either by himself, or his son. That hundreds, or thousands, of poor people should be shot, or mutilated, or starved, was a matter of very little consequence to the cunning and selfish politicians of those times. Blair Castle, the chief residence of the Marquis of Athole, was the most important point in Athole, or in Perthshire, or even in the Highlands; for it commanded the Pass between the Highlands and the Lowlands on the West of Scotland. Blair Castle was then a rude, lofty tower in the valley watered by the Garry, and was about five miles from the northern end of the Pass of Killiecrankie. Through the Pass, in modern times, there is a fine road, much frequented by tourists and artists. But, in William's time, Killiecrankie was mentioned with horror by the peaceful and industrious inhabitants of Lowland Perthshire; for, through its dark ravines, fierce marauders sallied forth to plunder and to slay the people of the Lowlands. Two hundred years ago, the only road through the Pass was narrow and rugged. A horse could with difficulty be led up through it, and three men could hardly walk abreast along it.

State of affairs in Athole before the Battle of Killie-crankie.—The Athole retainers were on the side of James. They regarded the Whigs as synonymous with the Campbells, and hated them both with bitter hatred. Stewart of Ballechin, at the head of a body of the Athole retainers, now declared that he held Blair Castle for King James II., under a commission executed on the 21st of July 1689 by Dundee, as James's lieutenant-general.

He refused Lord Murray admittance into the Castle of Blair, and sent off messengers to Dundee to hasten to his aid. On the other hand, Murray sent off messengers to Mackay. Hearing of Dundee's approach to Blair Castle on the 26th of July 1689, Lord Murray retreated from the siege of Blair Castle, and retired to the southern end of the defile of Killiecrankie, where, on the 27th, he soon afterwards met 200 fusileers of Mackay's force as an advance guard. The remainder of Mackay's army soon followed the fusileers.

Dundee raises the fiery cross, and hastens to Blair Castle.—In July 1689, Dundee was with the chief of the Robertsons, at Struan, which is two miles north-west of Blair Castle. He had head-quarters at Struan, and also at Moy in Lochaber. He. tried to get Murray to join the Jacobite party, and failed. Having discovered Mackay's intentions as to Athole, he urged Lochiel to join him in Athole, at once, with all the men he had beside him, and to leave his eldest son to follow him with the rest of the Camerons. He himself hastened from Struan with all his available forces towards Blair Castle as soon as he heard that Mackay was hastening to Murray's assistance in Athole. But he waited for Cameron of Lochiel and his men, then numbering only 240, who marched in all haste to join him at the north end of the vale of Athole. Before this event, Dundee was joined by 300 ragged, half-starved, and badly-armed Irishmen, under an officer named Cannon, who had received a commission from James, as second in command to Dundee, now the chief-commander of the Jacobite forces in Scotland. This miserable and insignificant Irish contingent was all Dundee received from James in fulfilment of the glowing promises of succours from Ireland. Worse still, the men who composed it were ignorant of the art of war, and were poorly provided with necessary provisions. Unfortunately for them, some English cruisers, who had been stationed on the West coast of Scotland, although they had failed to intercept the Irish contingent, did succeed in seizing the provisions sent by James from Ireland. This loss was a serious one for Dundee ; for, at this very time, Dundee was very badly off for provisions ; and, for many days, his officers had no bread to eat, and had drank nothing but water. He was a bold and a sanguine man who could hope to succeed in a war with such materials against a foe fairly well-disciplined, and well-provided with all warlike necessaries, and commanded by a general experienced in the art of war. Still, Dundee had several advantages on his side. His men had perfect confidence in him ; they knew well the country round about ; and they were animated by the inspiring influence of a great, or, at all events, a strong, personal cause. Most people then thought that he must inevitably be defeated. But he was determined to fight out the contest to the last extremity. In March 1689, he was denounced as a rebel by William's Government in Scotland. In the following July, a reward of £20,000 sterling, offered by a royal proclamation for Dundee's head, had no effect on the loyal and devoted Highlanders under his command.

IX.—THE BATTLE OF KILLIECRANKIE.

Mackay marches to Killiecrankie: His and Dundee's forces.—On the 26th of July 1689,

Mackay left Perth with 3,000—some say 4,000—
infantry and with 100 cavalry.   About a half of
Mackay's men were well-seasoned English or Scotch
regular soldiers.   He had no artillery.   He had a few
field-pieces known as "Sandy's Stoups," which were
made out of a combination of tin, leather, and cordage,
and were warranted to burst after three or four shots
were fired.   His first object was to get possession
of Blair Castle ; and his second to garrison Inverlochy
Castle.   As we shall find, he accomplished neither of
these objects.   He reached Dunkeld on the evening of
the 26th.   At the break of day on the 27th, he began
his march from Dunkeld.   He reached the southern
entrance of the Pass at ten o'clock in the forenoon,
allowed his men two hours' rest, and then gave the order
to advance into the Pass.   He also sent forward
Lieut.-Col. Lauder with 200 men to secure the other
or northern mouth of the Pass of Killiecrankie in the
Vale of Athole.   The Pass having been reported clear,
Mackay's men marched through it from one end to
the other with the loss of only one man, who fell
at a place still pointed out as the Horseman's Well.
Mackay's movements had been too quick for Dundee
and his allies.   Not a single enemy was found at this
other end of the defile.   Very soon, a short way down
the Pass, Mackay was met by Lord Murray with a total
force of 200 or 300 Athole men.   But not one of these
could be depended on by Murray.   Dundee's total force
at Killiecrankie numbered about 2,300.   Unless to
the extent of about 400 men, they were all armed with
claymores.   He had about forty cavalry, and no artillery.

Dundee holds a council of war.—Early in the
day of Saturday the 27th of July, Dundee

arrived at Blair Castle, and was told that Mackay's troops were hastening to enter the Pass of Killiecrankie. He immediately held a council of war at Blair Castle. In this council, diverse views were advocated; but the advice of the wise and sagacious Lochiel prevailed. Lochiel said, "Fight at once. Fight, even if you have only one to three. Let the Saxons fairly through the Pass; and let us press home; and I do not fear the result. If once we are fairly engaged, we will lose our army, or gain a complete victory. We should dare to attack the enemy at odds of nearly two to one." Dundee, the commander-in-chief, agreed with him, and the council of war resolved to fight Mackay. When the council's resolution became known to the soldiers, the Highlanders were delighted. Lochiel also said—what turned out to be true—that he believed that Mackay had got through the Pass. As a matter of fact, Mackay was encamped in the vale of Athole when this council of war was held. Dundee had to fight, or retreat. To retreat would have dispersed his forces, and ruined his cause. He had, therefore, no alternative than to fight. He was not in a position to maintain a large force against his enemies. His insurrection against the new Government, unless aided from Ireland or France, was doomed from the first to absolute failure. James's opinion that William would soon be expelled from England, and that he himself would be restored to the throne, was a wild fantastic dream. Nothing less than a great victory and a rapid descent into the Lowlands could keep Dundee's army from dissolution or from starvation. Montrose, his great example, was victorious in the Highlands; but could not long keep the field in the Lowlands. At this

council of war at Blair Castle, Lochiel and the other
chiefs urged Dundee not to engage personally in the
impending fight. "You," said Lochiel, "ought to
command; and we to execute. On you depends our
brave little army, and the cause of the King." He
replied that he must charge at the head of the army on
that occasion; but that he would not insist on doing so
in the future. "Give me," said he, "an Shear Darg"
(or harvest day's work), "and he was content." From
the name of the house, then called Renrorrie, and now
called Urrard House, near which the battle was fought,
the battle of Killiecrankie was long known as the
battle of Renrorrie.

Mackay takes up his position near Urrard House.—
At noon, the whole of Mackay's column entered the
Pass of Killiecrankie. The Pass was then a veritable
valley of the shadow of death. The van was led by Brigadier Balfour's regiment; the baggage was in the centre;
and the horse and foot were in the rear. Beyond the
mouth of the Pass lies a considerable space of table-
land, forming the valley of Athole. On the right of this
valley stand the peaks of Ben-y-Gloe and Ben-y-
Vrachie; and around the mighty chain of the Grampian
mountains. Straight in front of the mouth of the
Pass stands Blair Castle. On the right of the
valley also stands Urrard House, with hills of some
considerable elevation at its back, and with a
considerable open space below and around it in the
direction of the mouth of the Pass, as well as towards
Blair Castle. Mackay meeting with no opposition in
the Pass, took up his position in a field near Urrard
House. He drew up his troops, as they emerged from
the Pass, on the large plain at its mouth. He afterwards
marched them up to the top of the rising ground on

which Renrorrie House stood. He had six battalions of
infantry and two troops of horse, and he divided his
infantry into right and left wings. He also divided each
battalion into two, and left a small distance between each
half-battalion. He placed his horse in the centre, and
left a large space between his cavalry and his right and
left wings. He drew up his men three deep; and had
no reserves. He intended his horse to fall out of line, and
flank the enemy on each side. He himself commanded
the right wing, and Brigadier Balfour commanded the
left. His baggage was placed by the side of the river.

Dundee does the same on hills above it.—In the afternoon, Dundee marched with his men from Blair Castle
straight down the valley. He led his main body across
the Tilt, which joins the Garry below Blair Castle, and
turned round to his left. He then suddenly and unexpectedly appeared on the right of Mackay's forces.
He posted his army upon the brow of the hill rising above
Mackay's forces. Attended by Lochiel, he drew up his
army in battle-array, and assigned each clan, or
division of a clan, to fight each separate division of
the enemy. His disposition was as follows :—Sir
John Maclean and his battalion of 200 men were on
Dundee's extreme right. Next to, and on Maclean's left,
were 300 Irish under Colonel Pearson. Next to Pearson
were the tutor of the Chief of Clanranald and his battalion of 600 men. Next to the men of Clanranald were
300 of the Macdonalds of Glengarry. In the centre
were a few cavalry, composed of Lowland country
gentlemen, and some of Dundee's old troop. Next to
his cavalry, and on their left, were Cameron of Lochiel
and his 240 men; and next to the Camerons were
Sir Donald Macdonald and his battalion of 700 men
on the extreme left. Though there were great dis-

tances between the Highland battalions, and a large
space in their centre, Dundee could not make his line
equal to Mackay's. Dundee was in danger of being
outwinged by Mackay. He was supposed by Mackay
to be intent on making an effort to get behind him,
and to cut off his means of communication with the
Lowlands, through the Pass of Killiecrankie, for
reinforcements and provisions. Before Dundee got his
men in order of battle, the afternoon was far spent.
While Dundee was arranging his men for battle,
Mackay's whole army began to fire in platoons, and
killed several of the Highlanders. A local tradition
that, on the night before the battle of Killiecrankie,
Dundee occupied the hill behind Urrard House is con-
tradicted by Drummond of Balhaldy, and also by
General Mackay, and is clearly without any real
foundation. After examining the ground, and com-
paring the accounts given of the battle by Drummond
and by General Mackay, who were both present at the
battle, I have come to the conclusion that Dundee took
possession of this hill behind Urrard House far on in
the afternoon of the 27th of July, and that it was from
it that his men rushed down upon Mackay's army.
Mackay says, in his Memoirs, that his position was
bad for making an attack, but a good one for defence.

Both armies drawn up for battle.—The clans were
drawn up in battle array on the hills; and Mackay's
forces were drawn up in the valley below. During
the day, an unsuccessful skirmish by a part of Mackay's
forces against the Highlanders stationed on the hill
above the field which Mackay had occupied, was made.
Another skirmish by the Highlanders was made, in
which they were defeated and were chased back to their

main body. Mackay's soldiers stood to their arms all day
long with stubborn patience.   The Highlanders calmly
looked down upon their foes in the plain below, and
calmly waited for the appointed time to rush down
the mountain side to destroy everything which stood in
their way, or opposed them in their onward course.
Each general addressed a few words to his men. Dundee
urged his followers to fight for their king, their country,
and their church.   Mackay urged his men to fight for
their king and their lives, and told them that, in the
event of defeat, their escape from utter destruction
was impossible.   The day wore onwards to its close, and
no serious attack had been made on either side.   As the
sun was setting behind the hills, Dundee passed along
the front line of his soldiers, who vigorously and
defiantly raised their war-cry of victory; while down
in the valley below, anxiety filled the minds of Mackay's
soldiers, who were tired and wearied, and had their
minds filled with anxiety and fearful forebodings.

The Highlanders defeat the Lowland forces.—
Then the pipes sounded the call to battle; Dundee rode
to the front; and the clans rushed down the hill
against their enemies.   As the Highlanders advanced
against the Lowland forces, Mackay's men fired a warm
volley into the Highland ranks. The Highlanders,
however, did not fire till they had reached the plain
below, and were close upon their opponents.   They
then fired a single volley; flung away their muskets;
and, with their swords in their hands, they bounded
forward against their foes. Before Mackay's men had
time to fix their bayonets, the Highlanders were in
the midst of them, and were flourishing their broadswords and their battle-axes, and were dealing

out death and terrible wounds on every side upon their enemies. Mackay says that he tried to rally his men; but all in vain. He says that the shock was terrible. He also says, and not untruly, that his men never had a chance to fix their bayonets, which were then fixed inside of the muzzles of their fusils after the men had ceased to fire at their enemy. Mackay afterwards improved on the bayonet by fixing two rings on the outside of the barrel of the fusil. After a few minutes from the shock of battle, and, as Mackay writes in his Memoirs, in the twinkling of an eye, the battle was practically at an end. For a few minutes, nothing was heard except the clashing of swords, and the sighs and the groans of wounded and dying men. After the battle, Mackay wrote that, "All his men, except Leven's and Hastings', behaved like vile cowards." His left wing had been scattered to the winds. His cavalry in the centre had fled at the sight of Claverhouse's cavalry. His right wing alone stood anything like firm, and alone escaped utter destruction; and yet, at one period of the fight, it also must have been driven from the field. Mackay's left wing was quickly driven backwards by the right wing of the Highland army towards the river, where his baggage was. His officers fought like heroes, and many of them were slaughtered. But the ardour, skill, and endurance of Mackay and his officers were all in vain against the terrible shock of the Highland soldiers. The Highlanders had obtained a complete victory over their opponents. Man for man, the Highlanders were then the best irregular soldiers in Great Britain. Their rush took the Lowlanders by surprise, and their flaming and rapidly-used swords drove terror and dismay into their enemies, unaccustomed to their mode of fighting. When successfully resisted and defeated in a battle, the Highlanders fled with precipitation from the field.

Mackay's men fled, and the Athole tenantry and the victors slew and plundered them.—Many of Mackay's men, foot and horse, rushed down the Pass of Killiecrankie. The Athole men, stationed on the hills above it, then rushed down upon the flying soldiers, and slew them in large numbers, and plundered nearly all of them. Dundee's men also pursued the fugitives, and slew and plundered them, and did not return to their encampment till about midnight. On the following day, they found a rich booty in horses to the number of about 1,200, and a large store of arms and provisions.

The scene after the battle.—Although the darkness of the night partly enshrouded the field of battle, vast numbers of the conquered were seen to be strewn over the field of battle, stripped, mutilated, and dead. The loss of the Highlanders must have been about 600 or 700. Most of them fell as the Highlanders advanced to the attack, and before the armies were engaged at close quarters in a' hand-to-hand struggle. Cameron of Lochiel alone lost 120 of his men. In the Highland host, the loss of officers was heavy, but greatest of all was the loss of Dundee. "The vanquished conquered, and the victors mourned." At one and the same time, it had carried death to the Lord Viscount of Dundee, and also defeat in Scotland to the cause for which he died. The victory at Killiecrankie, in fact, overthrew, for the time, the Jacobite cause in Scotland.

The fates of the two armies.—Unarmed, bewildered, without martial spirit or discipline, Mackay's forces were reduced to a rabble. Some fled for their lives into the deadly Pass of Killiecrankie. About 700 men, who had been placed on Mackay's right in the field of battle, were led off the field by Mackay, who crossed the Garry, and were afterwards joined by about 150 men. They were all led over the mountains to Strath Tay, and along the foot of the hills to Weems Castle, and to the Castle of Drummond, where Mackay had a garrison, and then on to Stirling. They reached Weems Castle in the morning and Drummond Castle in the evening of the 28th, and Stirling Castle on the 29th of July. Those who arrived at Stirling with Mackay, and those who arrived there after him, did not exceed one-half of the force with which Mackay had left it about a week earlier. Drummond of Balhaldy says that not one-sixth of Mackay's men escaped, and that 1,800 men of them died on the field of battle. His authority, on this point, cannot be accepted. Indeed, nothing in this Lecture has caused me such trouble and anxiety as the wild exaggerations as to the numbers engaged, and the number of the dead and wounded in the battles to which I have referred. But, let us proceed. The Highlanders had performed great feats of strength and courage, and had proved, at the battle of Killiecrankie, that the old martial spirit of the High-landers of the time of Montrose had not disappeared. The battle of Killiecrankie caused a terrible ferment in Scotland by arousing the fears of the vanquished party, and by exciting the hopes of the victorious Jacobites. In Edinburgh, the greatest alarm prevailed amongst the courtiers, till the news arrived that Dundee had been killed in the battle. The Jacobite cause in Scotland, however, was, in point of fact, dead for the present. Want of provisions, jealousy, and pride broke up the camp of the victors as soon as the breath was out of the body of the only man who could give life, cohesion, and success to James's cause in Scotland. King William quickly, accurately, and decisively gauged the position of Scotch affairs at that time; for, when urged to send a large army into Scotland, he answered: "It is needless; the war is ended with Dundee's death."

New Era.—Immediately after the battle of Killie-crankie, a new era sprung up all over Scotland. Agriculture, which was then the mainstay of the country, began to revive and flourish, and men's minds began to revert from rapine and civil war to industry and the arts of peace. By the revolution of 1688-89, peace, liberty, and freedom of conscience were brought to all in Scotland, and the priceless boons of civil and religious freedom were then established, and are being gradually secured and consolidated in every part of the wide dominions of the British Empire as they have never been before in this Empire, in any age or in any country, either in the history of the world.

I now come to the last branch of our subject, and propose to give you some further details as to the death of the Viscount of Dundee, and to conclude my observations by giving you a brief summary and exposition of his life and character.

X.—DEATH AND CHARACTER OF DUNDEE.

Dundee killed in the battle.—At the beginning of the battle, Dundee took his place in the front of his little band of cavalry, and bade them follow him. As his men appeared to hesitate, he turned round, and stood up in his stirrups, and waved his hat to encourage them to follow. On lifting up his arm, his cuirass rose and exposed the lower part of his left side. In this way, he received a deadly wound from a musket shot. His horse then bounded forward in a cloud of dust and smoke. Mortally wounded, he swayed from his horse, and fell, it is said, into the arms of a soldier named Johnstone, who saved him from falling with a crash to the ground. He asked Johnstone: "How goes the fight?" "Well: but I am sorry for your lordship," was Johnstone's answer. "It is," replied the dying general, "the less matter for me, seeing the day is well for my master." Dundee expired soon afterwards. According to a common tradition, a rude stone in the middle of a field marks the place where the victorious general fell. According to another local tradition, Dundee fell near a clump of trees on a mound at the back of the garden of Urrard House. I do not believe in either tradition. However, be this place where it may, Dundee's body, when recovered on the field of battle, was wrapped in a plaid; and carried to Blair Castle; and buried in the old church of Blair Athole. Truly, and well, writes Burton, "Never vaulted roof or marble monument covered the last abode of a more restless and ambitious heart than that which slept in this quiet spot amidst peasant dust." Here I could not do better than quote

some of the beautiful lines of Aytoun's *Burial March
of Dundee*.   I shall read the first, fourth, and fifth
stanzas, which are in the following words :—

I.

Sound the fife, and cry the slogan—
  Let the pibroch shake the air
With its wild triumphal music,
  Worthy of the freight we bear.
Let the ancient hills of Scotland
  Hear once more the battle-song
Swell within their glens and valleys
  As the clansmen march along !
Never from the field of combat,
  Never from the deadly fray,
Was a nobler trophy carried
  Than we bring with us to-day—
Never, since the valiant Douglas
  On his dauntless bosom bore
Good King Robert's heart—the priceless—
  To our dear Redeemer's shore !
Lo ! we bring with us the hero—
  Lo ! we bring the conquering Græme,
Crowned as best beseems a victor
  From the altar of his fame ;
Fresh and bleeding from the battle
  Whence his spirit took its flight,
'Midst the crashing charge of squadrons,
  And the thunder of the fight !
Strike, I say, the notes of triumph,
  As we march o'er moor and lea !
Is there any here will venture
  To bewail our dead Dundee ?
Let the widows of the traitors
  Weep until their eyes are dim !
Wail ye may full well for Scotland—
  Let none dare to mourn for him !
See ! above his glorious body
  Lies the royal banner's fold—

2 D

See ! his valiant blood is mingled
　　With its crimson and its gold—
See how calm he looks, and stately,
　　Like a warrior on his shield,
Waiting till the flush of morning
　　Breaks along the battle-field !
See—Oh never more, my comrades,
　　Shall we see that falcon eye
Redden with its inward lightning,
　　As the hour of fight drew nigh !
Never shall we hear the voice that,
　　Clearer than the trumpet's call,
Bade us strike for King and Country,
　　Bade us win the field, or fall !

IV.

And the evening star was shining
　　On Schehallion's distant head,
When we wiped our bloody broadswords,
　　And returned to count the dead.
There we found him gashed and gory,
　　Stretched upon the cumbered plain,
As he told us where to seek him,
　　In the thickest of the slain.
And a smile was on his visage,
　　For within his dying ear
Pealed the joyful note of triumph,
　　And the clansmen's clamorous cheer :
So, amidst the battle's thunder,
　　Shot, and steel, and scorching flame,
In the glory of his manhood
　　Passed the spirit of the Græme !

V.

Open wide the vaults of Athole,
　　Where the bones of heroes rest—
Open wide the hallowed portals
　　To receive another guest !

Last of Scots, and last of freemen—
  Last of all that dauntless race,
Who would rather die unsullied
  Than outlive the land's disgrace!
O thou lion-hearted warrior!
  Reck not of the after-time:
Honour may be deemed dishonour,
  Loyalty be called a crime.
Sleep in peace with kindred ashes
  Of the noble and the true,
Hearts that never failed their country,
  Hearts that never baseness knew.
Sleep!—and till the latest trumpet
  Wakes the dead from earth and sea,
Scotland shall not boast a braver
  Chieftain than our own Dundee!

Estimate of Claverhouse's life and career.—Having now gone through all the chief events of the life of John Graham of Claverhouse, Viscount of Dundee, and, as far as time would permit, explained the chief historical events involved in his life, all that now remains to be done by me, on the present occasion, is to sum up the life of this remarkable man as a private individual, as a public servant, as a soldier, and as a politician.

Claverhouse was quick, dauntless, and ambitious. He was brave and honourable, stern and relentless. He was neither selfish, nor mean; but was self-sacrificing and generous. He was gentle and urbane in his general manners. He hated cant and hypocrisy. He was loyal to his King, true to his religion, remorseless to his enemy. In his social relations, he was a perfect Christian gentleman in a licentious age, and at a licentious court. He was very ambitious of military glory, and was stern in enforcing discipline amongst his troops. He was reckless of human life, and fierce and ardent in the pursuit of military glory. But the worst crime which has ever been imputed to him is perfectly insignificant when compared with the cool and deliberate blood-thirsty cruelty inflicted by King William and his chief Scotch ministers in 1692 on the Macdonalds of Glencoe. With him, martial enthusiasm became an abiding and permanent principle of action. In the hour of battle, he did not fear death. In espousing the Stuart cause, he risked life and fortune, and lost both at a time when he might easily have made advantageous terms for himself.

His work in the South-west of Scotland amongst the Covenanters was not at all to his taste. In its execution at first, he was uncommonly moderate. But, after Archbishop Sharp's death, he remorselessly executed his civil and military commissions against the Covenanters. He was not a wanton oppressor, or a blood-thirsty man. He was the staunch supporter of the order of things—civil and ecclesiastical—then established by law. If he violated the considerations and scruples of individuals in acting in this manner, he did so in the performance of his duty as a soldier, and, as he thought and believed, in the interests of his King and country. He looked upon most of the Covenanters, not as men acting on high conscientious principles of action, but as men who were mere crazy fools, or selfish villains. His contest with the resolute, undaunted, and head-strong Covenanters at Drumclog was a huge blunder, brought about by his own rashness and impetuosity. He treated them with contempt, and was defeated by courage, energy, and foresight, which were equal to his own. With the gaining of the victory at Bothwell

Bridge he had practically nothing whatever to do. At this battle, Claverhouse's sole duty was to slay and capture, and this duty was relentlessly carried out by him.   At Killiecrankie, he gained a great victory by making the very best use of the soldiers under his command. The battle of Killiecrankie was a soldier's hand-to-hand fight.   The death of the general at the outset of the battle prevented the possibility of any display of brilliant tactics during the battle.   In out-manœuvring his opponent, and in drawing up his own men in the most advantageous position, and in the most skilful way, he had done all that a great general could do.   The Viscount of Dundee never had an opportunity of displaying the genius of the great commander.   What he might have done, if he had survived Killiecrankie, would be a profitless and idle speculation. He died at the early age of 46.   Previous to this battle, he had for months, and from first to last, gained the unstinted confidence of his officers and men by his frank and disinterested conduct.

As a politician, he allowed personal devotion to the monarch to usurp the place of a rational devotion to the interests of his country and his religion. On grounds of personal and affectionate gratitude to King James, whom he considered as his Sovereign lord and King, he refused to vote at the Scotch Convention, in 1689, that the Scotch throne was vacant.   His loyalty became a crime, and the Covenanting writers have blackened and defamed his character and reputation.   The title of bloody Claverhouse is a historical myth, and has sprung from the lies and exaggerations of his political

and religious opponents. He was an honourable
man, whose word could be implicity trusted. He
was the prince of the Jacobite cavaliers. From
loyalty to the cause of King James, he never swerved.
In adversity, as well as in prosperity, he was faithful
to the cause he had espoused. As a civil administrator he had a high reputation among his colleagues
and contemporaries on the Bench and at the Board of
the King's Privy Council.

Opinions of Macaulay and others.—Macaulay
says that Claverhouse was high-minded, high-
spirited, and courageous; but rash and not
far-seeing or prudent. Burton says that he was
a fanatical cavalier, devoted to the royal House
of the Stuarts and their allies. He also says that
he was educated in the ideas of high Toryism, aristocratic and monarchical, and in those of hereditary
monarchy, which, in the abstract, involve the doctrine
that the King can do no wrong under any circumstances. Scott says that he was terror and awe-
inspiring, and that he had the reputation of being a
keen observer of men, and of accurately divining
their inmost thoughts, and of using his wonderful skill
in this respect for the execution of his own ends.
Drummond of Balhaldy, the author of the life of
his father-in-law, Lochiel, and a man who knew the
Viscount of Dundee better than Macaulay, or Burton,
or Scott, thus writes of the Viscount: His lordship
was true to his word, and was never known to break
it. He was a man of high principle and religion.
He was a good Christian, an indulgent husband, an
accomplished gentleman, an honest statesman, and a
brave soldier.

In conclusion, let me hope that I have fulfilled my promise at the outset; and have placed before you a true and just account of the life and character of John Graham of Claverhouse, Viscount of Dundee.

[Before the Lecture on Claverhouse was delivered at Kew on 25th June 1889, the proof sheets of the Lecture up to the end of page 376 were printed and finally revised.

The proof sheets of pages 377 to 399 were finally revised on 24th July 1889.]

DANEBURY HOUSE, KEW GREEN, KEW,
SURREY, 27th July 1889.